Consuming People

Consumption is widely regarded as one of the most important phenomena in contemporary society, but there has been very little analysis of how consumption patterns evolve, transform and proliferate. *Consuming People* provides an incisive treatment of consumption on a global scale from a cultural, philosophical and business perspective.

Beginning with an analysis of how a dominant form of consumption pattern took hold in modern, capitalist, market economies, *Consuming People* explores the contemporary changes and paradoxes in our consumption patterns during the transitional period from the modern to the postmodern. The text focuses, in particular, on the forces shaping American consumption patterns, from corporations to Hollywood. The authors argue that as modernity wanes, consumption is replacing production as the fundamental process in the economy and society. Consumption exhibits multifarious postmodern tendencies but, paradoxically, the shaping of consumption patterns continues under an expanding hegemony of the market which is a quintessentially modern institution. The text concludes with an analysis of the emerging trans-modern possibilities of the new 'theatre of consumption' where communities with a variety of consumption styles will flourish.

Consuming People is an original and radical analysis which will be of great interest to students and researchers of consumer behaviour in business and the social sciences, as well as intellectuals concerned with contemporary cultural transformations in general.

A. Fuat Firat is Professor of Marketing at Arizona State University West. He is Co-Editor in Chief of the journal *Consumption, Markets & Culture*.

Nikhilesh Dholakia is Professor of Marketing, E-Commerce, and Management Information Systems at the University of Rhode Island. He has published extensively in the field of marketing, e-Commerce and consumer culture.

Consuming People

From Political Economy to Theaters of Consumption

A. Fuat Firat and Nikhilesh Dholakia

Routledge
Taylor & Francis Group

LONDON AND NEW YORK

First published 1998
by Routledge
11 New Fetter Lane, London EC4P 4EE

First published in paperback 2003

Simultaneously published in the USA and Canada
by Routledge
29 West 35th Street, New York, NY 10001

Routledge is an imprint of the Taylor & Francis Group

© 1998 and 2003 A. Fuat Firat and Nikhilesh Dholakia

Typeset in Times
Printed and bound in Great Britain by TJ International, Padstow,
Cornwall

British Library Cataloguing in Publication Data
A catalogue record for this book is available from the British Library

Library of Congress Cataloging in Publication Data
A catalog record for this book has been requested

ISBN 0–415–16680–2 (hbk)
ISBN 0–415–31620–0 (pbk)

To Omer Fehim and Fahrünnisa Fırat, my parents, who gave me the courage to explore

AFF

and

To the memory of Navrang Dholakia, my father and first teacher

ND

Contents

Preface

The idea for this book started in 1975 as a treatise in the political economy of marketing. Our purpose, then, was to explore and present the history of the development of marketing, particularly as part of the growth of the consumer culture and the modern capitalist consumption pattern. Our intended audience was the marketing and consumer research community. We wanted to illustrate that marketing was more than a business activity, or even a social process, that it was becoming a culture of our time. Also, we wanted to explore the consumption–production nexus, recognizing that new conceptualizations of old categories were becoming ever more necessary to understand our world.

Over two decades, the purpose and the content of the book, as well as its intended audience, evolved and transformed in significant ways. Given the long period since its inception, this may be expected. Furthermore, the years in-between this book's inception and completion have been very active years in the social sciences and the humanities. This dynamism in the discourses of many different disciplines is reflected in our work. The growing interest in consumption and consumer culture in an increasing range of social science disciplines has influenced our work. What we realized along these years is that in the humanities, social sciences, and the business disciplines, the leading phenomena of interest have tended to converge. One phenomenon of common interest arising from such convergence is consumption and its impact on all facets of life in contemporary society. Another is culture, which seems to be (re)gaining a central place in understanding other phenomena. For some time, culture had lost its primary position and seemed to be relegated to a secondary, "superstructural" position. We discuss this dynamic at some length in this book. Culture's place in human history was substituted by the economy, which took center stage as the engine of society and human relations. As a result, from being regarded as a determining moment, culture got demoted to a determined moment in human society. It became increasingly synonymous with degrees of "cultivation" and the institutions that represented cultivation. Several trends in intellectual discourse, particularly postmodernism, feminism, and globalism, have reversed this diminished role of culture in determination.

Finally, a third phenomenon of interest increasingly common to many disciplines today is marketing. Understandably, everyone is becoming interested in this mode of social influence and persuasive communication, especially as practiced by powerful corporations. Furthermore, many are recognizing that marketing is becoming more than a mere business or communication practice; increasingly it is the dominant mode of discourse in the contemporary global society.

Recognizing this convergence of interests, and influenced by the different literatures of humanities and social science disciplines, we gained confidence in our long-held position that compartmentalization of science into disciplines was and is a misguided tendency which often serves a dominant interest. We were convinced that the topics we were exploring spoke to an audience much larger than our immediate disciplines of consumer research and marketing. Plus, as is evident from the last two chapters of the book, the conclusions from our analyses of the development of consumption in modern culture and of the transformations observed in contemporary life relate to much more than marketing and consumer research. In effect, these are conclusions regarding the organization of society and human life in general. The reason is that consumption, culture, and marketing—phenomena we study throughout the book—are the central phenomena of our day. Consequently, our conclusions have wide implications, and our intended audience now covers people from social sciences, business and humanities disciplines as well as intellectuals interested in contemporary social issues.

Thus, the book has transformed from being a treatise in the political economy of marketing to a treatise about consuming people—people in the act of consumption, and consumed by the act of consumption. The first five chapters examine the evolution of the concept and practice of consumption in modern–specifically, capitalist—history, and its elevation to great significance in everyday lives. Our analyses in these chapters are informed by many theories and research in different disciplines. Therefore, some of the discussion in these chapters may be familiar to some of our readers. We have striven, however, to provide an integrative analysis from a relatively unique perspective that constitutes a foundation for our discussions about present and future potentials and possibilities in the remaining chapters. The analytical tone of the first half of the book, and the discussion of possibilities in the second half, may initially give the impression that this is a prescriptive treatise, that clear and conclusive diagnoses and prognoses are being offered. While we trust the insights of our analyses of modernity and the contemporary conditions, our purpose in this book is to promote a creative multilogue on the potentials and possibilities for meaningful human lives rather than to provide conclusive theses.

In many ways, therefore, this is an unfinished work, exactly as it should be. The work of life is always unfinished, always seemingly in the process of completion, moving from the meaningless to deliberate, from produced meanings to yet more meaninglessness. This quality makes life exciting. Therefore, we cannot—and do not wish to—establish a conclusive analysis nor a final possibility for the modes of life. We can, however, try to examine the past and the present from various perspectives in order to forge different modes and meanings of life for the possible futures. By choosing from among these perspectives and meanings, we may arrive at modes of life that we deem to be preferable. Furthermore, we can explore ways that may make this quest relatively more feasible under the contemporary circumstances.

Today, the looming task seems to be to find the ways to escape or subvert the totalizing stranglehold of modern ideologies and the socioeconomic systems they have reinforced in practice. To do so, it is imperative to produce new visions through new categories that open alternatives to hegemonic ways of being and living. We argue that today the hegemonic system is the market system. We explore the (hi)story of how this came to be, and the possibilities of playing with its potential and yet transcending it.

Many influential observers of current affairs agree that we are living a time of substantial—perhaps even epochal—transformation, widely acclaimed to be from the modern to the postmodern. Transformation is always difficult and full of hazards, bewildering yet exciting. The world is in a quandary and the search for ways out is fully open with potential as well as laced with many unanswered questions. Much of the transformation we observe at the end of the twentieth century, especially in the "transition economies"—those in transition from communist systems to market-led ones—seems to be toward marketization. Yet, in the already marketized economies, we observe that many are beginning to feel the most troublesome effects of the market—pollution, depleting resources, endangered and dying species, runaway corporate power, poverty amidst plenty, homelessness, and multiplying costs and failures of essential human services such as health care and education. The role of the nation state is also increasingly in question, having historically evolved from a provider of rights, security, and opportunity to an irresolute protector of the consumer from the excesses of the market. Today, the nation states find themselves increasingly "marketized" and somewhat irrelevant as politics itself becomes marketable.

Culture itself is becoming marketable. Cultures that discover or invent qualities that are marketable flourish, at least until competition brings forth substitutes. Cultures that fail to do so fall into oblivion or become museum relics. Thus, the market is becoming the arbiter of all success and failure, the sole locus of legitimation in the world. This development has many downsides and shortcomings as well as potentials. The major shortcoming is the unidimensional commercialization of life.

This shortcoming seems to be one of the major reasons behind the universal search and quandary. Crass commercialization leads to much disappointment and the disenchantment of life. People, we find, are in search of a rejuvenation of the multiplicity and multidimensionality of life and life experiences, a re-enchantment of life. As the market becomes universal, so does this search. Consumers, people in general, seem to be looking for forms and modes of consumption that will enable them to become players in the construction of meaningful life experiences, rather than follow given models. Resilient and inventive, the market itself continually proffers a chimerical array of new experiences, tantalizing yet ultimately disappointing.

It is times of such search and quandary, characterized by loss of commitment as well as indubitable trust in the present, that also open up the possibilities of alternatives, of experimentation, of taking some risks. We may be living such a period in human history. The communication technologies available today enable us to negotiate, sample, and experiment with many alternative possibilities and to reflect upon them. Yet, the same technologies that may enable this are signalling greater speed—leaving less and less time to reflect—and, consequently, greater difficulty for large portions of the global human population to become literate in their use. The response to the issues that we encounter at this juncture (of epochal change?), therefore, is not likely to be technological but cultural. We must playfully, yet critically and consciously, negotiate creative cultures, or else relinquish our fates to market technologies.

Tempe, Arizona   AFF
Kingston, Rhode Island   ND

September, 1997

Acknowledgments

We wish to thank our family members, especially our spouses Linda and Ruby, for the emotional and intellectual support they generously provided during the development of this book. We found much joy and inspiration in the experiences they offered us. Alladi Venkatesh is a colleague and friend who has been a constant source of intellectual growth for us through the many discussions we have had and, to our great delight, continue to have. Thanks go to Dominique Bouchet and the Bouchet family. They may not be aware, but during two months of reading and reflection in their beautiful home, in the long and cold winter nights of pastoral Fyn, some of the important ideas for the last two chapters were developed. Also thanks to collegues at the Marketing Department, Odense University, especially, Søren Askegaard, Lars Thøger Christensen, and Per Østergaard. Discussions with them have given us much energy. Maggie McFadden has been a mentor through the many women's studies programs she organized. Russell Belk was patient and kind to read the final draft for the book and point out errors, as well as provide encouragement and guidance about literature to read. Thanks also go to the production staff at Routledge who did an excellent job of copy editing and scheduling. Finally, but not least, thanks to Ozan and Ritik who spent many hours with us proof-reading the manuscript! Without the help and understanding of those mentioned above, and many others, we could not have completed this book.

1   The consuming society

When one of the authors of this book first arrived in the United States to start his graduate studies in marketing, a classmate persistently asked what he thought of America.[1] Being from a culture that finds it difficult to be directly unflattering, and experiencing a culture shock due to the difference between what he expected of America and what he found, he chose to elude this recurring question for almost two months. Finally, squeezed into a corner, having run out of elusive responses, and finding the courage, his answer was:

> You know, Richard, I don't think there is a culture in America. When I visit Italy, or France, or England, the air is thick with culture. The buildings, the people, the way of life tell me this is Italy, or France, or England. Here in America, the atmosphere is thin. There is no character to the things I see around me that tells me it's a distinct culture.

This reaction could partially be understood since he had grown up with Hollywood movies and yet had landed at Chicago's O'Hare Airport, and his first glimpse of America was Skokie, Illinois, on his way to Evanston. The Hollywood movies of his childhood did not much reflect Skokie!

But it was when he went back to Europe for the summer months, after spending a year in the United States, that the naiveté of his initial reaction to Richard's question struck him. The impact of American culture was now apparent to his senses; so strong a culture was it that it had permeated the aspirations of entire masses of European and Middle Eastern consumers. So, on his return to the States, he confided in Richard, now a good friend,

> I was so naive. I was observing America with expectations shaped by traditional ideas and indicators of culture. There is a very strong culture in America, and it is taking over Europe and the world. In material terms, three things define this culture: the television, the car, and the credit card. The television tells people what to buy and where to find it, the car gets them there, and the credit card allows them to buy—even if they don't have the money now.

He had encountered *the* consuming society. Not that other societies did not consume. This one, however, was consumed with consuming. For over a century in America, and today all over the globe, we find so many others expressing the same idea.[2] The concepts of culture of consumption, consumer culture, and culture as consumption are now moving to the very center of many social discourses.

But are our constructs, the terms we use, and the categories we employ in distinguishing things from each other, really able to reflect the nature of what is taking place today, in America and around the world? Or do they—like the naive author coming to America for the first time—belong to an old order, not allowing us to "see" the culture around us and the changes that are occurring? After all, "consumption," "consumer," and "society" are not new terms arising from novel circumstances at the end of the twentieth century. They have been around for a long time. So have many others that we employ to understand the world around us, or, as postmodernists may suggest, to construct the world around us.

The purpose of this book is to discuss and present an explanation of what has happened and is happening to us, the consumers. One may even argue that understanding ourselves as people who consume may explain much of what we are about as human beings since, in late modernity, many claim, consumption is much of our life.[3] Students of contemporary culture often state that as advertising becomes the primary mode of discourse in our culture, the consumer becomes the representation of the individual, as opposed to, say, the citizen in a political society.[4]

The project of this book, explaining what has happened to the consumer and what the possibilities are for the future, is a complex one. It is made even more complex by the fact that so much seems to be changing around us. Many claim, for example, that modernity has come to an end; that we are either living the final moments of the modern era or are already in a post-modern era.[5] And postmodern discourse is quite different from one dominated by modern science. As a matter of fact, most of what constituted the language and idea systems of modernity that made life intelligible for members of modern society is being challenged by a series of "post-" movements: poststructuralism, postindustrialism, postmodernism. So, when we want to explain what happened to the consumer, which language, what kind of discourse, which categories and terms should we employ? Do we study the phenomena that mostly occurred during modern times using modern or postmodern constructs (terms, words, categories, concepts)? How would each approach enable us to grasp the meaning of what happened to the consumer? How might each approach potentially limit the varied possible insights? By utilizing any one discourse we are going to tilt the scales in favor of one insight and against others.

For the authors of a book such as this, a dilemma exists as to whether to adopt a modern or a postmodern perspective. In the absence of a better idea, we have chosen to provide as scientific and structuralist—in other words, modernist—a perspective of the phenomena as possible in the first part of the book. We chose this approach while being cognizant of the many postmodern currents that are sweeping aside established forms of consumption culture.[6] Our major defense for taking this route is that much of what we will try to explain took place in modern society. Consequently, to understand the phenomena, the best vocabulary may be modernity's own. Even from a postmodernist perspective, it is the modern simulacra that constructed modernity.[7] What better tools to use, then, to understand something than those which constructed it!?

Modern society believed in the existence of an order and the existence of structures that constituted this order.[8] Consequently, modern society (re)produced many structures. For example, at the heart of modern society were first the urban structures, and later the suburban structures. Modern society gave us the structures of nation states. For the modern(ist) sensibility, such structures existed and enabled order. Governmental structures maintained the social order. Kinship structures maintained the family order. Whether the order was "observed," found to be "real," taken as "preordained," and reinforced to sustain the order human society "naturally" sought; or whether the order was constructed based on historical narratives or otherwise, modern society was indeed *structured*.[9] To the members of modern society these structures were real. People found themselves stuck within an order of structures, difficult to get out of or get away from. They depended on these structures to maintain their livelihoods. And if people did try to get away from these structures, they hurt: psychologically, socially, financially, and physically. For example, an individual could not easily walk away from the educational structure. To do so meant illiteracy, inability to access well-paying jobs, exclusion from "good" society, and possibly poverty. One could not walk away from the legal structure; that meant, possibly, incarceration. In modern society, a discussion of whether these structures truly existed or were in the social imaginary, or a construction of (meta)narratives did not make much sense.[10] Either way, they were very real for the people experiencing them. Anyone challenging them felt the jaws of reality closing in. The (hi)story of consumption and the consumer is not independent of these structures of modernity. We shall study these structures in this book, their formation and transformation. But before going into details let us look into some of the facts which may inform our (re)search. The consumers of the United States consume over five times more than their percentage of the world's population.[11] In effect, this has made the United States the primary market of the world—a consuming colossus that drives production systems globally. It is no accident that most of the world's new products first get introduced and tested in the United States, especially if these products require substantial financial investment on the part of the consumer unit. The notion of substantial financial investment is relative, depending on whether the consumer unit is an individual, a household, or an organization. No matter which consumer unit we talk about, it is the American market that determines substantially which new products will be developed or invested in. It is, again, for this reason that in the last three or four decades we have seen the transfer of products from the US that are now very popular in Europe, Latin America, Asia, and elsewhere. America is the beacon of consumption for the world at large. That is why the author, with whose saga we started this chapter, observed the growing aspirations in Europe and the Middle East for products such as the car and the television set, both initially popularized in America. There are other examples: the washing machine and dryer, the dishwasher, the microwave oven, etc.[12] By 1989, 87 percent of all urban American households owned automobiles.[13] Other numbers are equally striking: 98 percent owned color televisions (64 percent had two or more sets), 99 percent had refrigerators (15 percent had two or more), 94 percent had home audio systems, 76 percent had washing machines, 79 percent owned microwave ovens, and 77 percent had VCR decks.[14] The interesting thing is that for established durable goods, these high ownership levels had been achieved two decades ago. In 1974, the last year for which ownership statistics were published in the *Statistical Abstract of the United States 1978* by income categories, 84 percent of all households in the US owned automobiles. The proportions of ownership in the same year for television sets was 97 percent, for refrigerators 98 percent and for washing machines 72 percent.[15] In Europe and elsewhere in the developed world the proportions of ownership were not as high in 1974, but have been catching up.

Because of this transfer from the United States to other markets of some of the products which have become important in people's everyday lives around the world in modern times, concentrating our discussions on market developments in the US is not unusual. In fact, we will argue that the consumer society in its fullest form was created in America and the rest of the world is in the process of catching up.

Many students of American society tend to consider the period following the Second World War as the period when the "consuming society" became entrenched. Although a full-blown consuming society manifested itself as a post-Second World War phenomenon, this had much to do with social trends such as automobilization and suburbanization that had begun before the war. By the early 1940s a substantial proportion of the urban population was living in the suburbs. In a study of eight metropolitan areas, Stanback and Knight found that during the 1940s urban population grew at an annual rate of 0.80 percent while suburban population grew by an average of 4.19 percent.[16] By the 1950s urban growth rate in these eight metropolitan areas had turned negative (−0.21 percent) while suburban population growth had leaped to 6.78 percent per year. The trend continued into the 1960s: urban growth rate was −0.54 percent while suburban population continued to expand at an annual rate of 3.35 percent. This fast-paced suburbanization meant, in many ways, a withdrawal into the home. Access to public spaces, mostly in urban centers, had become difficult due to distance, physical as well as social. Movie theaters and movies, which were more easily reproduced and therefore able to spread into the suburbs, thrived, while less easily reproducible public entertainments such as live theater, opera, and symphonies atrophied.[17] Outings from the home increasingly began to gravitate towards shopping centers, movie halls, and restaurants.[18] Increasingly these outings took the form of consumption activity rather than participation in public affairs. The activity at home had already become "consumptive" with the change from homesteads to accommodation dwellings, and the increasing use of products acquired in the market for use in the home. As we shall discuss later, modern society had already separated the domains of consumption and production and the activities at home had been signified as consumption.

Following the Second World War, household durables and consumable items to maintain these durables (cleaners and the like) both improved in quality and exploded in variety.[19] The household's success was very much represented in the amassing of these products. Specifically for the "middle class," success came to be measured through the ability to own a home and to furnish it.[20] Government policies and the media (both advertisements and other forms of programming on television or articles in magazines and newspapers) reinforced this popular culture.[21] In a relatively short period of time, the United States was transformed into a consuming society where one worked in the public domain to acquire coveted, meaning-laden consumer items, while the inherent meanings or value attributed to one's work, career, or job largely lost importance. Except perhaps for the wealthy, the primary purpose of work became its potential or ability to generate disposable income for consumption. For the wealthy, also, consumption was no longer something to be hidden or to be prudent about. Nor was it, as in the middle ages, particularly to be made conspicuous, since most of the erstwhile "conspicuous" products were re-signified in the modern, industrial society as necessities, or at least desirable and accessible luxuries. Like attire, consumption of all kinds became something to be flaunted—not to establish a conspicuous imprimatur of class and style, but to dazzle for the moment.[22]

We are now in the era of the "Lifestyles of the Rich and the Famous." Consumption is good, out in the open, for everyone to partake in, whether actually or vicariously. That this is the case is hardly contested. American literature has an abundance of expressions of this revolutionary transformation in the public mentality.[23] But why is it the case? And why are the consumption items, the car, the television set, the telephone, the washer and dryer, the dishwasher, the refrigerator, etc., so central and important in the public sensibility; in definitions of good life and success? This book is an attempt at providing answers to such questions for the modern society, and a commentary on the emerging postmodern consumer culture.

2 Consumption patterns

In his early work, Jean Baudrillard, one of the most prominent postmodernist philosophers of our day (although a self-proclaimed modernist), argued that consumption items were not independent of each other, but that consumption is a system.[1] Indeed, in some ways, what a pervasive and iron-clad system it is. One wonders why it is that the products we find so diffused in the consuming society were the products that became so popular: why, for example, the car, the television, the telephone, and the washer-dryer? Why not the train, the theater, the neighborhood soda fountain, and the community laundromat? Are these popular products, which define so much of our daily lives, there just by chance or force of technology, or is there some rhyme and reason behind their popularity and diffusion?

Our argument is that these products are not so unlike each other, that certain common dimensions underlie them. As is usual with most aspects of modern society, a structure seems to be present within the character of these products which binds them. In poststructural terms, there appears to be a code to the prevalent consumption system that can be discerned and interpreted.

This brings us to the discussion of consumption patterns. It needs to be recognized at the outset that consumption choices occur at different levels. For example, there is the choice of consumption mode: car versus public transportation. Then, there is choice among product forms: small truck versus automobile, family sedan versus sports car. Then, there is brand choice: Ford versus Toyota. For a consumer, these choices may be made simultaneously or there may be some order. For example, a consumer may know that s/he wants a private transportation vehicle, decides on buying a station wagon, and then checks out the brands that offer station wagons. Further, some choices may be socially rather than individually made, and the consumer may be highly constrained. Again, consider transportation choices. Many cities, large and small, as well as country towns in the United States, do not provide adequate public transportation, and whether one is in Dallas, Texas; Muncie, Indiana; or Boone, North Carolina, not having (access to) a privately owned car generally means an inability to get to many places.

With technological advancements and economic growth, consumption experiences have changed for individuals and households in modern society. These changes may best become apparent when transformations along some common dimensions are considered. As we discuss later in this chapter, we identify four dimensions: the social relationship dimension, the domain of availability dimension, the level of participation dimension and the human activity dimension. We call the different configurations of relationships among these dimensions consumption patterns. These patterns correspond largely to choices along the modes of consumption, as in the case of public versus private transportation. They indicate historical, cultural, and social trends.

Consumption patterns have changed through history. Over the span of history, different products, or consumption items and activities, have come to correspond to different configurations of relationships along the core dimensions of consumption patterns that we will elaborate in this chapter. In the process of evolution of consumption, some of these products, items, or activities of consumption become popular and desirable. These changes were largely reinforced by major transformations and trends in modern society. As modern society developed, one major transformation was the increasing separation of the activities called production and consumption from each other. We are all largely aware of this transformation from the popular media. Earlier, human communities did not much separate work and play, creation and recreation.[2] Everyone in the household had to participate in production (and rather constantly) to ensure a decent livelihood in agrarian or hunter societies.[3] Pure consumption or recreational social activity rarely ever existed. Every entertaining or recreational activity had a social, ritual, or functional purpose: the harvest festival, the medicinal ceremony, the rites of spring, the prayers for rain, etc.

The clear demarcations between "productive" and purely "consumptive" activities seem to be products of modern society. With such demarcations, of course, came the distinctions in definitions of consumption and production, consumer and producer. These demarcations occurred in time and in space. Modern society defined and demarcated work shifts, work hours, and work places. With the industrial revolution and public organization of production came the separation between the workplace and the home. The home became the domain for consumption, and the factory, the office, the plantation, etc., the domains for production.[4] These demarcations changed the lives and dreams of many consumers rather abruptly. Many who dreamed of a homestead and a life on one's own land soon found themselves in fast-growing urban landscapes, in housing complexes, and in work environments far removed from their dreams of the country. On the other hand, at the societal level, the transformations took time, confusing the classical economists trying to categorize and classify economic activities. How were cooking, canning, sewing, weaving, and gardening at home to be categorized? Was this consumptive production, productive consumption, or consumption proper?[5]

Indeed, for a long time, activities that "produced" continued in the home, and to much lesser degree still do. Even up to the Second World War, some of the most popular household items acquired in the market were those that enabled "production" in the home, such as the sewing machine. But, increasingly, such activities at home were substituted with products bought in the market, such as ready cooked meals and ready made clothing. Even much of the household maintenance activity was complemented and partly substituted by market-bought products such as the washing machine and dryer, the dishwasher, and the like. Then, using these major household products required other products, such as detergents and other cleaning and upkeep items. The private domain, the home, was increasingly "invaded" by products bought in the market. All these products were continually improved, new features were added and major novelties were produced.[6] Consequently, these products were not disconnected, they made sense together and supported each other's existence. They produced lifestyles and supported patterns of life. They represented consumption patterns.

THE CORE DIMENSIONS

Earlier we mentioned that consumption patterns are identified by a set of configurations or relationships along dimensions that underlie the products which become popular and dominant in different historical periods. We find that four dimensions best describe these configurations and relationships. These four dimensions characterize the most critical trends in modern consumption. We call these dimensions the social relationship dimension, the domain of availability dimension, the level of participation dimension, and the human activity dimension.[7]

The social relationship dimension

This dimension defines a consumer's relationship with other consumers during the act of consumption and ranges from collective to individual consumption. Consumption reaches an individual extreme when a consumer unit (person, family, or household) has no relations with other consumer units during consumption activity. A good example is a person eating a meal alone, without sharing any planning or food or space with another. On the other hand, a picnic planned together with neighbors where cooking, transportation, and food are shared is an example of a somewhat collective consumption. The Israeli kibbutz with its communal kitchen and dining space is an example of a highly collective consumption pattern.[8]

As the transformations briefly mentioned above took place, where the public and private domains became increasingly separated, and production and consumption also became demarcated in time and space, the relationships along the social relationship dimension became increasingly individualized. This trend has been reinforced with the growth of nuclear families, mobility across space with industrialization and urbanization, and with suburbanization and individual housing. First, families were drawn away from others, into their own homes, with the advent of radio, television, and air conditioning.[9] Later, each family member largely withdrew from the rest of the family with multiple televisions, telephones, stereos, TV dinners, microwave ovens, which reinforce fast and individual cooking, and multiple cars that allowed each family member to commute separately to their jobs and workplaces.

The domain of availability dimension

This dimension defines the availability of a product to the members of society and ranges from private access to public availability. The private extreme is reached when a single consumer owns or possesses a consumption item and allows no availability or access to anyone else. Consumption is public when the consumption item or process is available to all. An example of private consumption is a clothing item belonging to and worn by a single consumer. If this clothing item is worn by others in the family or friends to whom the owner lends them, its "publicness" increases and the level of private consumption is reduced. Public consumption examples are public parks, movie theaters, public libraries, museums, and public telephones— items which are available to anyone who can get there or who can pay for them. These access conditions attenuate the degree of "publicness" of the consumption experience.

It is reasonable to think that the two dimensions discussed are somewhat related. The more private a consumption activity, the more likely it is that it will be individual, as in the case of a privately owned automobile. Yet this is not necessary. Much public consumption may be, and indeed is, individual. While public transportation vehicles such as buses, public telephones, and movie theaters are public, for example, their consumption is generally individual in that individual consumers neither share decisions to consume nor interact much during the consumption of these public goods, services, and spaces. The reverse may also be true. A consumer may privately own and control a consumption process or item, but share it and interact with others in the act of consuming it. During the Christmas holiday season, for example, some American homes put up elaborate lighting displays which they expect others to "consume" in terms of driving by and admiring them. As another example, consider the established family in Kingston, Rhode Island that opens its five acres of azalea gardens one Sunday every spring and arranges the popular "Azalea Tea" for the community. The exceptional nature of these examples needs no comment.

The history of western (and by extension global) culture represents an increasingly privatized consumption pattern. Consumers use and spend longer hours with products which allow and induce private consumption. The trend is clear, for example, in entertainment activities. People have increasingly gravitated from consumption in public spaces—movies, dances, and social gatherings—to consumption in private spaces, for example, television, home videos, stereo systems, and especially the Walkman, which provides a private and isolated listening experience even in a crowded Tokyo commuter train. Similar patterns are observable in transportation. In the United States, for example, the percentage of personal consumption expenditure for public transport fell from 3.6 in 1910 to 0.92 in 1990.[10] Again, technological developments, sociological tendencies, and work and living conditions have reinforced this trend.

The level of participation dimension

This dimension defines the direct participation by a consumer in determination of the different aspects of consumption items and consumption processes. In the case where consumption revolves around a product, for example a television set, this dimension relates to how much a consumer has participated in the production and development of the features, programming, etc., of television. In the case where consumption revolves around an activity or a process, for example, visiting the Grand Canyon, this dimension relates to how much the consumer has directly determined the rules and procedures of the activity or process.

This dimension ranges from participatory to alienated consumption. The greater the direct contributions by consumers in the determination of products and activities consumed, the more participatory is their consumption. The less a consumer contributes to such determination the more alienated consumption becomes. Examples of participatory consumption are a household planning and building its own dwelling from scratch, or developing recipes as a family and cooking meals based on these recipes from scratch. An example of alienated consumption occurs when a consumer uses a microwave oven to prepare a pre-cooked frozen meal or a video machine to watch a pre-recorded movie. In either case, the consumer is largely a follower of instructions which have been dictated by the way technologies were developed by experts or by mass production requirements. The consumer usually cannot change the procedures of use indicated in the instructions without encountering serious problems. In fact, in some cases, not following the instructions may even result in fatal accidents.

Over the last century our homes, the private domain, have been increasingly invaded by products manufactured for a mass market, such as television sets, cleaning machines, VCRs, computers, and video games, and the resultant consumption experience has become more and more alienated. Many of these products bring with them their own time use patterns and procedures for use, turning us into a society of instruction-followers. When technology makes possible new products that can possibly *increase* the participatory aspects of consumption, such as interactive television, the markets plunge into deep uncertainties as to whether people will buy and use such products.[11]

The human activity dimension

This dimension defines the level of combined human physical and mental activity during the act of consumption and ranges from passive to active consumption. The typical example of passive consumption is the act of watching an entertainment program on television. Many interpret this activity as one of being a "couch potato." In the process of such consumption, the consumer is largely in a state of being a receiver audience, with physical and mental activity greatly reduced. On the other hand, participating in a sports activity, say, playing basketball with neighborhood friends, represents an increased level of mental and, especially, physical activity in comparison to watching television. Different television programs may induce different levels of activity, but the general level of activeness will be low in non-interactive programs. Other examples of relatively passive consumption include the use of washing machines, pre-cooked meals, driving instead of walking, and the like. Active consumption activities, on the other hand, are, for example, hobbies or do-it-yourself home improvements.

An active consumption does not automatically indicate participatory consumption. Many hobbies and home improvement kits, for example, are largely pre-configured by their manufacturers, and the consumers simply follow instructions.[12] The opposite is also true, therefore. Passive consumption does not have to be alienated. Yet, in a majority of cases in the contemporary culture, passive consumption will require the use or presence of products produced for a mass market. The growing role of time and energy saving products at home, the domain of consumption, has increased passive consumption in the last century.

THE GROWING TREND IN CONSUMPTION PATTERNS

A study conducted in the United States supported the presence of a trend toward an increasingly individual-private-alienated-passive pattern of consumption in the last couple of centuries.[13] In this study consumers were asked to list consumption items and practices that were popular in North America before the middle of the nineteenth century, from the middle of the nineteenth century up to the Second World War, and after the Second World War. Then, an expert panel made up of a historian, a women's studies scholar and a literary criticism scholar evaluated the lists of items to construct the final list used in the research. Finally, a random sample of respondents were asked to plot these items[14] onto graphs that represented the dimensions discussed above. With incredible consistency, the consumption items that play an important part in the life of consumers following the Second World War came up very high on the individual-private-alienated-passive scale, with items popular between the middle of the nineteenth century and the Second World War less individual-private-alienated-passive, and consumption items and practices from before the middle of the nine-teenth century relatively more collective-public-participatory-active.

Our examples during the discussion of different dimensions also indicated such a trend towards an increasingly individual-private-alienated-passive consumption. In fact, the exceptions to these patterns in America and else-where are becoming so difficult to find that, when they do occur, they are featured as newsworthy "human interest" stories in the media. Why this trend towards individual-private-alienated-passive consumption? What were (are) the forces that induced and influenced this trend in modern society? What can we expect to see in terms of this trend in a society that may be starting to run a postmodern course? These are some of the questions this book will address.

3   The making of the consumer

In the preceding two chapters we frequently used the terms consumption and consumer as well as some others such as consumption item, consumption process, and consumption activity. None of these terms are strangers to the readers, they are terms of everyday usage. But sometimes, such terms are the most difficult to understand and define.

One might think that a term like consumer or consumption is clear-cut. Yet, as recently as Adam Smith and David Ricardo, economists had difficulty in defining these terms. Consequently, they were forced to develop several terms, including productive consumption, consumptive production, and consumption proper.[1] No "production proper," however. Production was the core activity of the modern classical economy: its propriety was not an issue. Consumption, however, played varied roles in relation to production. It was clear to classical economists that any human productive activity requires consumption; consumption of time, energy, tools, materials, etc. Production, therefore, always has a "consumptive" character. How did the economists who formulated the definitions of the main terms of the classical economy define consumption? It is the process where value is used, devoured, or destroyed. If nothing of value is created in this process, then it is consumption proper. If, however, something of value is created while some value is used, devoured, destroyed, then this is productive consumption—since all human creation of value requires consumption, in short, this is production. With time, the other terms initially used to overcome definitional difficulties were dropped and forgotten, only consumption and production remained. And, of course, consumer and producer.

Why go through this rather obvious, though brief, discussion? To show that any definition of what consumption and production are, their distinction, depends purely upon the meaning of value. If the community of definers see the outcomes from a process of consumption as something of value, production has taken place. Otherwise, it is a rather profane act of consumption, the so-called consumption proper— pure use, devouring, and destruction of value.

What has value, however, is not so easy to decide. Nor is it possible to have an absolute definition. Rather, the notion of value is quite relative, to be defined by the culture of the time and the prevalent "values" of the society. And culture constructs this definition in myriad ways: through the market, politics, social relations, or a complex combination of such things.

Classical economists were fairly satisfied with their categorizations, but Marx introduced further difficulties when he extended their labor-value thesis.[2] Exchange-value was not just an attribute of commodities produced by labor for the market. In a capitalist economy, the labor-power that produced these commodities was itself a commodity. Like textiles and corn, labor-power was traded and exchanged in the market and, thus, had an exchange-value. Was consumption of food at home, then, a productive act since it "created" labor-power that had exchange-value in the (labor) market? Marx's conclusion was that capitalist ideology would not count such consumption as production because exchange-value for labor-power entered the capital equation merely as a cost and did not, therefore, afford the capitalist any surplus-value toward realization and accumulation of capital. Calculations of the gross national product (GNP) in contemporary capitalist economies are a continuing attestation to this conclusion. These calculations do not account for production of labor-power at home as part of the GNP. Because it does not enter any firm's balance sheet, all the work done at home to keep body and soul together, to raise and maintain a family, represents the destruction of value—consumption proper.

How did value come to be considered what it is in capitalism? Marx's implied answer was that were a capitalist to have a farm for breeding human beings to sell their labor-power in the market, thus getting surplus-value within the exchange-value of this labor-power—surplus that would accumulate as additional capital at this human-breeding farm—*then* the food, clothing, etc. that these laborers consumed would have been considered productive, and the eating, sleeping, etc., that went on in this farm would be considered production.[3] When similar activities went on in the homes of the laborers, however, not affording surplus-value for capital, such activities were considered consumption proper. The efforts of the home-maker to feed and sustain the laborer were not productive. The home-maker was a "consumer proper," as was the laborer when at home. The laborer became a "producer" in the factory, working for the capitalist, producing commodities and, of course, surplus-value for the capitalist. The differentiation between work and home was not just a differentiation in accounting and economic terms. It had its social, cultural, and psychological correlates as well. When at work, one was not at home—literally and figuratively. And "work" at home was not work—it was trivial activity, gender-stereotyped as "women's work" and reduced to unproductive (but nonetheless essential) drudgery.[4] The above "narrative," the story of value, work, home, production and consumption in capitalist society, is specific to just that, the capitalist society. This narrative, however, became very much that of modern society, built on capitalism, scientific technology, and the ideology of the market economy. But the development of the market itself has a history. This history is intertwined with the separation of the public and private domains, articulation of gender categories, the growth of commodity production, and legitimation of private property. It is also the history of the emergence of the concepts of consumer and consumption, as well as producer and production, and, of course, the system of values which produces these concepts.

A COMMON HISTORY OF CONSUMPTION AND GENDER

While human beings have always consumed, the concept of consumption as separate from production seems to have its roots in other separations: separation of home from workplace, separation of time for work (job) from time for play (recreation, leisure), separation of the public from the private. With these separations came the separation of consumption from production in concept. Increasingly, activities at home, during play, in the private domain, came to be considered consumptive. Production was done in the public domain, the factory, the mine, the docks, the plantation, the office, the workplace.

Historically, in many cultures work and play, toil and recreation were largely merged.[5] Consequently, concepts of leisure and recreation are relatively new.[6] Rather, for many human beings, before the appearance of societies where substantive and persistent specialization took place and some decided while others labored, life was a continual and perpetual series of tasks, some more enjoyable than others, but all required for subsistence as subsistence was known to be. With growing commodity production, carried out in corporate settings and geared towards the market, tasks began to be performed not just when and where needed, but to accumulate for future needs or for trade and barter. Especially with the development of vast regional and national markets, the separation of work time from consumption time, or the separation of when commodities were produced versus when they were used, became recognized and socially legitimized phenomena.[7]

Industrialized modern society brought greater specialization, with production increasingly organized in mass quantities. The home(stead) became separated from work(place), a clear separation of the space where family or household matters were practiced from the space where social or public affairs were run.[8] Production (laboring to produce commodities to be exchanged in the market) increasingly became delegated to the public domain, the factory, office, agency, etc. In this domain, the truly "important" matters—rising over and above the mundane individual and family issues—were organized, formulated, and carried out. Increasing numbers of "useful," "creative," and "value producing" activities left the private domain, the home—which was left for the mundane, playful, light, and value-devouring activities of recreation, leisure, and consumption. The people in the private domain did not "work," they rested, played, consumed. Chores to be done at home were frivolous, banal, profane, and worthless. They were unproductive, petty tasks that required no expertise or "knowledge of importance." These meanings were signified mostly through the valuation practices in society, that is, acts which promoted or demoted, rewarded or condemned, dignified or degraded, glorified or oppressed, remunerated or exploited the tasks done, and those who did these tasks, in the private and public domains.

In many cases, actual practices contradicted the rhetoric about the importance of the tasks relegated to the home, mainly because these tasks were essential for the reproduction of labor-power. Thus, women—who had the primary responsibility for household chores—were praised as devoted mothers, loving wives, and caring sisters but this rhetoric did not translate into valuing the work they did. Important things were going on in the public domain. People there were producing, contributing to the economy and the society, to the welfare and wealth of nations. In the public domain people were making decisions that influenced nations, society, humanity. In the private domain people played, and did other insignificant things such as eat, clean, cook, sleep, rear children.

Consumption, activity attributed to the private domain, was considered selfish, solely for the individual or the family. It did not create anything of significant (economic) value for society, and humanity. Its sole purpose was to replenish the individual to carry out the really important, meaningful, and valuable activities in the public domain, for production. Production was creation, it added something of value to human lives. It was, therefore, treated as a sacred activity.[9]

In societies which later formed the western civilizations, women came to occupy primarily the private domain and men the public domain. This, in fact, may have been largely due to many chance occurrences and accidents as evidenced from other cultures that did not specialize in the same way.[10] With time, these accidental occupations were reinforced by the resulting structures. In other societies, the separation of the public and the private did not occur, or women and men occupied the domains in different proportions, or women dominated the public domain.[11] In many such cultures, especially in Africa, the western colonizers—the men who set out on expeditions that started with trade and culminated in conquest—would not recognize the economic centrality of native women and would refuse to deal with them, forcing the native men to take on public roles mirroring those of the colonizers. Thus, traditions that were different from the ascendant and powerful western colonial values were forced to change under colonial pressure.[12]

Following the colonial and mercantilist periods, commodity production exploded and market exchange began to dominate and largely determine all other forms of socioeconomic relations. That is, capitalism entrenched itself as the defining social system of the industrializing societies of western civilization and its colonial outreaches. Categories of gender were constructed on the meanings that were generated from the roles attributed to public and private domains. Given the sex specializations into the two domains, the feminine and the masculine collapsed into female and male respectively. Sex and gender became inseparable. Sex defined the biological qualities but gender afforded them their meanings, roles, values, and status—in short, their culture. Feminine (female) was the consumer: located in the home, the private domain. Masculine (male) was the producer: located in the work-place, the factories, the offices, the political arena, the public domain. Consequently, given the values and meanings attributed to production, masculine qualities were positive in the culture that developed. Males did things that counted in the calculation of national wealth and income. Female activities at home were worthless, consumptive, and economically discounted. Masculine activities in the public domain were worthwhile, and therefore merited payment. Feminine activity at home did not contribute to national income, and therefore did not merit payment.[13]

The female, specifically the female body, became the representation of the feminine which was the "ideal" consumer in western culture. She "went shopping" while he "worked." She spent his money or earnings. Her frivolousness in buying and consuming became a major topic for jokes in the culture. She was such a "consumer" that he had to always restrain her appetite for consumables. In the cultural ecstasy of constructing these mean-ings, the fact that the privacy of the private domain was a sheer myth, an illusion, went unnoticed. Indeed, the structure and forms of what went on in the "private" domain were determined by the politics and culture of the public domain. This determination became more and more forceful as prod-ucts bought in the market played an increasing role in the home, replacing things made at home.[14]

THE MARKET AND THE PUBLIC AND PRIVATE DOMAINS

The separations discussed briefly above, which engendered and entrenched the concept of consumption separate from production, and contributed greatly to the modern concepts of gender and value, were paramount in the formation of the market as we know it in contemporary society. The impor-tance of these separations in the development of modern culture cannot be overemphasized. Without the separations of home and workplace, public and private, work and recreation, the "market" is merely a site—a location, where trade or barter takes place between tribes or communities. The conceptualization of the market as the population of actual and potential customers, consumer units (individuals, households, organizations, etc.) that may span regions, nations, and even continents, can only make sense given such separations.

The market was not instantaneously the focus for activities in the public domain, however, when the separations first occurred. Neither was it the dominating force in legitimizing culture, meanings, values, and socio-economic practice that it is in contemporary society. The primacy of politics and social (kinship) relations continued and did not become subordinated to the market for quite some time. This subordination has increased with the growing transfer of creative activity from the home (private domain) to the socially organized workplace (public domain). As we already discussed, creative activity at home has been increasingly substituted by products bought in the market. Correspondingly, activities such as gardening, weaving, cooking, baking, and knitting—production activities historically performed at home—have diminished and have been substituted by canned foods, ready made clothing, frozen dinners, packaged bread, etc.[15] In a sense, creative labor at home is substituted by "productive" labor in the public domain. This is good, from a capitalist perspective. Labor-power in the public domain is productive; it creates surplus-value, contributes to realization and accumulation of capital and, thereby, to the wealth of nations. The more labor is transferred from the private to the public domain, the more products of labor in the public domain are purchased in the market to substitute labor at home, the healthier becomes the gross national product, and the larger grows the national wealth.

The transfer of labor-power from home to the public domain, however, did not mean that people (women, who primarily occupied the private domain) were always transferred from the private to the public domain. The transfer was in terms of what Marx called abstract labor, not concrete labor. The actual history of this transfer, of course, is much more complex, with women and children being pulled into the factories as cheap labor during the initial phase of the industrial revolution and then returned to the home as "pure" consumers, their labor in the workforce being substituted by machines and male workers as industrialization advanced. The co-optation of "family wages" and other labor demands for benefits into the industrialists' political agenda seems to have had as much to do with the necessity of ensuring mass consumer markets to keep up with growing mass production as it had to do with any benign, humanistic, or progressive political impulses of the industrialists.[16] Indeed, with increasing efficiency of factories, households had to be (re)populated during the daytime in order to have continual consumption to absorb the increasing production capabilities in the public domain. So, while they used more and more products produced in the public domain and channeled through the market, substituting for the productive chores they earlier performed at home, women were simultaneously returned to the private domain in order to "consume" the products.[17] With the growth of industrialization and the necessity to sell more and more products in the market, the character of consumption at home indeed changed, as mentioned earlier, from "productive" to "consumptive" types of activities.

Women, the consumers, returned (forced back?) to the private domain through social policies in industrialized western economies, lived extremely paradoxical lives and confronted paradoxical rhetoric and behaviors. First of all, the so called "private" domain was not private at all. It is the practices in the public domain, in terms of political-legal outcomes, and their consequences, in terms of products for consumer markets, that largely determined life patterns and relationships in the "private" domain. Women's lives were not private by any means. They were, in many respects, the private properties of men. Husbands owned them and all other "assets" in the household.[18] A woman could do little without the man's permission.[19] This happened at the same time that much praise of women went on in public rhetoric. As mothers, especially, women were put on pedestals; for raising the stout sons and looking after their needy men—sending them to glorious wars? Being on a pedestal, women became objects of desire and of voyeuristic gaze, and as consumers they became objects of study in order to increase consumptive activities at home.[20]

Other paradoxical circumstances in the private domain were perhaps more telling in terms of consumption culture. While women were praised for undertaking their important social tasks of childrearing and taking care of men, they were belittled for being consumers. Consuming, after all, was valueless; a profane and banal act. But, if they did not consume, their prudence would stunt the expansion of the market and, therefore, limit the wealth (read as capital accumulation) of the nation. They were criticized, made fun of, devalued for being "consumers"; and yet, if they were not "good consumers" they hurt national economic growth. This contradiction in rhetoric and economy has produced much paradoxical indoctrination of women as consumers. They have been given contradictory signals regarding what they ought to be, how they should look, and more recently, the images they should represent.[21] To a large extent, such contradictory signals— although unleashed disproportionately on women—seem to be an inevitable part of the general state of being a "consumer" in modern society. Thus, the consumer is fickle, frivolous, and faddish; yet a drop in consumers' buying activity, or even a dip in consumer confidence, can send a contemporary advanced economy into a tailspin.

Modern society, while predicated on the premise of improving the lives of "knowing" human subjects by controlling nature through scientific technologies, nevertheless imposed much responsibility upon its consumers (the subjects). They had to keep up with the times and insure the health of the economy through their prudent yet ever-increasing consumption. According to the diagnosis of the pre-Second World War era offered by Keynesian economics, the producers of modern society were doing well, improving their mass-production capabilities and expanding the economic base. Consumption, however, had difficulty catching up. Consumers needed guidance and incentives. Demand needed to be spurred to catch up with supply capacities. With government aid and active entrepreneurship on the part of marketing organizations and financial institutions, structures were developed to perform the tasks of guiding consumer expenditures and increasing demand. Especially following the Second World War, the media and other cultural agencies joined in this effort full-force to institute a culture of consumption. Techniques of marketing and advertising were honed and fine-tuned and, in the field of business as well as in fields that aspired to be businesslike, listening to the voice of the consumer was made into a religion.[22] The following two chapters provide an insight into this culture of consumption and its modern structures which constructed the consumption patterns we discussed earlier.

4 Consumption in modern society

The model of a consumer in modern society was of an individual who had needs, seeking to satisfy them in some rational order to improve his/her quality of life. Modernity made this quest for quality of life a central one, turning it into *the* project of modern society. Improving human lives by harnessing nature in the service of human needs through scientific technologies was a leitmotif of modernity. In many ways, then, the modernist project was a marketing project as modern marketing has come to be defined: Find out the needs of the markets (actual and potential consumer segments) and provide for these needs using the most efficient and advanced scientific technologies of product development, communications, promotion, distribution, and pricing.

Needs, therefore, were central to modern society. Despite this centrality, needs, specifically their genesis and transformation, have not been made the focus of study in any discipline. Rather, even including consumer research and marketing— disciplines for which the consumer is central— all social science disciplines have pretty much taken needs for granted. That is, needs have come to be considered largely as given, as well expressed in Abraham Maslow's hierarchy of needs, widely used and accepted in mainstream western social science literatures.[1] Even when the impact on needs of social and economic organization of human society is recognized, the genesis and transformation of needs have not been made the focus of study. A reading of the literatures in social sciences seems to indicate that the reason for this lack of interest is the rather common assumption, which largely goes unsaid, that needs are derived from human nature, a rather stable phenomenon. What changes with changing social and economic organization of society, therefore, is not the essence or content of the need but its appearance or form. Such dualistic, binary categorizations, such as essence versus appearance and content versus form, very prominent in modernist thought and rhetoric, enabled formulations of stability and change to coexist, as well as enabling other resolutions of paradoxical circumstances in modern discourse. We shall address this character of modern discourse in later chapters. For now, let it suffice to say that, generally, mainstream modern social science, including the applied fields of marketing and consumer research, worked with the assumption that needs were universal, given, and stable.

Needs arose from the nature of human physiology and psychology, generally considered to be more common than different across segments of humanity. In modern society, humans were considered to have higher purposes to be achieved through hard work and perseverance, that is, through productive endeavor and creative action. Humans had the intelligence, and the insight and wisdom, to conceptualize and seek such higher purposes; both material and spiritual. The human being was, therefore, the subject, the one who acted upon other things. As such, s/he deserved to lead an improved, better life where s/he was physiologically and psychologically well maintained, nourished and nurtured, to allow the pursuit of higher purposes. This maintenance was consumption's domain, the pursuit of higher purposes being the domain of production. Relative to production, modernity assigned consumption a subservient, supporting role.

As such, in disciplines such as consumer research and marketing, the basic problematic was one of how consumers in different cultures, societies, and market segments chose among alternative offerings (product categories, brands) to satisfy their needs. Specifically in economics and in marketing, various models were developed to try and explain consumer behavior in terms of making such choices among need-fulfilling alternative offerings.

NEEDS AND WANTS: THE CLASSICAL MODEL

Especially in economics, a major issue was the allocation of resources to the development of alternatives to satisfy different needs. That is, answers were sought to the question: Which needs, and which alternatives to satisfy these needs, would (or should) get priority in society? Here again, the assumption that human needs were inherent to human nature played a role in the structures of the models. Need is internal to the individual, it was believed, and unless one perceived or felt the need one would not seek to satisfy it.[2]

As a result, resources could only be allocated to those needs which were perceived and for which satisfaction was actively sought. In a market economy, the expression of seeking need satisfaction is found in buying power, or effective demand, and unless a production unit supplies what is effectively demanded in the market, it is bound to lose its livelihood, for it will not be able to sell its products and, thereby, collect funds for further production. As long as the individual is assumed to be the source of needs, this is a logically consistent argument. Based on this premise, the appearance of new needs in an individual was attributed to the satisfaction of more basic needs such as, in terms of Maslow's hierarchy, physiological needs. In an affluent society, where the basic needs have been largely satisfied, individual consumers seek to satisfy "higher order" needs. The environment acts as a constraint or stimulus, but not as a determinant of needs.[3] Whatever need is felt is the result of innate processes, although the stimulant may be an environmental condition.

Here it may be useful to discuss the distinction made between needs and wants. In modern philosophy needs are thought to be more closely related to physiology, whereas wants are viewed as more closely related to the cultural environment. As Philip Kotler, one of the foremost marketing scholars, puts it:

> People require food, clothing, shelter, safety, belonging, esteem, and a few other things for survival. These needs are not created by their society or by marketers; they exist in the very texture of human biology and the human condition. . . . While people's needs are few, their wants are many. Human wants are continually shaped and reshaped by social forces and institutions, such as churches, schools, families, and business corporations.[4]

The usefulness of this distinction between needs and wants becomes somewhat fuzzy when the issue is considered from the point of view of the individual consumer. When a consumer prefers to travel or buy expensive, high fashion clothing items instead of fulfilling the "need" to eat required amounts of nutritive food, and this consumer's actual consumption behavior reflects this preference, can we say that this person has consumed what s/he does not need? Or, are we to accept that for this consumer the "need" to travel and wear fancy clothes was greater than the "need" for "required" amounts of nutritive food? Even further, are we to say, as one often hears, that what we have here is an "irrational" consumer, one who puts wants before needs?

One cannot help but recall a televised interview in which a rather fashionably dressed young woman was telling the correspondent on the program that she regularly had to go without one of the two basic meals about five or six days a week. She just did not have enough money. As she was saying this, viewers could not help but notice how well groomed she was, her heavy use of cosmetics, and her pretty leather jacket and her designer jeans and purse. Observing the same, the correspondent inquired how she could afford all that if she could not afford adequate food. Her response was, indeed, telling. She informed us that had she not consumed those seemingly extravagant items she would have been unable to hold down the job that provided her at least her one meal of the day. Given recent episodes, such as the case of a news anchorwoman on a Kansas television station who was fired because she did not fit the image of a "good-looking" woman, could we fault the young woman's reasoning? When bread and beauty aids become competing and complementary consumption items in the game of survival, it is hard to categorize one as satisfying a "need" and the other a "want."

The simple but important conclusion is that the macro rationale (the rationale that is accepted and imposed by those who assume a detached perspective on the situation and assess it according to so-called "objective" criteria) is in contradiction with the micro rationale (the rationale of the individual consumer living in the situation). As long as what is a want, according to the macro rationale, is preferred and traded over what, according to the same rationale, is a need during the actual consumption of a consumer, we cannot make a clear-cut distinction between wants and needs. Therefore, in this book we shall use the terms needs and wants interchangeably, and accept the fact that they are transformed both in kind and in priority across time and socioeconomic contexts.

CLASSICAL MODELS OF CONSUMPTION

As we already mentioned, however, classical modernist models of consumption assumed needs to be innate and not transforming in essence. To set the stage for the discussion of the social construction of consumption patterns, let us first discuss briefly how some important questions of consumer choice were answered within this classical framework. Given the variety and abundance of needs in society, the question arose as to which needs would be satisfied. Earlier it was pointed out that in a market economy consumers express their needs in the market by exerting pressure on the suppliers through their choices in the marketplace, buying what they perceive to be good satisfiers of their needs and not buying what they don't need. Here we observe *consumer sovereignty*. The market serves the needs of the consumer through mechanisms of competition. This philosophy of consumer sovereignty is derived from the classical economics framework of perfect competition. Although certain imperfections have been observed in actuality, and theories of monopolistic and oligopolistic competition have been developed, the basic assumptions of consumer sovereignty and the belief "that economic activity is directed to and by human wants and needs" still stand.[5] Two questions arise: (1) What if consumers feel a need for something that is not already available?, and (2) What happens when some consumers have greater buying power than others and, therefore, their demands are more *effective* in the market? The second question is especially important when consumers' needs are not homogeneous, and when conflicting needs and interests are present.

The answer to the first question within the mainstream philosophical framework is the innovative entrepreneur who is receptive to consumer needs and has the right antennae. Innovative entrepreneurs work on products for which expressed needs or effective demand do not exist. Many fail, but the few who succeed keep the wheel of technological change rolling.[6] The "marketing concept"—managing an organization so as to meet consumer needs and deliver consumer satisfactions in a cost-efficient, profit-maximizing manner—is the marketing interpretation of this entrepreneurial function in society.[7] When this function is performed correctly, the productive organization of the innovative entrepreneur creates and supplies the best commodity to satisfy consumer needs, and thereby achieves the best returns. Consumers, being fully informed about the market, buy this commodity. Competing producers, again fully informed, try to match this product or service. Of course, there is a trade-off between the quality of need satisfaction and price. Still, through perfect, or close-to-perfect competition, consumers are able to get the commodities they need at a reasonable (normal) rate above the cost to the producer.

The cost (or price) structure is a basic part of economic thought. According to this frame of thought, a new commodity competes for the consumer's budget on the basis of its price, or "cost" to the consumer. The new and more satisfying commodity will be selected by a consumer only if the additional cost to the consumer is not higher than the cost of the satisfactions forgone because of the sacrifices made from other consumption.[8] For example, a torrent of new information technology products and services started entering the market in the 1990s. The selected group of successful products and services were those that the consumers were willing to accommodate in their discretionary budgets. The concept of cost is used in explaining the choices made in the market. In social sciences other than economics, an effort is made to incorporate costs other than economic costs, such as psychological and social costs, to better explain choice behavior and structures. Economists have also made some attempts to incorporate social costs into the framework through the concept of external economies and external costs, but difficulties arise in the measurement of these external and social costs.[9]

Although the cost structure is an important factor in choices among different patterns of consumption, what lies at the base of it is the preference structure, and consequently, the *perception* of costs by the consumers. Through the development of need perceptions within a culture, a commodity which has high social and economic costs may very well have acquired an inelastic demand[10] and, therefore, may still be chosen by the consumers—as in the case of the automobile.[11] The perceived costs of *not* having such a commodity may be far higher than the perceived costs of acquiring and maintaining it.

One answer to the second question—What happens when some consumers have greater buying power than others?—has been provided by Pareto, a leading economist of the neo-classical school. In his discussion of the *Pareto optima*, he showed that some consumers can reach optimum points that define higher satisfactions (or welfare) than others. Pareto argued that as long as none of the consumers was *worse* off than before, it is economically and socially desirable to move towards the point where resource allocation is efficient, even if this resulted in some of the consumers being better off than before. However, an efficient utilization of resources, or "allocative efficiency," is not sensitive to the consideration of a socially desirable income distribution. That is:

> A competitive equilibrium, even if it is also a Pareto optimum, may involve a more unequal distribution of income than is regarded as desirable from a social point of view.[12]

The logical conclusion to be drawn from this is that although from a naive economic standpoint an allocative efficiency is reached, the Pareto optimum may be highly inefficient from a social, political, and public policy perspective. Furthermore, economic efficiency is measured in terms of certain specific criteria which need not be, and according to different schools of thought indeed are not, the only criteria that could be considered.[13] According to alternative criteria even economic efficiency may not be obtained, or a new Pareto optimum may have to be found. The only certain criterion to which classical economics adheres is the criterion of capital accumulation. That is, only economies of capital are considered.

When affluent consumers (who generally also have relatively higher levels of satisfaction) have sufficient buying power to support the production of the patterns they have a preference for, they can influence greatly the structure of available alternatives in the economy. In the 1935–1936 Consumer Expenditures Survey in the United States, for example, it was found that the upper third of the households with highest incomes accounted for 50–75 percent of purchases in different consumption categories such as food, housing, clothing and transportation.[14] This might be a rough indication of such influential buying power by the upper income groups. Although there seems to have been a redistribution of income since then, in the 1960–1961 Consumer Expenditures and Income Survey 37.3 percent of the households with the highest incomes still accounted for 51 percent of the total ultimate consumption market. This percentage is higher in the discretionary consumption categories, which grow at rates higher than basic consumption categories.

Pareto's suggestion raises the question of power in the marketplace, with the possibility of a privileged, affluent group of consumers controlling the innovations because they have the discretionary incomes that can be allocated to (and risked in) new patterns of consumption. Other consumers with lower incomes are usually just catching up with and maintaining the contemporary dominant pattern of consumption.[15] Therefore, buying power seems to affect the *structure of available alternatives for consumption* in the economy.

It may be important, as we introduce the concept of the structure of available alternatives for consumption, to mention that it expresses more than the mere availability of certain consumption alternatives. The term "structure" contained in this concept posits that there are relationships among the alternatives available for consumption. These are significant relations that the consumption alternatives have with each other. Among others, they include relations in terms of complementarity, higher or lower visibility, varying degrees of importance to living standards as signified in the culture, and costs of acquisition. Thus, the concept of the structure of available alternatives for consumption involves the *meanings* that relate the alternatives to each other, to the culture, and to consumer values which in turn influence choices that consumers make for consumption. This is important because it is all these meanings that render the structure of available alternatives for consumption to become a part of the environment to which a consumer's need and desire formation is subject.

Economic models of consumption have rarely included variables other than costs and utility—utility being defined rather strictly in terms of satisfaction of physiological necessities, and costs in terms of prices. Attempts at inclusion of social costs and community benefits have been admired but largely neglected.[16] Disciplines other than economics, such as sociology, anthropology, psychology, social psychology, consumer behavior, and marketing have been more fertile grounds for exploring other variables. Sociology, for example, has provided insights in terms of reference groups and conspicuous consumption claimed to be rising out of the desires to fit in or be different. Psychology has provided insights into the workings of the subconscious and the emotional states, especially the fears and joys which tend to impact heavily on consumption choices. Consumer behavior discipline has tried to present integrative frameworks to provide multifaceted explanations of consumption choices.[17]

From these contributions from various disciplines we know that consumers behave not only in ways which minimize economic costs while maximizing economic utility (i.e. they are not purely a *homo economicus*), but that psychological and other factors also enter into their decisions of consumption. Yet, although the rationale for consumption has been thus enlarged and made more "real," it is still an individual rationale. That is, in mainstream philosophies the individual consumer is still the source of needs. Perceiving these needs, the consumer is still searching for maximization of utilities and minimization of costs, this time not only economic, but also psychological, social and cultural utilities and costs as well. The consumer still has a rationale but now one that is much more complex than a simple economic rationale.

As more and more variables enter the process of decision-making, but consumer needs and consumption patterns still remain unexplained, we ought to become skeptical of an individual rationale and wonder about the extent to which outside factors influence the perceptions of individual consumers about the utilities and costs of different consumption patterns, products, and brands. This takes us back to the question of *subjection*. Does the moving force in the determination of human needs lie within the human being, with the social, political, economic, and cultural environment acting as a set of constraints and stimulants, or is this environment a determining force, determining not only what needs the consumers will perceive, but also how they will satisfy these needs, specifically, from our point of interest, in terms of consumption patterns?

There have been observations which tend to support the case that the structure of available alternatives for consumption in society is not only a result of the need structures of consumers and their buying power, but also a determinant of need perceptions.[18] A good example of the dependency of preference patterns on the structure of available alternatives occurred in

Canada when a strike caused a change in the structure of postal services. When the strike ended, a number of consumers did not return to their earlier patterns of usage because the change in the structure of available alternatives during the strike had enabled them to recognize feasible substitutes for services heavily used before the strike.[19] Another example of the impact that the structure of available alternatives has on the preference and need perceptions can be found in the energy crisis which occurred in the United States as well as in other parts of the world during the early 1970s. When the shortage first started, some consumption effects (such as a switch to smaller cars, better maintenance of cars, and some limited car pooling) occurred, but they were minor. Despite significant price changes, changes in behaviors of usage of transportation alternatives did not follow. This is because changes in the *structure of available alternatives* did not follow the oil shortages; a situation different from the Canadian postal strike. Consequently, almost as soon as the shortage seemed to be over, there was a return to earlier levels of consumption (somewhat bigger cars, neglect of maintenance, and abandonment of car pooling) although the price of energy was now much higher. This seems to have occurred because of the scarcity of available and feasible alternatives in the socioeconomic system.

Conventional models of choice seem to have oversimplified the character of influences on human need perceptions and desires by largely assuming that needs are in the nature of the human. As well exemplified also by Schmookler,[20] this is indeed an assumption that suppresses the complexity and reality of how individuals tend to make choices in contemporary society. As we shall further explore in the next chapter, the culture and conditions encountered by individuals in society, well represented in the structure of available alternatives for consumption, are as important, if not more important, determinants not only of how needs are satisfied, but how they are constructed and recognized.

It can be said, then, that despite some attempts to enlarge the foundation of influences upon consumer choice, the mainstream model of consumer choice in modern science, one derived from classical and neo-classical economics and enlarged by other social sciences, has largely continued to work with the basic assumptions discussed above:

1 the consumer comes to the market with a set of needs given by her/his nature and constrained by the nature of the economic environment;
2 the innovative entrepreneur in the marketplace senses these needs and puts together creative packages at attractive prices to satisfy them;
3 the consumer makes choices from among the alternatives so provided; and
4 as long as no one is worse off, increasing consumption by the affluent increases overall social well-being.

DEVIATIONS FROM THE CLASSICAL MODEL

There have been deviations from the above classical model of consumption. These deviations differ in their degree of rejection of the basic assumptions listed. Some largely accept the assumptions but point out conditions which hinder their effective operation. Others go as far as rejecting the basic assumptions of the classical model completely. For the sake of simplicity and brevity let us discuss these as non-radical deviations and radical deviations.

Non-radical deviations

Three models that do not radically deviate from the classical explanations of consumption are the Naderian consumerism, the Veblenian, and the Galbraithian models. In some ways all three take off from the issue of differential power in the marketplace. The consumerist model, brought into prominence by the work of consumer advocate and activist Ralph Nader,[21] raises the issue of power differentials in terms of the inequality of power between buyers and sellers (or consumers and marketing organizations, especially big business). Several authors perceive that the consumer protection movement was a consequence of unequal power between buyers and sellers.[22]

The consumerist model has been interested mostly in deceptive promotional (especially advertising), pricing, and packaging practices by producers and distributors as well as low quality, unsafe, and unreliable products.[23] In their approach to these problems, consumerists usually do not make any discrimination among consumers along the lines of income, social status, and other differences. Their basic discrimination is between sellers (producers and distributors) and buyers (consumers). The consumerist model does not disagree with the basic philosophical assumption of consumer sovereignty, but it blames imperfect competitive conditions for not allowing this sovereignty to be at an ideal level. Because of imperfect competition, consumers partly lose their ability to communicate their needs to the producers, as well as their ability to audit the institutions which theoretically still serve them. Therefore, although these institutions cater to the needs of consumers, they can get away with shoddy products and services as a result of imperfect and/or deceptive information flows. The consumerist view has influenced public policy in the United States and elsewhere, leading to consumer protection legislation in areas such as product safety, truth in advertising, and truth in packaging.[24] By preventing the power balance from tilting too far towards the side of the seller, consumerism has provided an important safety valve for capitalism.[25]

Deviations from the classical assumptions underlying consumption models which were more substantive yet have had some contemporary impact on conventional social science approaches are found in the works of

Thorstein Veblen and John Kenneth Galbraith.[26] Veblen, rather than analyzing the formation of consumption patterns, was interested in the impact that the consumption activities of what he called the "leisure class" (wealthy and high income strata) had on other strata of society. He argued that through emulation the lower strata acquired the consumption patterns of the leisure class. If this is so, then individual determination of need perceptions is not true for the lower strata, because they acquire the needs of the upper strata. But what is the mechanism by which the need perceptions of upper stratum consumers are determined? Veblen's work does not provide an answer to this question. We return to this issue in the next chapter.

Galbraith, not making the distinction between upper and lower social strata in society, claimed that the producers were in the driver's seat: they were the determinant actors in the process of need formation.[27] Galbraith has been a strong influence in the discussion of corporate power in the United States. In an address to the American Economic Society, he pointed out the importance of including power in economic analysis:

> The decisive weakness in neoclassical and neo-Keynesian economics is not the assumptions by which it elides the problem of power. The capacity for erroneous belief is very great, especially where it coincides with convenience. Rather in eliding power—in making economics a nonpolitical subject—neoclassical theory, by the same process, destroys its relation with the real world.[28]

Galbraith argued that the power of corporations in the marketplace is not only a decider in the mechanism of price, but that through this power, corporations create the need for their products. That is, supply creates its own demand, instead of the conventional logic of demand creating supply.

According to Galbraith, the power of the producers—or more precisely the power of big corporations—comes from their size and their control over economic resources and information sources such as the communication media. Their control over the economic resources also provides them with political clout and influence over government policies. Thus, big corporations, and the technostructure which runs them, become the *de facto* social planners in the economy. They control demand indirectly through their influence on government policies and directly through marketing practices, such as advertising and sales promotion.[29] In this way, rather than producing products that meet consumer needs, they create needs for their products through the management of demand, and manipulation of need perceptions.

Galbraith also argued that consumer demand is controlled by the relationships that products in the marketplace have with one another. Adoption of certain products both necessitate and facilitate adoption of others. That is, products come with a system of their own. Having an automobile, for example, means that the consumer has also adopted directly a system of gas stations, automobile accessories (such as tires, seat covers and wipers), highway and road systems, but also indirectly, suburban housing, parking structures, air conditioning, etc.

Galbraith's arguments continue to find supporters in various disciplines. Several studies have recently investigated the influence of giant corporations in the field of communication and their impacts on cultural values. Studies such as Herbert Schiller's examination[30] of mergers among giant corporations which produce cultural products (films, magazines, etc.), tend to show how the commercial requirements of business influence and commercialize the consumption of cultural icons (Mickey Mouse, for example) and, in general, values that impact upon the meanings of life and consumption.[31]

These arguments have been challenged by conventional economists, business people, and marketers. The manipulative power of advertising, in the sense of creating needs that are not already latent, is still under discussion. Large corporations' control over government has also been questioned but more and more examples that support this control arise. Specific examples that could be given are the influence of the oil (or energy) companies on governments' energy programs, and the ability of steel and automobile industries to stand against and change environmental policies of the United States government.[32]

Other similar arguments, which have not had as large an impact as those of Veblen, Galbraith, and Nader, can also be found in the literature. Potter and Packard have separately argued that corporations have become powers which control consumer tastes.[33] Caplovitz, in his studies of shopping patterns of the inner-city poor, has examined the processes through which consumers are forced to pay more for commodities which represent the wealthier consumers' patterns of consumption that the poor emulate.[34] He explains the emulation in terms of "compensatory consumption" in which the poor compensate for blocked social mobility through the purchase of material goods. He goes on to say:

> The low-income consumer is trained by society (and his position in it) to want the symbols and appurtenances of the "good life" at the same time that he lacks the means needed to fulfill these socially induced wants.[35]

Duesenberry is another scholar who has presented consumption and savings in terms of interdependencies among individual consumers.[36] Following Duesenberry, Brady was able to demonstrate that consumption is a function of the income level of the community in which the consumption unit resides.[37] These works tend to discredit assumptions of independence in need perceptions and consumption choices. Duesenberry has also mentioned the presence of certain value judgements prevalent in US society, such as the goal of a rising standard of living, the desirability and importance of consuming high quality goods, etc., which contribute to the determination of consumption patterns. More radical departures from the classical models of consumption build upon this recognition of interdependence of need perceptions to further propose the origins of major influences on consumer choices.

Some radical departures from the classical consumption model

The most important radical departure from the classical model of consumption is the marxian model. Marx's model is clearly based on class analysis.[38] The differences in power regarding determination of what is to be produced among different classes play a very important role in the marxian model. Especially significant are the differences between the bourgeoisie (capitalist class) and the proletariat (working class), tied largely to ownership of capital and, thereby, to access to disposable incomes. While Marx and marxists have not much elaborated consumption issues, the following seems to represent the logic of marxian analysis extended to the domain of consumption. Capitalists control much of what will be available for consumption through their control of decisions as to what will be produced in the factories and lands they own, through their substantial personal expenditures for consumption from their large disposable incomes, and through the many ways they can influence state policies and expenditures. Domination through all such avenues enables them to be the trend setters in consumption.

Two issues are of interest regarding the above brief summary of the marxian framework on consumption. One is that Marx did not necessarily see the capitalist class in total control of things despite the fact that he saw it as the major instrument of capitalism, running its course. That is, the capitalist class was the main believer in and defender of the interests of capital. Capitalists clearly benefited from the maintenance and flourishing of these interests, mostly to the detriment of other classes, especially the working class. The capitalists themselves, however, were also ruled by the economics of capital; in a way they were servants of capital. Thus, the economic and social structures which guided consumption in capitalism were determined by the material conditions of the realization and accumulation of capital. The ideology of the capitalist class that ruled the political, economic, and social life in capitalist society was itself determined by these conditions and simply reflected the rationale for and the interests of capitalist growth.

The second issue of interest is that the marxian analyses seem to hold onto the idea that there are some natural qualities to being human while recognizing the possibilities that such qualities may be distorted by the socioeconomic systems and ideologies (such as that of capitalism) which are antithetical to these qualities. Consequently, the system may alienate human beings from these natural qualities to the detriment of humanity. Marx argued, for example, that workers were alienated from the products of their own labor because, despite the fact that the values of these products were created by the sweat of their labor, it was not the workers but the capitalists who appropriated this value. Furthermore, what was to be produced was not decided or controlled by the primary producers (the workers) but by those who owned the capital (the capitalists), an idle class which exploited the true producers by virtue of its ownership of capital. In these capitalist relationships (relations of production) lay the foundations of both exploitation and alienation.

Marxian analysis was a powerful and insightful one, both conceptually and politically, moving masses to action in order to stop the claimed alienation and the exploitation. Therefore, the capitalist class and its intelligentsia developed counter-arguments and organizational methods as well as engaged in military and political actions to counter the tide. Much of the conceptual defense relied on the idea of the creative entrepreneur who sensed the needs of the market, worked hard and took risks, financial and otherwise, to develop and organize the resources which would allow production of products for these needs. Without such entrepreneurial effort, the products to satisfy the needs of society would not be produced. Without entrepreneurship, new economic activity (vitality) would not be created which enabled a better standard of living for many, including the workers who found employment in this activity. So, these theoreticians argued, the entrepreneuring capitalist deserved a big piece of the pie, the capitalist was not an exploiter but a deserving shareholder in the wealth created.[39] Even in spawning massive counter-arguments, marxian analysis achieved a theoretical opening. It necessitated a recognition of classes and power differentials among social and economic groups and thereby enabled the inclusion of these important factors in the theoretical models.

While Marx and most marxists did not, as we mentioned earlier, directly discuss issues of consumption, marxian analyses have inspired other, not necessarily marxist but still radical, departures from classical consumption models. Maybe the most important and relatively contemporary departures are the theories developed by Simmel, Barthes, Bourdieu, and Baudrillard. For Marx and orthodox marxists, consumption was basically a determined domain, determined by the conditions of relations of production. The major difference between the works of Simmel, Bourdieu, and Baudrillard versus mainstream marxian analyses is that these recent works, while informed by marxism, nevertheless argue that consumption plays a very important part in the determination of human life. According to these thinkers, consumption is not only determined by other factors, but is also an important determinant of socioeconomic relationships in society.

We will articulate these theories very briefly here, since implications of these theories will inform discussions in the rest of this book. Simmel argued that consumption constituted the process in which human beings (consumers) became cultivated (cultured) individuals. It was consumption that enabled the consumers to attach meanings to and act upon the objects in their world. Thus, consumption determined much of their values and experiences regarding life and being.[40] Barthes further problematized the whole notion of true and false needs through introducing the concept of the symbolic code of consumption.[41] According to him, consumption has two aspects: it satisfies needs but it is also embedded within the social, cultural and symbolic structures. Satisfaction of needs cannot be separated from the symbolic meanings of commodities and consumption activities; what Barthes called "significations." Consumption is, thus, embedded in systems of signification, in making and maintaining distinctions. Bourdieu's theory, taking the structures of signification to new dimensions, indicates that "structurations,"[42] construct the social "reality" for the human being through processes that are crucially determined by the economic, which, in turn, has to be mediated by the symbolic. As a result of structuration, then, consumer tastes develop by being socially, not privately, determined. These tastes, as much constructed by consumption experiences as by the economic condition, reflect and represent a symbolic hierarchy which further determines consumption choices. Bourdieu argues that through these processes of structuration and determination, classes and distinctions in society are constructed. The struggles for symbolic appropriation among the classes create what some may call "overdetermination." That is, material structures may greatly determine the actions and practices of social classes, but, in turn, members of the social classes have some room to improvise and, thereby, affect and transform structures.

While recognizing and articulating the influences of consumption on human life, its meaning(s) and direction(s), thereby rejecting the solely production-oriented explanation of how human society is organized and consumption choices are determined, Simmel's and Bourdieu's theories may be interpreted as belonging to the structuralist social science school, because structures play the crucial role in determinations of consumption, preferences, tastes, and styles. Baudrillard, on the other hand, is a representative of poststructuralist, postmodernist thought,[43] especially in his later works. In his earlier works, he was informed by a marxist orientation, but later he thoroughly rejected marxist theory, and with it the determining role of structures. While at first he argued that a system of objects and their functional rationale largely determined consumer meanings and choices, later he abandoned both the possibility of an innate human nature and the idea that any structure, material or otherwise, exists and determines things. His later work explores human society in terms of simulacra (symbolically signified set of simulations) and nothing else. We shall discuss Baudrillard and his ideas at greater length later in our examinations of postmodern consumption.

The radical departures from the classical models of consumption briefly reviewed above have re-established the complex nature of human needs, desires and consumption in scientific discourse by challenging the unrealistic assumptions of the classical models we have discussed earlier in this chapter. It was a difficult task, given the influence of classical and neoclassical economics on social science disciplines that have human behavior as a core subject matter, to challenge these assumptions. Quite interestingly, members of these disciplines have found it politically necessary to maintain the idea that the human subjects are independent in their actions while, at the same time, they have continued studying the human subjects with the purpose of increasing the influences on them in order to improve their behaviors to be more *rational*, or, in some cases, to be more susceptible toward certain points of view.

On the whole, both the classical model of consumption and the more conventional deviations from it were inadequate in representing the complexity of the foundations of human consumption by

(a) not problematizing human needs (that is, in assuming that they were innate and physiological);
(b) not taking into consideration the power differentials among consumer classes;
(c) not sufficiently recognizing the role of social structures and dynamics in the determination of consumption tastes and choices; and
(d) not articulating the important impacts of the different roles the human being plays as a consumer and producer, and the interaction between these roles.

The next chapter will discuss how consumption was socially constructed in modern society, by trying to recognize the complexities through integrating some of the important insights contributed by all of the theories of consumption briefly discussed in this chapter.

5 The social construction of consumption patterns in modern society

Let us begin with some simple but meaningful facts about consumption under any circumstances. What do or can people consume in a society? People can consume what is available for consumption, within the limits of their resources. To consume anything that is not already available for consumption, they have to be able to visualize or imagine what it could be. People would have to initiate processes whereby such imagined things could be produced or made available; they would have to innovate. This process could take several forms. A consumer could self-produce what s/he wishes to consume, have others produce it, or organize a combined productive effort with others.

If we were dealing with a simple subsistence economy, the issues of production and consumption would be correspondingly simple. The forms of production, how they are initiated and completed, who does what, and who gets what, would be much simpler and easier to follow than in a complex, hyperindustrial economy. When we are dealing with a huge economy with many players and layers, and many different forms of institutionalized operators and organizations, the understanding and description of the processes get very complex. One thing remains unchanged, however. People can only consume either what is already available in society or find means of developing new consumables.

THE STRUCTURE OF CHOICE

In a large economy where a very large portion of what we consume is not what we produce ourselves but what we can obtain or acquire, the importance of the *structure of available alternatives for consumption*[1] is clear. In order to carry on our day-to-day existence we, the consumers, have to acquire many things. Much of this acquisition begins to take on routine characteristics where we do not (re)consider our options and what else could be possible, but just select from among what is already there. Rarely do we spend time thinking and planning new ways and means of maintaining our teeth, for example. For most of us, it is just a matter of acquiring toothbrushes and toothpastes, and maybe dental floss. That is what has become the acceptable means of dental care, those are the consumption items available for dental care, and that is what most of us will consider. We just do not have the time, energy, willingness, and information to consider what alternatives now *un*available could be there.[2] As a result, for a very large portion of our consumption lives, our horizons are limited by the consumption alternatives that are already available.

There may be times when we wish we had alternatives other than what is available. Consider, for example, that you are living in Phoenix, Arizona—in 1997 the eighth most populated metropolitan area in the United States. You wake up in the morning and need to go to work. Let's assume that you wish that you could take a short walk to the corner of the block you live on to get public transportation (preferably a fast, quiet train) to work, find a newsstand and a nice coffee shop on your way to the train stop and get a newspaper that has good coverage of East European news and analysis, and your favorite blend of Costa Rican coffee. These may be your wishes, but the options to satisfy these wishes do not exist. What do you do? You do what is *reasonably* available: get in your car, grab a donut and tasteless coffee, and *drive* to work. The newspaper has to wait for later in the day. Consequently, you end up consuming private cars, gasoline, roads and highways for such private transportation, and, occasionally, services for car repairs and maintenance. You contribute to the sales of such things and your expenditures get counted as choices you have made, as *your choices*. But are they really your choices, or are they merely indicative of *your preferences among what is available*? Clearly, it is the latter, but they can easily be *mis*read as your choices, since you have no practical way of making your *wished-for* choices known. You would have to initiate some drawn-out political process or some promotional campaign, or some such action that would be involved and costly (economically, socially, psychologically) to make your *wished-for* choices known and perhaps, eventually, if the stars are right, your wished-for choices may be available.

How many of us can afford to engage in such committed (and probably hopeless) political struggle, and for how many of our wished-for consumption options, during a lifetime? Let's face it: the logical course for the vast majority of us is to buy into the fable of free choice and to consume what is available. In a developed modern economy, therefore, where each individual is involved in many, many different consumption situations, the potential for any individual consumer to influence the structure of available alternatives for consumption that s/he encounters is very low indeed. Under the circumstances, choice is limited to selecting from among those alternatives that are already available. We may find that there is quite a range of choice among brands in a highly developed market economy. Yet, when it comes to consumption patterns, the choice tends to be highly restricted. While one may choose among many different brands and models of automobiles, the choice among modes of transportation—private automobile versus public transportation, for example—is rarely available, especially in a highly developed market economy, such as the Unites States. The structure of available alternatives for consumption has developed such that it has greatly suppressed choice at the level of patterns of consumption. In fact, a cynical definition of development could be "a great proliferation in the choice among brands at the expense of a progressive restriction of the available patterns of consumption."

If individual influence upon the structure of available alternatives for consumption is so limited, how has this structure developed in modern society in the first place, and what forces have acted or can act upon it to change it? Understanding the formation of choice and the structure of consumption patterns in modern society requires an investigation into the historical transformation of the structure of available alternatives for consumption.

Currently, in the economies of advanced nations, consumers encounter an enormous range of products and brands. The production and distribution of these products require huge amounts of time, energy, and material resources. This is quite different from times, that we can now only imagine, when a small consumer community gathered, hunted, or raised whatever it needed for immediate consumption, and perhaps for the very near future. While such a system clearly must have had its complexities for the people who lived through it, and while even then there were limitations to choice— some will argue that choice was much more limited then—the complexities of contemporary national economies far outstrip the complexities of such primitive[3] economies. How decisions get made as to what will be produced and how these decisions are put into practice to produce and distribute an almost infinite number of products across a country, indeed the world, is truly a wondrous phenomenon. Yet, these decisions do get made and the resources that nature has made available to us as well as the resources that human society has created do get allocated to make certain things available for consumption. How did it all start?

Whatever history we provide regarding how it all started is, surely, biased. We really do not know how it all got started. Given a very limited amount of historical evidence, clearly biased—by those who kept the records and by those for whom they were kept—we develop stories that seem most plausible given our own biases influenced by our own conditions of existence. In essence, therefore, we construct myths about our history and current situation(s) which enable us to survive the circumstances we encounter. The (hi)story of modern society, therefore, is no different. Possibly, the most distinguishing quality of modern society is, however, the amount of trust and faith it puts in its ability to expand its material resources.[4] Consequently, this accumulation of material resources and products is what one needs to understand most in order to comprehend modern society on its own terms.

Indeed, the structure of available alternatives for consumption today is largely what has been produced through the social organization of humanity, not what Earth's nature provided for us. Even the Earth's nature is constantly being shaped by what has been socially produced. In any event, what is interesting to us is not what was available *by nature* but what is made available from it, and the uses to which what is available—by nature or by culture—is put, for purposes of consumption. After all, as we shall discuss further in later chapters, everything that is available for consumption can be put to many different uses, many of which may be far from the use initially intended in making it available. In fact, every alternative for consumption is independent or autonomous of the function(s) it was or is originally intended for. Consider, for example, the automobile. The function for which it is commonly produced is to provide transportation and status. Yet, many have and still do put it to unintended uses. A subculture has developed, for example, based on demolition derbies even though cars are not intended for crashing into each other, to be wrecked for pleasure. Some use automobiles as places to live in, others make art pieces of them. Still others consume them as collectibles, not to drive but to show. Given that so many unintended uses exist, and many more that people have not yet thought of or put into practice, what is amazing is that, in modern society, there has not been much subversion of initial functional intent of products in the act of consumption. Indeed, what is surprising is that modern society has been so successful in instigating or instilling such order, such structure, for so long on the consumption modes of available alternatives.

MODERN SOCIETY

Modern society, most agree, came into being with the Enlightenment, the entrenchment of the capitalist market, and of science, generally around the seventeenth century, and basically in Europe. Humans took a long time getting to this stage. There were, undoubtedly, many varied paths and forms taken until then in terms of people relating to each other and to the items (made) available for consumption. Since our focal interest in this chapter is to explain the development of the modern consumption pattern, we shall start our (hi)story from around the seventeenth century; the time of entrenchment of modern social order in, specifically, the First World.

In the seventeenth century, emerging economic and social conditions in Europe were paving the way for major transformations in structures of society and culture. In exploring the developments in the scientific enterprise, for example, Bertrand Russell, a mathematician and a respected historian of western philosophy,[5] points out that while the methods and the philosophy that were later to become institutionalized science were present in both eastern and western cultures before the seventeenth century, they did not become influential until then.[6] The earlier systems of knowledge-generation were rather varied and included scholastic discourse, oral traditions, and (as in eastern medicine) experiential learning.[7] Modern scientific knowledge-generation methods, or the methods that became adopted and labeled as such within the science establishment following the seventeenth century, were initially merely alternative and complementary ways of generating knowledge. Why and how did they become institutionalized and privileged as "science" while others were excluded and demoted? One is likely to find the answers in the history of the revolutionary intellectual struggle which accompanied the revolutionary social, political, and economic struggles in Europe at the time.

The seventeenth century in Europe witnessed the breaking down of the political and economic hegemony of aristocratic rule. Changes in land systems, commercial relations, and state organizations that had started before the seventeenth century resulted in the development of an urban culture, freer markets, mercantilism, the beginnings of industrial activity, and laborers free from serfdom.[8] Such developments boldly challenged the aristocratic social order. The representatives of the new order were pitted against the powerful spiritual and traditional teachings of the Church.

The messengers of the new order needed a language, an idea-system which could successfully question the theological assertions and serve as a credible alternative philosophy to faith in supernatural powers. Such a system was presented to them, especially by a series of gifted astronomers who were able to create doubts and confusion in the beliefs of the masses by contradicting the heavenly word through their discoveries. Moreover, they seemed to present observational evidence that people could easily, inexpensively, and commonly experience and verify. Galileo's telescope, for example, had very much become a mass-marketed item. Tycho Brahe's extensive and meticulous observations were difficult to refute through faith. Kepler presented a system consistent with these observations.[9]

For the progressive social elements who wanted to break the repressive stranglehold of the conservative, stagnant elements over the people, facts based on empirical evidence became weapons for change. Precise observations contradicting the old doctrine became powerful rallying points for a social revolution the masses could relate to. In social terms, these revolutionary elements in the seventeenth century were primarily mercantilists, small urban trades-people involved in commodity production and commerce, and burgeoning bankers and industrialists for whom the bourgeois concept of freedom was found in independent observation as well as in Luther's and Calvin's challenges to the Church's teachings.[10] As the Church responded with reactionary ideas and practices to suppress the new elements, these elements retorted with weaponry of empirical findings to challenge the Church. This process of challenges and counter-challenges created the need for the revolutionary forces to develop a complete systematic alternative ideology to offer to society. This was achieved through the institutionalization of science on the basis of those precepts that had already won some battles for the challengers of the Church.[11] Thus, on the one hand, the sociopolitical elements that were seeking freedom in economic activity to develop what they saw as their potential in improving the material conditions for humanity, and, on the other hand, the scientific enterprise, found mutual interests and supported each other in building an order that became the modern era.

Enlightenment, science, small-scale industrial and commercial growth, lessening regulation (restriction) from religious and guild establishments, the greater belief and trust in the abilities of individuals to take fate into their own hands—these were, to many, liberating experiences and themes in seventeenth- and eighteenth-century Europe. With these influences, a more liberated attitude also affected consumption and consumptive activities. While, clearly, some restraint and prudence in consumption was commonly preached from all quarters, both the religious and the new entrepreneurial sectors,[12] evidence shows that these sermons were rarely heeded. The amassing of goods and conspicuous consumption, mostly for reasons of representing status and its achievement, both to self and others, began to take hold among the wealthy and the middle classes as early as the seventeenth century,[13] and perhaps even earlier.[14] Consequently, many scholars argue that the consumer culture started as early as the seventeenth century, almost as early as capitalism and market economies, which began with the Enlightenment.

ECONOMIC CHANGES AND GROWTH OF CONSUMPTION

The onset of modern society coincided with and was integral to the revolutionary liberation of market activity, and increased private ownership and private control of productive forces. Before the seventeenth century many restrictions were imposed on business activities, financial transactions, and commerce. The struggles to free human social existence from the restrictions and dicta of monarchies and religious institutions were partially related to the liberation of business activities, and free entrepreneurial creativity and inventiveness from restrictive laws and regulations of the old regimes. The justification most often asserted for this was that it was to free economic vitality in order to enhance wealth and betterment of human lives, an aim well in line with the project of modernity. As the students of economy later realized, the setting free of productive creativity had to go hand in hand with the liberation of consumptive capacity. Yet, at the onset of the free market economy, consumption was a term and an activity that carried much baggage with it. It was practically synonymous with sickness and waste.[15] Despite its negative connotations, however, early in the history of the market economy consumption grew and became a favorite pastime for many in the wealthy and middle classes. The favorite consumption items linked to status and to hedonic meanings were beverages such as tea and coffee, fabrics such as silk, mostly imported into the western markets, highly cultivated gardens, accessories such as umbrellas and hats, and certain household items such as clocks and other furniture items that had ornamental as well as utilitarian functions. In the seventeenth century, certain skills, such as literacy, numeracy, and playing a musical instrument were also status items.[16]

The tremendous explosion of consumptive appetites, however, occurred later, with the explosion of mass-production technologies in industry and in agriculture. Initially, much of the increase in mass-production capabilities was absorbed by population increases and the extension of markets through commerce and colonial expansions. But colonialism also expanded the production of consumables available for the European markets,[17] requiring an expansion of demand for consumption. With the explosion of production capabilities in the domestic markets through industrial technologies, further growth of wealth and capital accumulation became increasingly dependent upon increasing domestic consumption, especially because the consumers of foreign markets generally lacked the resources to exchange for marketed goods. As mass-production technologies exploded the capacity to produce, consumption began to fall behind and to create a bottleneck for economic growth. Production of consumables was of little use without consumers willing and able to purchase them. This realization hit the students of the economy with greater force at the turn of the twentieth century. The First World War acted to relieve this bottleneck of overproduction (or underconsumption) temporarily, but the first major business cycle *depression* (the Great Depression) followed when the war was over and forced war-linked social consumption no longer existed.[18] Keynesian economics was developed to deal with this problem of underconsumption in market economies, and the United States government adopted these policies under Franklin Roosevelt's presidency. Yet it was the Second World War and the forced mass consumption of the war economy that finally pulled the world economy out of the effects of depression.

The history of business cycles in market economies and the experience of the Great Depression made many policy makers realize the necessity of demand management. Governments have developed monetary and fiscal policies to manage demand (and partially supply), but it is mostly the marketing organizations that have invented numerous promotional and other techniques and strategies for this purpose. Certain historical relationships, along with these marketing strategies, have helped the development of the modern capitalist consumption pattern, especially in the twentieth century. This is the (hi)story we would like to relate in order to explain and understand the social construction of the modern consumption pattern.

MODERNITY, MATERIALISM, AND INDUSTRIALISM

The (hi)story we wish to relate is one of modern society. Already, we have mentioned several defining aspects of modern society: the central role of science and scientific technology, the belief in the ability of human individuals to take their fate into their own hands; the existence of and commitment to a modern project of improving human lives by controlling nature through scientific technologies; the freeing of the human individual and, especially, the unfettering of economic activity from restrictions; and the growth of reliance on material consumables as a sign or indication of prosperity, wealth, and greater mastery over nature and life.

As is clear from the aspects of modernity already mentioned, modernity put the human individual at the center of things and in control—as opposed to nature or supernatural powers—as the *subject*: the one who acts upon his/her environment and the *objects* in his/her environment. The independence of individuals from their nature, to become the *knowing* subjects, that is ones who can be and are aware of the conditions they are in with validity and objectivity, was conceptually achieved through the Cartesian separation of the mind and the body. According to Cartesian thought, the human body is still restricted by its nature, but the mind can separate itself from the natural restrictions of the body and take a detached and distanced perspective, study the conditions of human existence from this objective point of view and attain knowledge. Through this ability, the human being (the subject) can rationally act upon things and improve life by taking control of her/his own fate. The most clear and objective evidence of this ability is in the material impact one has upon one's environment. The increasing abundance of material objects (products) for consumption to make human life more comfortable and to attenuate the effects of nature on human life was the best evidence of such material impact upon the natural environment. Consequently, in modern society, materialism understandably became a revered value. It was a logical extension of the modern idea system (including science which took a positivist turn in modernity) and the modern project. Material comforts sustained through material consumption logically became the clearest indication of achievements promised in the modern project.

Early in the twentieth century, with the great strides in industrial mass-production technologies, the opening of new frontiers through colonialism and commerce, the importing of new resources into the modern economy by explorations, mining, etc., especially in North America, and integrating these new frontiers with the markets through railroads (a major technological breakthrough),[19] the modern society was substantively transformed. Consumables became the focus of all economic activity, not just indicators of success or achievement. Increasingly, the health of modern society came to depend upon ever growing production and consumption of consumables, upon an ever growing market. It is, therefore, not a coincidence that modern society and industrial society became almost synonymous. Modernity came to be judged by the industrial productive capabilities of a nation. Consequently, all modern nations, including the United Kingdom, Japan, the Soviet Union,[20] and the United States, strove to maximize this capability.

CONSUMPTION IN CAPITALIST MARKET ECONOMIES

One difference did occur, however, between the Soviet Union and modern capitalist society. The Soviet Union tried not to rely on the market as the criterion of economic success. It chose a path of state planning, arguing that human lives could better be improved through human rationale than through market performance. While Soviet socialism did not repudiate the market, it relegated it to a marginal economic role. Consequently, it is not surprising that capitalism and market economy historically came to mean one and the same thing. Politically, usages such as the *free* market were often preferred in the west. Our interest in this chapter, and in this book, is to understand the dynamics in the market economies, that is, capitalism. There are at least two reasons for this interest. One is that the market economies seem to have greater control over the world economy. The second reason is that we, the authors, live in capitalist societies, and, therefore, have greater insight and investment in what they are and what might become of them.

The capitalist modern market

In the modern world, without a doubt, economic strength has become the major source of influence on the world stage. Those countries which amassed the greatest economic wealth have had the greatest impact upon the economies and cultures of other countries, not only through colonization and trade, but also through military might based on industrial (economic) strength—therefore, the ability to expend on armaments, military technologies, etc. It is interesting that almost all large economically strong nations have elected to expend so much of their societal resources on the military. Of course, many will attribute this to the historical development of the Cold War between east and west, or the First and Second World, capitalism and communism, but rather convincing arguments have also been made regarding the necessity of creating military expenditures in order to absorb the economic surplus due to overproduction (or underconsumption).[21] These arguments gain greater credibility considering the fact that both the First and the Second World Wars helped market economies to come out of business cycle depressions. It is also quite scary to think that wars may be found somewhat attractive when economic depressions hit. Such points aside, the close relationship between economic growth and modernity is, however, clear. In modern times it was economic power that determined and influenced so much of international and global affairs. Again, this is under-standable, since material wealth and signs of success or achievement in modern society had become one and the same.

In modern market economies, therefore, production of material wealth—meaning consumables that were sold and bought in the market—creating economic vitality, increasing financial resources, expanding money supplies, and growing capital accumulation, became of paramount interest. This meant strength, it meant global influence, it meant awe and admiration by others. Furthermore, it meant becoming a superpower, as in the case of the United States and the Soviet Union which were the two largest economies for most of the twentieth century. Of course, the United States represented the market economies (capitalism) and the largest economy in the world. As a result, the United States became the leading influence and the leading economic model for the rest of the capitalist world. Especially since the First World War, and even more so after the Second World War, the United States has played this leadership role quite actively. Consequently, our focus in understanding the developments in modern market economies will be the United States—or in its leadership and model role, "America."

Twentieth-century America

In terms of moving into an era of immense mass-production capabilities, enlargement of the market, and the consumption ethic beginning to take hold, the beginning of the twentieth century was, indeed, a turning point in America. The exploitation of natural resources discovered in the rush to the western regions, the industrial successes in the eastern states, and the linking of the eastern and the western United States through the railroads, all played an important role in this turning point in America. There was a large accumulation of wealth, capital, and a substantial rise in incomes. This released the desire and the ability to consume more, not only among the very wealthy but also the growing middle classes, especially in the urban centers. This was the time when sociologists such as Veblen[22] began recognizing the consumption ethic and the transformation in the meaning of consumption in society from one where it had utilitarian meanings to one where the symbolisms attached to consumption beyond utility began to take center stage.

One very important piece of the symbolism of consumption in modernity was to signify success in furthering the goals of the modern project. The more items for consumption were made available to consumers, the more this meant that the nation had attained greater control over its fate by improving its productivity. And the more a consumer unit, such as the household or family, owned and consumed such items for consumption, the more this family was considered to have made it: improved its quality of life, achieved greater strides towards the modern project—the improvement of human life and arriving at and maintaining a comfortable "standard of living." Consumption became, thus, the yardstick for modernity's success. Consequently, all efforts concentrated on increasing, improving, enlarging and expanding consumption, consumables, and the medium through which they were made available: the *market*.

The history of consumption in twentieth-century America

There are several important factors in the development of consumption, and especially the consumption pattern, in America in the twentieth century.

One is what we have already been talking about: the growth of the consumption ethic, that is, the idea that the level of consumption achieved is the measure of the quality of life attained. As a result of this consumption ethic, consumers judged their own and others' degree of success on the basis of their ability to consume, with different consumables representing success at different times—for example, one's own home, automobile (brand), neighborhood of residence, clothing (brand), etc. Another very important factor in the growth of consumption, specifically as it relates to preferred life styles, has been the media, in the broad sense of the term, including film and television (industries), the star and celebrity system, and the information/news system.[23] A third factor is the sector of production, constituted, specifically, of businesses of all kinds. Since in large part, corporations historically played the leading role in the business sector in the construction of the modern consumption pattern, we will frequently use the term corporation(s) to represent the business sector of the modern capitalist economy. A fourth factor has been the wealthy and high income households or families, specifically due to their relations with the corporations and the role they have played in the corporations, and, as a result, in their communities. The state, used here to define the complete institutionalization of political governance apparatuses (i.e., including the government(s), administrative offices and agencies, legislative and judiciary bodies), was another major factor in the construction of the consumption pattern through the politics and policies it promoted. Other factors include technological and social trends, such as suburbanization and automotive technology.

THE SHAPERS OF AMERICAN CONSUMPTION PATTERNS

The image of Hollywood

Just before the turn of the twentieth century, railroads had united the whole country and agricultural commodities as well as mined resources could now be found in all the markets in the nation.[24] Chicago was very much the creation of this era; it stood at the most important railroad junction and, as a result, hosted the commodities market. Yet, by the First World War and into the 1920s, the railroad had already begun to lose its image of the future, which had been taken over by the automobile. Based on this new vehicle, which was qualitatively different from the trains due to its individual ownership potential by masses of consumers, a new urban structure epitomized by Los Angeles was beginning to develop. This was the urban metropolis of suburbs and freeways, of expansive and dispersed city and architecture, an urbanization that sprawled in flat forms rather than being centered in the form of skyscrapers.[25] The most exciting medium of the period, the film, was also developing in Hollywood, a suburb of Los Angeles. Both the new urban structure and the film industry apparently needed to start in an area free of earlier structures in order to flourish free and unrestrained. And they did. As the radio was beginning to create a mass culture and a mass audience (market) where anyone in any part of the country could relate to some common experience (such as radio shows and news programs), the film industry was poised to make the common experience richer, specifically by making it visual.[26] Photography, another visual medium, had already excited the imagination and substantially changed tourism patterns through visual representations of the wonders of the west—such as Yosemite and the Grand Canyon.

Cinema presented not only an exciting new technology but a totally new experience of vicarious (or virtual) transportation into, and participation in, wondrous and exhilarating worlds (scripts, scenarios, sceneries).[27] These vicariously experienced worlds also presented a whole set of new *acquaintances*: faces, voices, and personal lives that were well "known" by mass audiences, and both admired and followed with interest by very large segments of the population. These new "friends" were the stars, some big and some small. With time, this star system grew from those who were only "seen" on the screen to those whose presence was not necessarily on the screen but in stories and scenarios as exciting and as grand as any in the cinema: the celebrities. Recognizing that vicarious living of incredible lives, and the virtual friendships and relationships were attractive to a large market, all media presented the "personal (interest) stories" of the "exciting" people, especially those of great *fortune*. Fortune came in many forms. Stardom was fortune, hitting a gold vein was fortune, creating a newspaper empire was fortune; and fortunate were the blessed few who were cast or projected into these roles. At a time when the ability to buy more and consume more meant success, any rags-to-riches story was a story of fortune and of the fortunate. The people of fortune were celebrities and (almost) everyone wanted to know them, and to be acquainted (for most, of course, vicariously) with them. Celebrities, stars and others, who became the acquaintances of all, sold things. They sold media (radio programs, films, magazines and newspapers), they sold life styles and consumables (to people who wanted to be like their "friends"), and they sold ideas, values and attitudes.

The image of wealth

Then as now, the life styles and patterns of consumption the "public" aspired to were those of the rich and the famous.[28] They represented the good and virtuous examples and became role models. They were the "successful" people, like Hughes, Hearst, Ford, Kennedy, Rockefeller, as well as the stars who especially represented consumptive life styles with a high public profile.

A very large proportion of the stars and celebrities were business people; they were in business (acting, producing, managing, etc.) and they all had a great interest in the growth of their markets. Their livelihoods and increased fortunes depended on their business. Some had greater control over the businesses they were in than others: specifically those who had ownership or top management responsibilities. They made the fateful decisions and guided the activities of their organizations, and when their organizations were successful they made, indeed, fortunes, had high incomes and accumulated wealth. In a culture where such a "fortune" was *the* sign of success and prowess, others admired and looked up to them. Plus, they had and/or controlled the wealth and the money to promote what they did, how they lived, and what they believed in. They had much control over what was to appear and become visible in the media.[29] They were successful, they believed in themselves, and they wanted to promote the idea that they could be examples for everyone to become a similar success. All this excitement about promoting their way of life was not necessarily selfish or self-serving. Many (must have) believed that what they had was good for everyone, and that everyone could equally benefit from what they could do.

This system of emphasis on being materially wealthy, the ability to consume, and the like, did create its criminals—organized crime, illegal avenues to becoming rich[30]—but those were aberrations, or they were treated as such. The dominant image and information was that the celebrities mostly came from moral and legal backgrounds. Ford was legal and moral, yet the company was a great success,[31] so were General Motors and Disney. The media, especially television and film, created an ever increasing awe and admiration for the entrepreneurs and the families who "made it," which meant only that they had become rich and wealthy. Outside the war movies and the westerns, the films that were most popular were ones about these celebrities of fortune; the great managers, people (specifically, men) of wealth, the business tycoons.[32]

However, the wealth and consumptive power of the wealthy, especially the families who constituted less than one percent of the population but owned about 50 percent of the wealth in the United States,[33] for example, could not be sufficient to absorb the production capacity that had developed. For mass production to continue adding to economic wealth, mass consumption had to occur; everyone had to develop the consumption ethic. Thus, the major role of the "fortunate," the stars and the celebrities, was to act as models, as examples to follow as much as possible. Through the media, the advertising industry, as well as political leaders and other public figures of America, all declared and promised that, if committed to the system of free enterprise and individual initiative, everyone could have "the good life" they were well acquainted with thanks to the exposure in the movies and other media.[34] The celebrities just showed the way and the media were especially fond of exhibiting the "rags-to-riches" stories. America was the promised land, where everyone could make it and become part of the affluent melting pot—they clearly could see enough examples of those who did, both real and fictional. But this was the land where fiction became reality and the wildest imaginings came true.

The rise of the middle class

For many, indeed, what they could only have imagined did come true. Some people who came to America as immigrants, with nothing to their names, did become rich. Not only rich, these hard working and fortunate few became important leaders of their communities, admired and revered.[35] Yet, still, they were a very small minority. A larger proportion became the *middle class*, the backbone of the consumer revolution in America.[36] They came from many different backgrounds and occupations, and they were committed to the material betterment of their lives more than to anything else.[37] They were well poised to follow the celebrities in wanting to own their individual homes,[38] have well-equipped kitchens, automobiles, fashionable clothing, etc. They were making a good living in a fast growing, affluent economy and market, and therefore, had the buying power; their families were becoming nuclear and with fewer children, resulting in higher discretionary incomes. They largely believed in freedom, interpreted as individualism and as little (inter)dependence (with) on others as possible. To them, therefore, a housing structure totally independent from others meant freedom; an automobile, an individual and independent method of transportation, meant freedom. Freedom was doing what you wanted to do when you wanted to do it, as far as possible. Consumption of certain things, like the private car, provided this. Therefore, consumption—the ability to consume—also became closely linked to the meaning of freedom.

Media as message

The media were not only (re)presenting the celebrities and stars, mostly business people as already mentioned, but the media had integral links to the corporations. Of course, the media, such as radio stations, television networks and newspapers, were corporations themselves. But, especially in America, they also found their greatest sponsors and major sources of revenue to be the corporations that advertised. Advertising-oriented corporations began by sponsoring specific programs, similar, for example, to *Hallmark*'s television movies. On television, the daytime series received the popular collective name "soap opera" because they were originally sponsored by corporations that sold soap and other cleansing products. Corporations were keen on sponsoring television and radio programs that represented situations and contexts which displayed and promoted consumption experiences, especially those that included the consumption of their products. This made good business sense. Both through the programs they supported and directly in their advertisements and the informational/ news segments they produced, the corporations informed the consumer households of the trends that were developing in American every-day life, trends into which the acquisition of the products these corporations were marketing fitted quite well.[39] Often, of course, these new trends and life styles were exhibited through the experiences of the stars and celebrities, the fortunate ones, who were the models and (vicarious) friends imitated by the middle class(es). And, again, often these new trends and life styles were related to and were represented by the introduction of new products into the market; new styles of clothing, new appliances such as television, air conditioning, suburban housing, and more recently, microwave ovens, video cassette recorders, and computers.

Innovation and trickle down

The introduction of a product that represents a new style, a new way of life, is usually an expensive undertaking. Imagine, for example, the introduction of television in the United States.[40] This was a new technology which had required large amounts of investment to develop and then adapt to a form which could be utilized by households. At the beginning, there were not many programs or channels to watch. Development of programming networks required huge investments. Corporations first involved in the industry were taking risks and investing much. People were not rushing out to buy the television sets immediately. As a result, those who were early purchasers of television sets had to pay quite a price for their sets, yet could see few original programs, and often with some difficulties. Not many could afford such expenditure and not many did until the development of technology and programming which allowed lower prices for higher values. This is typical when truly novel products which represent substantive differences in life patterns and styles are introduced to the market and added on to the structure of available alternatives for consumption. When only a few will initially buy the new alternative and substantive technological research and development have gone into its production, originally the product will (have to) be introduced to the market at a higher price. Given the level of risks taken and the costs undertaken to initially get the product on the market, and the small number of buyers in the market, the initial higher price is understandable and it makes business sense (especially when business is based on capitalist logic and requires economic viability). As the product begins to find a greater market, it then becomes less expensive, or less expensive versions of it are developed. Economists explain or rationalize this through the concept of *economies of scale*. As more and more numbers of a consumption alternative (product) are produced and supplied, many costs that are incurred to produce and supply it decrease per unit due to more efficient uses of capacity and greater specialization.[41]

The economics are different in the case of incremental innovations. When an organization introduces a new brand of toothpaste, for instance, the above relationship may not apply. There is already a large effective demand for this product category, it is relatively inexpensive, and the company producing the new brand can, through a successful advertising (promotion) and distribution campaign, capture a good portion of this demand, enabling it to afford to sell the new brand at a low price. Marketing a new brand at a lower price may, in fact, be a strategy to make more toothpaste consumers switch to the new brand. This is called a *penetration* strategy in the marketing literature.[42] It is possible to do this, because there is already effective demand for the product, and it is a low price product, so many people will be able to risk a small amount to try the new brand and see if they like it. When we consider a new product that represents a new consumption pattern—that is, a set of relationships, as discussed earlier—which is different from the currently dominant one, on the other hand, many conditions that make a penetration strategy or a low price possible are no longer present. Only a few people may be familiar with the new product representing a new consumption pattern. Demand for it, especially effective demand, will be almost non-existent. The complete novelty of the product will require development of a new production process, research and development costs, new production skills, etc., therefore necessitating a high price at the beginning. At least, this is the rationale of a modern economy; a rationale that was and is observed in the introduction of many new durables to the market. For example, radios, television sets, washing machines and dryers, refrigerators, air conditioners, microwave ovens, photography equipment, personal computers, video cameras and video players, electronic games, and on and on, all had the same history of arriving on the scene at prices that only the rich could afford or risk, then becoming more available to others. Thus, the advent of *trickle down* of life styles and consumption patterns, and products representing them in modern society.[43]

The weight of wealth in innovative consumption

The consumers who could first try such risky propositions—that is, products that were new to the market, representing new patterns of life, and commanding high prices—in early twentieth-century America, where production technologies enabled the presentation of new products at frequencies never known before, were the consumers who had greater disposable or discretionary incomes, the wealthier households. We know that incomes, and especially wealth, were distributed rather unequally, and still are, even in the economically most developed countries.[44] Consequently, there were many households that could not afford to spend their limited resources on consumption alternatives which represented novelties in the structure of available alternatives for consumption. Solely on the basis of what novelties they could afford to buy, and support the development of, these households could not influence any changes in the structure of available alternatives for consumption and, as a result, in the consumption patterns.

Could the wealthier, high income households[45] have this influence? They could, of course, if some common interest developed among them for supporting a new consumption pattern. Even at a time when fortunes rarely seen before were accumulated in America by industrialist, agricultural, and commercial families, it would have been highly unlikely that any single household could start changing the structure of available alternatives for consumption through its individual expenditures. The united expenditures of the richer households, on the other hand, could provide sufficient revenues for a marketing organization to undertake the production process. Therefore, in order to understand the role that wealthier households played in the construction of the modern consumption pattern in America, it is necessary to explore the factors which created such common interests among these households.

One of the reasons for the common interest among wealthier consumers was what Veblen called *conspicuous consumption*.[46] The wealthy, upper socioeconomic stratum households culturally developed an interest in differentiating themselves from others, and used consumption to indicate or express their status to others. That such an interest has played a role in wealthy households' expenditures for consumption has been argued and evidenced by many researchers other than Veblen.[47] Our interest in this book, however, is not just to reiterate these claims, but to try and bring an understanding about the direction which such expenditures have historically taken, in order to explain the development of the modern consumption pattern in market economies.

The wealthier or higher income households were, clearly, not going to be interested in just *any* consumption that differentiated them from others. In every culture ideas develop among the different social classes as to what signifies status, sophistication, privilege, and superiority. The wealthier households in a capitalist society, where wealth and fortune were already the major symbols of success and superiority, were going to look for consumption alternatives that signified their superior status, sophistication and high culture—at least, that has been the case in modern history.[48] What would such consumption be and how did these households acquire their values and tastes regarding such consumption?

This is one area where the modern project in modern society played an especially important role. The values and beliefs which revolved around the modern project directly influenced the consumption values of the wealthy, who were often the leaders of modern society in terms of their roles in the business community (specifically, the large corporations), or the state, or in the political arena in general. Those who did not get involved directly in the day-to-day politics of the community or the state were, nevertheless, involved in many sociopolitical decisions through the other influence they had: as business leaders, as *the* examples of success, as consultants in and to many decision-making bodies, as celebrities, as members of clubs, as leaders of social networks, etc. If they wanted something, the wealthy put their financial resources behind their causes, as well as their visibility and social positions, and were heard.

In modern capitalist economies, these households were mostly members of the business elite. They were business people concerned about their markets and the fortunes they made through their markets. Fortunes, in terms of accumulation of wealth, indicated what they had achieved. They believed in *progress* as defined largely by the modern project: improving human lives by controlling nature through scientific technologies. They were partial, therefore, to consumption alternatives which symbolized such progress. That is why many of the household durables, such as the refrigerator, dishwasher, vacuum cleaner, telephone, and the like, were signified as progress. They allegedly enabled human control over nature's chores, they enabled victory over the difficulties of nature, and furthermore, they signified individual conquest of one's every-day living conditions.[49] To such *achievements* were attributed the quality of freedom. In fact, that was how many of these products were advertised: as providers of freedom and control over one's life.[50]

The wealthy households played an important instrumental role in the development of a new consumption pattern in modern capitalist economies, therefore, through their choices of novel consumption alternatives; first by the fact that they had the discretionary incomes to risk and try new products, but also because they shared a common interest in modern progress, given their positions in society. That is, their choices were largely influenced by their positions and the interests that having these positions instilled in them. Their choices of new consumption alternatives, therefore, had some rhyme and reason. They were clearly biased toward certain consumption alternatives, the ones that, to them, meant or signified progress, development, improvement of life, achievement, etc. In modern society these were material goods. They were visible, tangible proofs of industrial might, of the conquest of nature. Where did they get these ideas from?

The production–consumption nexus

A major flaw in modern theories regarding the development of new products and consumption patterns has been that they often divided the society into producers and consumers. As a result, they concentrated on the needs of the *consumers* and the skills of the *producers* in providing for these needs. Theories critical of the way this system works in equating demand and supply,[51] then, have emphasized the power of the producers and the resulting manipulation of consumers' needs and wants. The more radically critical theories, such as marxist and elitist theories, further emphasize the role of class in the decisions made for and by the producers, the business organizations, as well as the state or government agencies. As we just discussed, class, wealth, and income did play a role in the decisions that consuming households made. When the role that members of these households play in the producer institutions is considered, a more complete picture of the influences in the development or formation and transformation of the structure of available alternatives for consumption and the consumption patterns emerges. To complete the picture, however, we shall further discuss the roles of the producer institutions and the state as consumers in their own right, not merely producers. First, let us discuss the connections between the powerful consumers, that is, the wealthy upper-class households and the corporations.

What individuals did within the producer organizations, such as the corporations, was and still is an important part of their lives and therefore it heavily influenced their values, world views, need perceptions, preference patterns, and consumption. In fact, the activities of producers in the public domain, that is, at their jobs, in their offices, boardrooms, etc., have constituted the major context within which people have come in contact with and learned from their environments in modern society, especially given the status of the public domain in modernity.[52] Many consumers, for example, had their initial experiences with computers in general, and more recently with personal computers in particular, at work or at the educational institutions which they attended. The uses and attractions of such a consumption alternative, the computer, therefore, were learned and felt in the roles these consumers had in public institutions. Their tastes and values were thus colored by their experiences with the computer in an environment of *production*, not in connection with their *consumption*. They became aware of such a product's existence through their roles in these organizations, and their ideas regarding the use or consumption of the product developed within this context.

Furthermore, the roles these consumers played in society, within the social stratification or class structure, as well as their incomes and wealth, were largely correlated with their roles in the organizations, specifically the corporations. Those who were at high levels of management within the larger and more influential corporations were also the higher income earners. Many times, those who had top management roles in such organizations as the Ford Motor Company, were also closely related to the families that owned the organizations or held the largest shares in them.[53] Large stockholders of all organizations clearly played important roles in the strategic decisions made for and by these organizations, whether they took direct or indirect roles in management and on the boards of directors. They also received the highest salaries and gained prominence and visibility in their communities, making them part of the powerful consumer households in these communities. Their power came not solely from their own incomes or wealth, but also from the fact that they became role models for other high income households, because they were admired for the positions they had achieved or the authority they wielded in their organizations and immediate communities. They were also admired for the types of consumptive activities they could afford or the visibility they had in the various media. They also had the latest information on the technologies that were developing, on world affairs related to their work, and they had the ears of the politicians who represented their constituencies.

All these afforded them a special role in the consumption choices their communities made.

Those who owned or controlled the corporations also participated actively in the decisions affecting the social, economic, and political environments, through their leadership roles and expertise in managing organizations, social clubs, and communities. They were often the people who were sought for advice or consultation by many other institutions, especially the state. They were the ones who were most often heard, for example, on Senate and House committees in the United States. They took active roles in policy formulations or even in government. In the United States, families such as the Rockefellers, Kennedys, Fords, and Hearsts, among others, are good examples of such lasting influence. There were, and are, others who may not have been born to great wealth but could also join the group of major role players by becoming leading managers and shareholders of large organizations. Among these, for example, one could count Iacocca and Perot. There is a close connection between power in the business community and in governments. While the business leaders have lasting and consistent influence on public affairs, political and social circumstances generally allow only limited and sporadic participation in such affairs by the less powerful and the underprivileged. Such limited and sporadic participation has had rather negligible impact on societal decision-making processes and their overall outcomes.[54]

The overlaps between those who controlled decisions within the corporations and those who had the buying power in the market, specifically in terms of discretionary incomes that could be risked on new products that represented new consumption patterns, was especially conducive to the development of consumption patterns that had a certain character. Because of their relations and interests in the corporations, the preferences of the powerful consumers were, understandably, biased toward the consumption pattern that best fit or satisfied the needs and efficiency criteria of the organizations they were connected with. Many may regard this association to be intentional and self-serving. Yet it is not necessarily a planned, purposive or, especially, self-interested behavior, but rather an understandable tendency resulting from every-day social and practical interactions. It is usual that someone who is working for the success of an institution adopts many of the approaches required for that success, believes in their necessity and purpose, and without necessarily having a hidden motive, values the outcomes such approaches will produce. This is especially so in the case of modern society, when the goals for which one strives are considered to be so meaningful and lofty.

In modern capitalist society, the central goal of a business organization striving to improve the human lot has been to provide products for consumers which improve their material living conditions, but in an economically viable way. The justification given for this economic viability is twofold: first, the scarce resources of society must not be wasted, and second, in order for the business organization to keep providing its products to the consumer it must maintain its livelihood. Both objectives can be realized through financial/economic effectiveness. In capitalism, the basic criteria for such effectiveness are profitability and return on investment. These criteria can be continuously met through the expansion and extension of the markets. The greater the expansion of the market, the greater the impetus for production, for development of technologies, for entrepreneurship, and, according to capitalistic logic, the greater the economic development and the improvement of human lives.[55]

The historical relationships among the powerful consumer households, the corporations, and the state in capitalist market economies discussed in this chapter have fostered a certain pattern of preferences and choices in modern market societies. Technologies that expanded and enlarged the market were favored and further developed through the research programs supported by the corporations and by the state, and managers and officials who were in decision-making positions in these institutions earned respect for the promise of such technologies and the products that could be produced through them. Consumers awaited the realization of these products and their introduction to the market with great anticipation, and they became admirers of what these products could do, choosing them when they appeared on the mass market in affordable forms. After all, these products were imbued with the images of success which are sought after in modern society. Thus, cycles of selection, expectation and preference occurred in modern society, resulting from the connections among the producers and consumers, and the values produced by a capitalist market system.

Capitalism and the modern consumption pattern

In a capitalist market economy, value systems that regard the markets as the most free and democratic means of supplying the needs of consumers reinforce the requirements of the corporation to expand markets. In such societies, those who are in decision-making positions within the corporations are influenced by those values that correspond well with the imperatives of success for their organizations. Therefore, they encourage marketing of those products that enlarge the markets. As consumers they foster a cultural appreciation of these products; as producers they develop a deep regard for the technologies that enable production of such products.[56]

Such an overlap among values, decision making, and consumers who can support the development of novel products that impact on life and consumption patterns, assures that in capitalist market economies changes in consumption patterns will be largely determined by the production technologies, the interests of those who provide products for the market through organized, corporate means, and the need perceptions created by them. These will be need perceptions that are first and foremost felt by the powerful consumers, because of their relations to corporations.

The model of the societal process of the development of consumption patterns sketched above is further supported by the historical observations made regarding the diffusion of products which were novel and which represented a transformation in consumption patterns when they were first introduced. For such products a definite trickle-down process is observed. That is, initially these products were adopted by and diffused among the upper socioeconomic strata, consisting of the wealthier households who held powerful positions and jobs, then later diffused to middle and lower socioeconomic strata. For a period, during the 1960s and 1970s, the United States Bureau of Labor Statistics collected and published statistics on ownership of household products that were, coincidentally,[57] representative of the modern consumption pattern. These were products such as automobiles, television sets, washing machines, dishwashers, and refrigerators. These statistics clearly showed the trickle-down process.[58] The last year for which these statistics were published by income strata was 1974.[59] It is evident, however, from other anecdotal sources, that if such statistics were available today for products such as microwave ovens, video cassette recorders, and personal computers, among others, the same process would be observed.[60]

Corporations as consumers

Yet this process is not the only one that confirms the influence of corporations over the formation of consumption patterns, although it is probably the most significant. The corporations themselves were, and are, major consumers in society. They were, both in theory and historically, developed and allowed to exist in order to provide for and serve the needs of people in the society. Their right to existence is based on the assumption that through such organization of affairs the needs of members of society can be provided for. In modern society, they have clearly become social entities in their own right, with legally organized rights, privileges, and responsibilities, just like the individual citizen. They have developed needs that required satisfaction, and, in modern society, they have become the largest consumers. By any measure, they are the largest consumers of energy, transportation systems, and the construction industry, for example. As the top managers of these corporations made decisions regarding what these organizations would consume in modern capitalist society, they used the criterion of economic efficiency, thus influencing the (trans)formation of the structure of available alternatives for consumption in a certain direction: toward products that *enlarge* the market, provide *material* improvements in human lives, and greater *accumulation* of capital for increased material wealth of human society. In the development of the automotive industry, highways, and electric energy, for example, it was the corporations that first subscribed to and adopted these consumption alternatives, not the individual consumer households. The same is true for the major components of consumption in contemporary society, the computers, the telephone networks, and now, in the 1990s, the information/communication networks. While consumption is generally considered as the domain of individual households, in effect the corporations have been and often still are the initial consumers of consumption alternatives that later get adopted by households. Not only do these organizations have the largest consumption budgets, they are also effective as lobbyists—both as consumers and as producers—in favor of government investment in the development and use of products that represent potential for market growth.

Role of the state

The allocation of state and government incomes (budgets) among different programs clearly has been and still is another major influence in the (trans)formation of the structure of available alternatives for consumption, and thereby the dominance of certain consumption patterns. Whether the states encourage spending on, say, highway transportation or suburban housing systems, is important because such decisions have influenced the socioeconomic structures of the housing and transportation subsystems directly and other subsystems (for example, shopping and recreation subsystems) indirectly. When resource allocation decisions by the corporations and the states are guided by the same criteria—that is, in modern capitalist society, capital accumulation and industrial and market growth—that guide the powerful, wealthy, high income, and influential consumer households and their values, choices, and preferences, and the admiration for the products that represent the consumption pattern which reinforces these same criteria, the cycle of influence upon (trans)formation of consumption patterns is largely complete. In modern capitalist society, it becomes clear that this (trans)formation is not guided by innate needs of human beings, but by the necessities of a system that has the goal of increasing the material wealth of human society through maximizing (or optimizing) the accumulation of capital by enabling maximum profits for the corporations.

In modern society where the original environment of human life has been changed immensely from simple existence on Earth to one where so much is humanly constructed—the cities, industries, work environments, shopping environments—it is impossible to talk of given human needs. Many, if not all, needs that human beings have are results of the environments that have been created—a house, a television, an automobile, and furniture are some of the main expenditure items that are needed in modern society for an acceptable standard of living. Not only do people perceive these products as needed, but the content of their needs are defined through their exposure to or encounters with these products.

The powerful consumers who also have significant positions in the producer organizations, specifically the larger corporations, are in the best position to know what technologies and what products are currently under development. They also have the best information as to which of these alternatives has the best potential for profitability and marketing. Adoption of these products by the socially more visible powerful consumer households, which extend the values and preferences of corporate management to the consumption sphere, influences both the structure of available alternatives for consumption and the aspirations of other consumer households who, in modern society, generally have learned to follow the affluent life styles with awe.

Impact on the poor

When the consumption pattern in modern society develops according to the needs and success criteria of the business organizations and the affluent social classes, its dominance over the whole society and adoption by other social classes has grave implications and consequences, especially for the poor. The implication of such a formation of the structure of available alternatives for consumption for the poor and powerless consumer households is that they get confronted with societal structures and subsystems of consumption which form and transform without their participation. This structure of available alternatives for consumption and the related subsystems (housing, transportation, health, shopping, etc.) largely determine what these consumer households will perceive as "needs" and which consumption alternatives they will value as acceptable, normal, attractive, and superior. When their incomes enable satisfaction of these perceived needs without major problems, they quickly and easily adopt products represented in the dominating consumption pattern. The poor have adapted to the changes occurring in the structure of available alternatives for consumption following the well-exposed consumption behaviors of the powerful consumers and, thereby, have helped in further reinforcing the transformations started by the powerful consumer households. When their resources run short, the poor aspire to consuming the products privileged by the structure of available alternatives for consumption and have to struggle to get access to them through improved incomes or saving programs.

Ironically, in modern literature, which on the one hand (re)presents this consumption pattern as progress and success, such aspirations and striving by the poor and the disadvantaged to emulate the dominant consumption behavior has been, at times, labeled as *irrational consumption*. This is because the powerless—that is, lower income—households, who do not have influential positions in the corporations or the state, will at times spend their limited incomes on products that the social, macro rationale, based on scientific and meliorative knowledge, identifies as "unnecessary," "frivolous luxuries," or not "really" needed. At the same time, the same households will be "saving" by spending less of their incomes on what the scientific literature identifies as essential products required for a healthy life. Consequently, many powerless consumer households will either exhibit imbalance in the satisfaction of their *basic* needs (resulting in malnutrition, inadequate sanitation, housing, medical care, etc.) or they will overspend, going into debt and financial dependency.

Thus, in modern capitalist society we have a very tight relationship between the corporations and the state, specifically through the role that wealthy consumers play in both institutions and through the communality of the values and visions that guided actions and decisions in the corporations and the state. It is understandable, therefore, that the consumption alternatives preferred by these two institutions, which command a very large proportion of all resources and their allocation in modern nation states, should dominate society. Also understandable, as discussed earlier in this chapter, is the direction and character of their preferences in resource allocation and in selecting consumption alternatives. The individual-private-passive-alienated consumption pattern is a logical result of these preferences; it is not accidental. Yet, in the diffusion of these preferences across practically all segments of modern society, the organization of information and communication media and systems, specifically the marketing systems and media, have had a tremendous role. Furthermore, the marketing systems have contributed to the (trans)formation of consumption values and preferences, not only to their diffusion.

The role of marketing in modern society

The marketing process is a leading force in the signification and representation of values, perceived needs, and preferences to the consuming masses. Generally, the marketing establishment has operated in modern society by taking the effective images, ideas, and concepts in society, and resignifying them in order to represent the products which fit the consumption pattern that has the best potential to enlarge and extend the market. Such products, linked to desirable values, people, and life styles are represented in a favorable light, making them attractive and desirable for greater numbers of consuming households. The role of marketing as an inherently postmodern institution which has flourished in modern society will become clearer in later chapters.

The typical modern marketing processes which help diffuse the modern consumption pattern involve product and price differentiation strategies along with the promotional processes. Differentiation enables purchase of products representing the dominating consumption pattern by consumer households with income constraints and different cultural backgrounds. While the same consumption pattern, which represented individual-private-alienated-passive consumption, diffused among the majority of consumer households, indicating increasing uniformity across these households, within the same consumption pattern there has occurred an abundance of product and brand differentiation, creating a great variety of consumer choice within this limited sphere. Again, examples include products such as the automobile, television sets, designer jeans and washing machines.[61] While almost every consumer household in the United States has one or more automobiles for going to work and shopping, for some households it is a Dodge van that serves the purpose, for others it is a Nissan sedan. Consumer households may feel a (false) sense of individuality in driving a brand of automobile that millions of others drive, doing the same things with their vehicles that countless others do using different brands. While product and brand differentiation helps this diffusion phenomenon, promotion makes the powerful consumer households' life styles and consumption patterns, as common reference points, more visible and attractive to all consumer households, reinforcing the dominating modern consumption pattern. In the meantime, price differentiation that goes hand in hand with product and brand differentiation helps each socioeconomic group afford a differentiated version of the product that represents the same consumption pattern.

Finally, it is important to explain why the individual-private-alienated-passive consumption pattern is the one that became dominant in modern capitalist society. It has already been made evident that in modern capitalist society there is a bias toward improvement of human lives through increasing the material wealth of nations, and that in such societies this goal was thought to be possible to achieve through the expansion and extension of the market. An individual-private-alienated-passive consumption pattern is most conducive to such extension and expansion of the market. If products are *individually* consumed rather than *collectively* shared, there will be a greater need to purchase and use more products. For example, as members of households increasingly have television sets for their personal use, in their own bedrooms, etc., each household consumes more television sets and the market for television sets correspondingly expands. Similarly, when products are *privately* owned by individuals or individual households rather than *publicly* owned and publicly usable, greater numbers of consumer households have to participate in the market, thus helping the market to grow. For example, when each household owns its own automobile(s) rather than shares in the consumption of publicly owned vehicles for their transportation needs, each automobile may be used less, but more automobiles will have to be bought, thus expanding the market for automobiles. Even the ownership of very infrequently used products, such as a rug shampooer, is promoted to some extent in American society. In order to enter all facets of life in order to expand markets, products have to substitute more and more for human labor in the consumer households and elsewhere. If members of households were to "produce" the products for consumption within their households, there would be less need to purchase them in the markets, causing markets to contract or have slower growth. Therefore, "labor saving" durables at home, such as washing machines and microwave ovens, have helped extend the markets by substituting for "productive" activities at home. As more and more products are bought in the market to substitute for activities at home, the industrial organization and production rationales of modern economies, such as economies of scale, have necessitated that mass-production technologies be developed and that large segments of consumers buy and consume the same products. Such standardization results in products that have the same use instructions and procedures developed by the necessities of their mass-production technologies rather than the different skills and needs or wants of their users. That is, the expansion of the market through modern mass-production technologies results in decreased participation by consumers in the specifications of the many products that they consume. Thus, the trend toward *alienated* rather than *participatory* consumption.

The dominant modern consumption pattern that favors the individual-private-alienated-passive relationships in consumption has not, therefore, developed by chance, but is a consequence of the logic of modern capitalism. It is one that coincides with the goals, values and necessities of modern capitalist society. This society has historically developed so that the relationships among the producer organizations, the state, and the powerful consumer households, which we have tried to investigate, assure the emergence and dominance of the consumption pattern which furthers the *modern project*.

6   (Post)modernity and consumption

Modernity established and entrenched the *market* as the most important and, in its later stages, the sole legitimizing force in society. The market played a central role in the legitimation of the modern capitalist consumption pattern, which developed in ways that enlarged the market and extended it into more and more facets of human life. This consumption pattern abetted the trend towards all consumption being performed through the mediation of the market. With the growth of modern society, the role of products bought in the market for consumption also grew. One by one, every activity performed in the home that could be called "productive," became substituted by a marketable product. With every passing moment in modern society, consumption activities slipped out of the productive modes prevalent in the homesteads of the past and became dependent on the market.

In principle, these products found in the marketplace were largely independent of their intended functions. That the automobile was produced to provide mobility for people did not prevent its use for other reasons and purposes. A light bulb or a salt shaker, similarly, could be used for many purposes other than lighting a room or sprinkling salt over one's meal. A child who got hold of these things, for example, could use them as make-believe toys, dragging them across the floor to make noises or imagining them as vehicles. An adult could make Christmas tree decorations out of light bulbs and salt shakers by painting them, in effect, turning them into art objects. Someone could break the bulb or the salt shaker and use the jagged edges as a weapon, turning them into objects of fear. These alternative uses of light bulbs or salt shakers, uses that have nothing to do with the intent of the producer, an intent only culturally attached to the product in the first place, are hardly unconventional. A truly creative (or destructive) individual could come up with a really astonishing array of unintended uses. The surprising thing is that given all the creative possibilities and alternative uses that consumption objects could be put to, modern culture was largely successful in ensuring that the objects did not get used in ways that subverted their original intents. This was achieved mostly through acculturation, and with little or no help from legal impositions. Indeed, in modern society consumption was the private business of the consumer in the private sphere (the home), and was mostly unregulated. The exceptions pertained mostly to consumption in the public arena such as driving cars and, more recently, smoking in public places. Why was modern acculturation so successful? The answer lies partly in the nexus of powerful consumer households, producer organizations, and the state, that we explored in the previous chapter. Partly the answer lies in the power that this nexus had over the ideological apparatuses in modern society, especially the media. Another part of the answer lies in what is becoming especially important in current (post)modern culture: the ability of the market to co-opt, usurp, and commodify, as part of mainstream culture, the subversions attempted by consumers. From the rags of the sixties hippies to the rage of the nineties rappers, the market responded quickly and resiliently by coming up with products (faded and torn jeans, rap music CDs and attire) that legitimized and de-fanged the subversions. The logic of the capitalist market is not adverse to any purpose that a product can be put to as long as this purpose can be transformed into a reason for marketing the product to increasing numbers of customers. Often, the original subversive intent and content may have to be emptied from the expressions of these subversions. All rebellions of our time—hippie, punk, rap, grunge, hip-hop and more—have been co-opted by the market.

THE WANING MODERNITY

Consumption patterns in transition

As the modern society increasingly takes on aspects of the postmodern "imaginary,"[1] and as we live through this transitional era, certain paradoxical, but historically and socially interesting formations begin to appear. Let us turn to some of these, especially as they impact or pertain to consumption. In previous chapters, we discussed the reasons why products which represented the individual-private-alienated-passive pattern of consumption were consistent with the modern capitalist system. These were mostly economic reasons, and understandably so, since modern society and modern culture established the economy as the prime engine of society, the determinant moment that gave direction to all others. Rational society very much came to connote a society that maximized its material wealth through efficiently using and allocating its resources; indeed, an economic feat.

Modern ideological systems, or *metanarratives*,[2] found strength in their internally consistent structures and unifying themes. The economic centering of social action in modern culture was internally consistent with the rest of modernist thought and especially with the meliorative modern project that gave modern society its purpose. Modern culture separated subject and object and gave the subject the central role of acting upon objects, purposefully, to employ these objects to improve the material conditions of life. Objects were squarely placed in the service of the subject, to be used and manipulated by the subject for his/her needs and goals. The fulfillment or satisfaction of the subject's (human) needs and goals, the improvement of human life, was accomplished primarily through objects—namely, products made available to the subject by a scientifically and technologically organized system of industrial mass production. As a result, the more objects a person possessed and utilized, the more accomplished was her/his goal, in terms of the modern project. A consumption pattern which individualized and privatized more and more objects (products), putting them under the direct control of the individual subject(s), therefore found philosophical, ideological, and moral support. Such a pattern had allure—after all, that was the dream, the vision of modern culture. When these products, the objects, were put in the service of the consumer subject, their purpose was to make life more bearable, livable, comfortable, free of chores, and to free up the subject's time for endeavors of higher meaning and purpose. In effect, objects were to serve the subjects, to carry out functions and chores for them. Hence, the "passivation" of consumption came to be the prevalent mode of consumption in modernity. Let the machines do the washing, the cleaning, and the cooking, and let the consumer subject engage in meaningful endeavors. Allow freedom from chores, from having to think about chores, so that people can devote their lives to higher pursuits. Yet, leaving the "thinking" about chores, and doing them, to products, not wanting to bother about how to do them, meant alienated consumption.[3] Of course, the primary reason for alienated consumption was the imperative of mass production and mass marketing to achieve economic efficiencies. Because such efficiencies also helped relieve[4] consumer subjects from having to think or bother about chores, alienated consumption became more acceptable, less objectionable, and, indeed, attractive. The consumption pattern that suited the modern economy also turned out to be ideal for modern culture.

What happens, however, when the same phenomena receive a different interpretation, when a culture, a social imaginary that idealized a consumption pattern, begins to lose its allure? This is, indeed, what is largely happening with the advent of postmodern culture. Many internally consistent elements of modern culture that sanctified putting more and more objects on the planet and in the service of consumers are no longer so readily accepted. The ongoing and even aggravated misery around the world, the depletion of the world's resources and riches, pollution, ecological disasters, endangered species, growth of serious crime in the most affluent societies, war and civil strife, and continued political repression around the globe, have eroded the commitment to the once-lofty modern project, despite the many scientific and technological breakthroughs in modern society. The ensuing disillusionment has, in turn, corroded the authority of many modern political and social institutions, including nation states (and governments), the "nuclear" family, and schools. As such institutions wither from the attack of anti-modernist ideologies, and a loss of commitment to these institutions and what they stand for continues, the only locus of legitimation that remains is the *market*. Yet the contemporary market is itself a very modern institution. It is the medium of economic interaction. It was in modern capitalist society that it reached its heyday thanks to the modernist discourses, ideologies and metanarratives. We will examine later the contradictions engendered by the overarching dominance of a modern institution, the market, under unfolding postmodern conditions.

Modern separation of spheres of activity

As Habermas explains,[5] and we have discussed in earlier chapters, modern society was very insistent on separating domains or spheres in searching for normativity and social order.[6] One major separation occurred among the spheres of science, art, and morality. Each sphere entailed its own norms, its own guiding principles. In modernity such separation was paramount. If the sphere of science—that of reason and objective knowledge, which together allowed the existence of the knowing subject of modern society who controlled his/her own fate through such knowledge—was to keep itself pure and free of contamination from emotion, partiality, and bias, then this sphere had to stand apart. The sphere of science entailed the norms of truth, knowledge and reason. The sphere of art entailed the norms of beauty and aesthetics, and the sphere of morality the norms of justice and ethics (normative rightness). Each sphere, then, could be governed according to its own internal logic.[7] If the spheres and their norms intermixed promiscuously, the progress of humanity towards the achievement of its project, the higher purpose of improving human lives, could be derailed.

These were not the only separated spheres in modernity. The separation of the public from the private domain,[8] and many related separations discussed in Chapter 3—of feminine and masculine, consumption and production, mind and body—were also modern constructions.

One other important separation was that of culture from nature. Originally, in modern thought, culture came to define all that was humanly created, while nature was all that was *given* to being human. And, originally, modern thought privileged culture over nature. This was apparent in the privileging of all that was humanly created and controlled over that which was given: mind over body, reason over emotion, production over consumption. Modernity, indeed, put the human being in the center, as the subject, as the most awesome entity in the universe and, thus, deserving of the good life. As such, everything else—objects, whether live (animals, plants) or inert (material goods)—was considered to be in the service of the human being. Animals could justifiably be used as guinea-pigs for testing drugs and other products to improve the living conditions of humans, for example. Anything could be done to a guinea-pig for the betterment of humanity. The conception of the human in modern society, that is, how humans perceived themselves in modern thought, is important for understanding much of modern life and, of course, modern consumption.

With the advance of modernity, culture partitioned into multiple domains. Most visible among these were the social, the political, the economic, and, rather ironically, in its specialized definition, the "cultural" domain.[9] Modern thought, always privileging the "real" and the material, assigned this specialized form of culture a secondary role, one that was not determinant but determined. Culture constituted the "super-structure" as opposed to the "infrastructure" which consisted of the material economic resources and relationships. The economy, the domain of material conditions and resources of life, came to be assigned the role of the engine, the determinant moment of modernity. The economic health of a society, of a modern nation, was, and in many ways still is, given paramount importance. Listen to the voices of the officials of international development agencies, government leaders, and business managers, and what you hear incessantly is the concern for the economy, economic growth, and the wealth of nations.

Tenuous centrality of the economic

The more important spheres of human life, the economic as the most determining moment, together with the social and the political, had their own guiding principles, similar to the norms specific to the spheres of science, art and morality, and their own media dealing with the affairs of the respective spheres. The political was guided by the principles of democracy. Modern society being a civil society, the social was guided by the principles of civics. The state, governments, the electorate, courts, the family, religious organizations—these were institutions that mediated interactions in and across these spheres. The economic sphere was guided by principles of resource efficiency and the medium of economic interactions was (is) the market. The norms and principles of the economic, political, and social spheres were distinct. As in the case of science, art and morality, these norms did not intermix. Each had its own logic and worked best when not contaminated by other's principles and norms.

As other modern spheres, their institutions and media, lose influence and disintegrate, the market fills in the gaps. The economic (and the commercial), which became the most central sphere in high modernity, ends up further strengthening its hold on society. This is highly paradoxical under conditions of transition, since postmodern discourse generally rejects the centrality of the economic. The "problem" tends to be the contemporary absence of another medium to substitute for the market. Fragmentation—sought and largely achieved in the non-economic, discursive domains—does not fragment the market. The market, in fact, is already a fragmented entity—it is *the* medium of fragmentation in modernity. As we discussed in the previous chapter in connection with the modern consumption pattern, the domination by the market was largely responsible for increasing fragmentation in modernity. The growth of the market fragmented the moments of life through the proliferation of products with autonomous functions,

causing consumers to spend specialized, separate moments on each—
watching television, heating dinner in the microwave, exercising on the
machine, driving the car, loading the dishwasher, and so on. The individual-
ization of consumption for fragmented families and households, each
bedroom with its own television set, each eating his/her own TV dinner,
further fragmented consumers' lives.

For the postmodern idea to supplant the modern in people's every-day
lives, this contemporary dilemma of increasing dependence on the market,
the medium of modern economy, must be transcended. The market does
fragment and, indeed, allows many life styles and experiences, at times
inconsistent and even contradictory life styles and experiences, to coexist. Of
course, this occurs as long as such life styles and experiences are marketable
and commercially viable, subject to the criteria of economic efficiency. Thus,
fragmentation in the transitional period to the postmodern is through the
market, which is still bound by modern principles. As the market increasingly becomes the only locus of legitimation in society, the modern principle
of economic efficiency together with commercial viability, and the fragmentation based on this principle, become the new metanarrative. The result is
that as long as the market takes over and remains as the arbiter of social
interactions, political choices, and other matters, the postmodernist idea of
the call for an end to metanarratives is not and cannot be actualized in
sociocultural practice.

Transition(s) from the modern to the postmodern

Our interest in this chapter is to explore (post)modern[10] consumption under
the limitations of the contemporary transition period. There are discursive
calls for an end to modern political and social institutions and practices,
which many feel were tyrannical in their insistence on the singularity of
purpose and rationality for all humanity. These calls have had some success,
and have caused some disintegration of modern political and social institu-
tional forms, such as the general distrust in politicians and state/government
apparatuses, as well as the general skepticism about the health of the environment, the social responsibility of business, and the family structure (with
resultant increases in spouse and child abuse, etc.). Such disintegration of
universalizing, totalizing ideas and institutions usher in multifarious changes
in consumption, despite, or perhaps because of, the domination of the
market over all else.

Originally, modern society emphasized and depended upon legitimation
processes other than the market. In early modernist discourse, the market
was not considered as part of the legitimation processes. Rather, legitimation was discussed mostly under the rubric of political institutions (state,
government, unions, etc.), and social institutions (family, social clubs, neighborhood, religious institutions, etc.). According to modernist thinking,
something was legitimate (acceptable, viable, do-able, legal) in society,

because some political process (hopefully democratic), based on economic and social criteria, circumstances and logic, resulted in some form of social consensus. Society, or at least a sane majority of the enfranchised that could coalesce and find the means to establish its will in society, came to some conclusion that a certain behavior was admissible, benign, or at least unobjectionable and, in some other cases, even highly desirable. Other behaviors were deemed, in the same manner, unacceptable. Behaviors about which a society felt passionately were sanctified (or proscribed) by law. Other behaviors, even if written into the law books, codified into regulations, or preached by society's leaders, were not so associated with passionate social feelings, and greater flexibility was allowed with regard to these.[11]

Crises of legitimation and commitment

The modern market was also influenced by these discourses of legitimation. Through political, legal, economic, and social mechanisms developed in modern society, attempts were made to keep products and behaviors with products—especially in the public sphere (such as bathing attire on a public beach)—"in line." Believing in the validity of these processes and mechanisms, which were carefully thought out, debated and *written* (the rules of democratic governance, for example), modern *citizens* tried to resolve society's affairs through such mechanisms. Modern discourse and rhetoric kept politics and social relationships, along with economics, alive as the loci of legitimation. As the influence of modern discourse wanes, however, these mechanisms have begun to lose their effectiveness in the resolution of affairs in society. Skepticism towards and distrust of political institutions and leaders seems to be at an all-time high. In the United States, for example, all post-Vietnam War presidents have had very low trustworthiness and believability scores. Their images were not helped by events such as the Watergate and the Iran-Contra affairs, marital infidelities, and campaign finance scandals. The same tends to be true in Europe and elsewhere in the world. In modern sensibility, entrusting the future of society to such untrustworthy people is highly paradoxical. In the case of Dan Rostenkowski, for example, a long-time Chicago politician and Illinois congressman in the United States Congress, many people expressed paradoxical sentiments such as "We know he is a crook, but he brings economic benefits to his district."[12] The sentiment that in today's political environment only a good crook or a wheeler-dealer can get things done, has also been widely expressed. Politics has become "dirty business."[13] The same can be said of social institutions, even a hallowed one such as the family. Modern society's depiction of the family is under growing attack.[14] So much child abuse, spouse abuse and the like has been hidden and victims have been allowed to suffer in the name of the sanctity of the family[15] that the trust in this institution's inherent and unquestioned import and necessity is eroded. No institution of modern society has a special immunity or impunity any more; all are open to skeptical and critical interrogation.

The failures of these institutions, and of the modern project,[16] in delivering the long awaited promises is one important reason for this skepticism and distrust. Another important reason is found in the postmodern discourses which have incisively deconstructed and demystified the hitherto unquestioned sanctimony of these institutions. Indeed, postmodernism and growing postmodern attitudes, especially among the younger generation (sometimes called Generation-X, Boom Busters, or the MTV Generation[17]) have created an increasing indifference towards these institutions, if not outright distrust or skepticism. The growing attitude among members of the postmodern generation seems to be that these institutions are generally irrelevant to their individual lives, that they rarely make any difference. Consequently, members of the postmodern generation largely ignore these institutions in order to do their "own thing." Reliance on and *commitment* to any of these institutions for support or for provision of care, rights, and services is greatly lost, and the individual *citizen* is increasingly left to her/his own devices. The void created by the dissolution or dismantling of institutions that, in modern society, provided for the many needs of the individual is now filled by the market. The *citizen*, who can no longer rely on the political and social institutions for such provision, has to morph into the *consumer*, and acquire things for the satisfaction of his/her needs in (or through the mediation of) the market.

Ascent of the market

This is by no means an unfamiliar experience for many in modern society. When, through urbanization or other forms of mobility, for example, members of modern industrial society had to abandon their traditional communities or their traditional ways of life, they realized that they had to provide for many of the needs earlier taken care of by their families and other social networks. Such provisioning of needs was generally achieved through purchasing services and goods (e.g., health care and food) in the marketplace. As people increasingly lost faith in the political and social institutions, as well as in their own abilities to influence these institutions, the marketplace moved in at higher and higher levels. In the United States, even a war[18] was run on the basis of employing the typical marketing techniques of polling and television campaigning. Every evening's news conference during the Gulf War was performed in high-tech promotional forms with well planned cuts to visuals of highly successful "smart bombs"[19] and other pre-taped segments. Furthermore, the distribution of war memorabilia, such as T-shirts and bumper stickers, by private entrepreneurs—very similar to practices of promoting major commercial movies—was allowed and encouraged by the state. In effect, the destiny of popular support for the war was not left to the workings of the traditional political processes, but was decided in the marketplace through well-crafted marketing strategies. The idea of the war was not debated through political institutions but sold through marketing campaigns in which the state and the corporate sector co-operated.

In the United States, at least, this is not unusual. It is widely known, for example, that political elections have largely become marketing events. When Ronald Reagan first met his marketing team, his initial remark was: "I understand that you are here to sell soap and wanted to see the bar."[20] In a way, one might say that political elections were always a market affair; that it was a competition for votes, a circumstance where each candidate was in the arena to sell her/his ideas and abilities to those who had votes (analogous to purchasing power). Modern discourse restrained this commercial quality of the political process. As the influence of modern discourse wanes, however, this quality comes to the fore and political parties openly begin to practice the "market(ing) game." Popular distrust in politics enables open discussion of the marketization of elections and politics in general. The public does not greatly resent this, finding such a state of affairs acceptable, inescapable, or inevitable. As a result, any legitimation of political ideas and practice increasingly necessitates the mediation of the market. This also seems to hold true in the arena of consumption activities of households. While in modern society public consumption activities were organized and controlled through the political and social institutions such as laws, regulations, family, social clubs and religious organizations, in contemporary society any control has to be realized through the market's ability to co-opt countercultural movements or subversive consumption practices. These differences between the role of the modern market and the contemporary market are in large part due to the fact that we are, indeed, living in a period of transition into what many scholars[21] of our time have called, postmodernity. Different perspectives on postmodernity have tried to capture and understand this phenomenon, which is likely to induce major transformations in consumption, transformations that are already being felt. To understand these changes in consumption, a brief discussion of how postmodernity is described and interpreted in an ever growing contemporary literature will be helpful.

POSTMODERNISM AND POSTMODERNITY

Modernity is defined by its central themes. Perhaps the most central theme, one that set modern society apart from its predecessor society, where an aristocracy ruled alongside religious institutions and set the ideological tone, was the idea that human beings controlled their own fate. The idea that came to hold sway in modernity was that the human being was not a subject *of* a supernatural power but a subject that *acts upon* nature to control its elements and impacts in order to improve life. This, in fact, became the *project* that guided modern thought and modern life: improving human life by controlling nature through scientific technologies.

To realize this project, the modern subject had to be a knowing subject, one who understood the conditions of existence imposed by nature, by the surrounding physical environment. As discussed in the previous chapter, this was achieved by the separation of mind and body, where the mind could distance itself from the everyday immersions into life and the biases that arose from such immersions, and assume an objective, detached perspective on reality, and be able to represent this reality as objectively valid human knowledge. The purpose of such knowledge, originally to control the impacts of nature on human life, quickly evolved into one of *producing* better conditions, specifically through the production of objects that mediated nature's power over human beings. Again, as we discussed in the previous chapter, in modernity the ability to produce objects and, through them, better living conditions, became the yardstick for judging the success of the modern project. Through the production of objects and living conditions, modernity began to construct the social environment of human life and thereby shape human reality in ever greater degrees. Yet the idea that reality was beyond human agency, that it was something given and could only be discovered, not constructed, remained intact as a cornerstone of modern thought.[22]

One of the major criticisms of modernist thought by postmodernists, therefore, is that modernism rejected the *idea* of the construction of social reality, while *in practice* carrying on at an unprecedented level the social construction of reality. Consider, for example, living in major cities such as London, New York, Mexico City, Tokyo, Paris, or Mumbai. All these are humanly constructed. Urbanization is one of the most impressive realities that modern people encounter. The construction of urban and suburban spaces and, thereby, (sub)urban life patterns and living conditions is an enduring legacy of modernity. Yet, in modernity, urbanization was not constructed but *happened*.

Hyperreality

The new sensibility regarding reality is called *hyperreality* by postmodernists. What becomes reality is based upon the imaginary visions of what could or might be. Such visions are originally represented as hype (or simulation, that is, exemplary reproduction) in the public rhetoric. These visions, when they are communicated powerfully, become the reality, especially when a community of believers in such powerful visions begins to behave as if these visions were real. In effect, hype or simulations that are commonplace and massively consumed become reality.

Examples of the hyperreal abound in our current world, especially in the sphere of consumption. Young consumers, such as teenagers and pre-teens, for instance, transform advertising hype into their reality when they imbue certain brands of shoes and clothing items with meanings of power, prestige, attractiveness, or sexiness. At school or among friends, not wearing these brand names becomes a reason for being excluded or ridiculed.[23] It is not only the young people, however, who consume hyperreal constructions. Thematization of many sections of our cities, based on an imagined past or future,[24] and (re)presented as powerfully communicated hype, attests to the society-wide occurrence of hyperreality. These thematizations range from the renovated city centers in the images of city life that once existed, to the attractive simulations of a city initially found in theme parks (such as Main Street, USA of Disneyland),[25] to the shopping malls built on thematized simulations of the marketplace[26] where, other than their homes and work-places, Americans now spend most of their lives. All of these spaces where we spend our *real* lives, including our homes and workplaces, are fantasy lands, except that we call them every-day reality, while we give the name fantasy to *Disney World* or the *Universal Studios* theme parks, which only provide simulations of how life could be (and if attractive enough, will be in the future). Yet each is equally constructed. A section of cafés in a Disney theme park is no more a construction of what life could be than a suburban neighborhood which—for example, in Phoenix, in the middle of the Sonoran Desert—replicates olive and citrus groves, lush lawns, and some-times even the desert itself.[27]

The identity of the real and the simulation in our everyday environments is well exemplified in the World Showcase section of EPCOT Center in the Walt Disney World complex in Florida. Here we find the simulated versions of London and Paris, of a Mexican marketplace inside a Yucatan Peninsula type of temple, of charming German and Norwegian villages—all as fantasy to experience and enjoy. While such fantasy seems to be the replica-tion of the real, in fact it is representing the real at its "best," including, for example, all the exciting and attractive elements of what a Mexican market-place is, but excluding all that is considered unattractive, unsafe, or unpleasant. To think that this fantasy remains confined to the World Showcase is a mistake, however. The very success of such simulations that attract millions of tourists and generate huge revenues acts as a signal to the "original" sites which are then recreated in a Disneyesque way to attract tourist revenues. The merging of fantasy and the real is complete, modern culture's continuing (but progressively feeble) insistence on their separation notwithstanding.

Difference

Postmodernist thought, then, recognizes both the freedom of the human subject from *given* social reality, and her/his responsibility in the *construction* of this reality. Modernist thought emphasizes the inevitability of this reality based, for example, on the inescapable consequences of technological devel-opments. Postmodernist thought emphasizes the potentials and the possibilities, as well as the responsibilities in making the choices among them. Postmodernists regard reality as a narrative (or a construction based on myths), without any absolute foundation or essentialist basis, onto which responsibility can be placed, or on the basis of which truth claims can be made. In postmodern thinking, all "regimes of truth"[28] are on an equal footing in terms of their construction.[29] Postmodern thought calls for recognition of difference as difference rather than in terms of superiority or inferiority. In this vein, the postmodern sensibility is to allow difference and also to allow the experiencing of different ways of being, living, looking, and acting.

Seduction

By rejecting the commitment to a singular way of life and being, postmodernism also seeks to liberate the human subject from commitment to a singular self. Furthermore, the idea that the human subject is centered, in the "know," in command of the environment and the objects (products) in the environment, capable of commanding such objects to improve life, is largely abandoned in postmodernism. Postmodernists recognize that far from simply being in the service of the human subject, to a large extent objects, especially products such as the automobile and the television set that modern society has so successfully mass produced, shape human life. Objects tend to take on a life of their own, and with the complicity of consumers, determine what kind of a life the human being will live.[30] How television has changed our lives, for example, has been well studied and documented.[31] In the postmodernist perspective, objects and subjects negotiate a reality. Paradoxically, in the process of producing objects to control life, the subject relinquishes control. Objects so produced acquire a seductive power.[32] They become objects of desire, due in part to the promise imbued in their creation that they will make life better, pleasurable, more exciting.

Decentering

Postmodernism thus posits a *decentering of the subject*. The human subject is removed from her/his privileged position and, as implied in the paradox just mentioned, can lay claim to power and control over life through objectification of self, that is, through presenting self as a marketable commodity —as an object of desire. In a market economy, for anyone who is not born into wealth, the only way to make a living and have some control over life is to market oneself as (having) something of value: a skill, as labor power, as someone with desirable traits and talents that can contribute to the economy or, in other words, to the accumulation of capital and material goods and to the wealth of those who own them. In our (post)modern economy, the "reality" of this condition is evidenced in the fact that, for example, in the United States, the most affluent economy in the world, millions of homeless are left "on the outside," figuratively and literally, since they have no marketable qualities. The phenomenon of homelessness also attests to the fact that, despite the insistence of modernist metanarratives on the value, importance and centrality of the human subject, it is the health and the rationale of the *economy* that is primary, and anything or anyone who does not contribute to it is indeed "on the outside."

It is not surprising that consumers have begun to regard themselves as marketables or as consumables. Evidence for such orientation abounds: increasing numbers of men and women are getting plastic surgery done to enhance different body parts to make themselves more marketable; increasing numbers of consumers are using publications and television programs that tell them how to make themselves more marketable in different situations;[33] people in advertising and fashion industries increasingly cater to consumers' desires for clothing and other consumption items for the purposes of *customizing* themselves for the various situations and contexts of their lives—workplace, home, recreational sites, fitness centers, and tryst locations (e.g., singles bars).[34]

Reversals

As customizing oneself as a situation-specific marketable entity becomes the mode of asserting oneself in the world, increasingly consumption (rather than production) becomes the domain where identities and values are determined and/or constructed. At the culmination of modernity into its highest form, there is a *reversal of production and consumption*. As we pointed out in Chapter 2, in early modernist thought production was revered and consumption slighted. Production, after all, created value while consumption merely destroyed or devoured it. Consumption was equated with waste; in seventeenth-century England, consumption was the popular name for tuberculosis, an illness from which people wasted away.[35] Postmodernists such as Baudrillard, on the other hand, claim that value is created in or through consumption, not in production.[36] It is consumption, or the desire for consumption, represented in sign-value, that affords the object its value.

Definitions of and meanings imbued in the terms consumption and consumer, as opposed to production and producer, constitute one of the defining paradoxes of modernism. The subject to be emancipated in the central project of modernism was conceptualized as the consumer, the individual who had needs that could be satisfied in ever-improving ways, allowing her/him to attain potentials and higher purposes for which human life was destined. As evidenced in declarations of the project of modernity by major philosophers (e.g., Kant, Descartes, etc.), the producer role of the human individual was only a means to support the existence of the central subject, the consumer. The producer self of the subject was the self in the moment of providing the *means* for the consumer self, the *end* for which all human action was justified. When, however, the consumer and the producer roles were separated and identified with the feminine and the masculine respectively, paradox and contradiction were injected into the system of modern signification and representations.[37] Since the consumer was identified with the feminine and the feminine was culturally attached with meanings of being an object—object of masculine desire, to be owned and kept at home, adorned, embellished and surrounded by other consumables[38]—she was also the objectified and the consumed.

The central subject of modernity, the consumer, was, therefore, also the consumed. She or he was consumed by the desire to consume more and more in order to reach or achieve a future vision of a life improved, paving the way for a self that attained actualization of its potential.[39] These objectives, however, could be endlessly redefined and reconstructed and what modernity really promised was, therefore, an unending cycle of desire and consumption. In this unending cycle was the consumption of the subject, as laborer, as manager, as owner, in the end, all in service of the system of the ever growing economy.

Modernity rarely, if ever, noticed its paradoxes. Modernity blithely ignored its central subject, whom the system was to work and provide for. The consumer ended up becoming the consumed. If the paradoxes were noticed, they were suppressed and repressed by the modernist rhetoric. At the same time that the consumer was the subject, the act of consumption, a feminine act, was profane; it did not produce any value but only devoured or destroyed it. As a feminine act, consumption was primarily a passive moment, one requiring little reason or the use of mind. Again, primarily a bodily act, consumption was sensual and emotional rather than rational. And, as we may recall, body, emotion, the sensual were considered to be the inferior qualities, unlike the mind and reason. Even the man, representing the masculine and, thereby, the mind that created and produced, became the performer of bodily functions and fulfiller of bodily needs and desires when at home, in the private domain, during consumption. If he identified too much with the roles at home, however, he was belittled with one of the most degrading labels in modern society: *effeminate*. Even though a mere consumer at home, the man at least had the redeeming values attached to being the producer in the public domain, as the active, rational, and *knowing* being. The producers, therefore, could be proud of their productive activity, but for the consumers what they consumed was not to be talked about or flaunted.

As the role of the products of the market, the products from the public domain, grew in consumption, lives in the private domain, representing the "feminine" increasingly required that women consume market-mediated products: fashion items such as clothing and accessories, or cosmetics. Furthermore, with the growth of *time saving* or *labor saving* products in the market, the expectations of the women at home, in terms of the frequency of washing, cleaning, and cooking, increased, causing them to consume more of the products made available by the market for these chores. The end result was a paradoxical increase in the physical and psychological pressures on women. Ultimately, time saving devices did not save but often elaborated the time required by women in consumption activities.[40] While being pressured to increase their consumption, consumers—particularly women—were belittled for *being consumers*. Far from being rewarded for their expertise in buying and consuming, they had to endure a pejorative public rhetoric that kept them silent and in relative shame for their existence as mere consumers. The imprinting of these significations and representations in the minds of modern people contributed greatly to the orientations in marketing— possibly the ultimate institution of postmodernity in contemporary western civilization—in terms of the representation of desire, of the consumer, and of consumption.

The paradoxical aspects of consumption are recognized, accepted, even embellished in postmodernism. Consumption is not underprivileged but embraced.[41] It is through what they consume or are able to consume, and through the process of construction of their consumption experiences that postmodern consumer-citizens lay claim to their identities and signal their worth to society. Modern culture, after all, had already instilled the idea that improvement of life lay in increasing the amount of one's consumption of products. It is not surprising, therefore, that in late modernity the marketing of a person's success and attainment in life would be based on how much and what s/he could consume. Postmodern ideas cut asunder the negative connotations (such as wastefulness) of consumption, and imbue it with notions of value, construction, and representation of self, and means of laying claim to power. Under such conditions, people begin to shed their cultural timidity about exhibiting their consumption patterns, habits, and styles. People increasingly judge an individual's status and value in society by what they see that individual consume—where s/he lives, what s/he drives, wears, eats. Individuals so judged increasingly represent themselves to others through what or how they consume, thus becoming "customizers" of self.

Recognition of these productive aspect of consumption (producing of self, self-image, physical and mental existence) further exposes the arbitrary and mythical separation of production and consumption in modernism's narratives. In fact, in every act of consumption there is production, as in every act of production there is consumption. It is our pragmatic assignment of values that conceptually sunders this otherwise uniform activity into separate moments called "production" and "consumption," moments that were culturally constructed in modernity. In postmodern thought, there is a 180-degree turn. Consumption subsumes production:[42] it takes over the importance attributed to production in modernity. Consumption comes to be regarded as a value producing process, and it becomes the domain that determines much of the significations and representations of the sign and the symbolic.

Modernism intensified, if not created, the paradoxical nature of the relationships between consumption and production by insisting that they were two separate and, in fact, opposite activities. Production was value creation, consumption was value destruction; two separate, distinct, oppositional processes. To think of two such opposing activities as one and the same was, understandably, not possible from a modernist point of view.

Postmodernism, on the other hand, argues that paradox is present (or may be waiting to be found) in every circumstance, every moment, every act. Rather than deny paradoxes, or if found, try to resolve, repress, or eliminate them—postmodernism embraces paradox and calls for playful, artful and critical utilization of it to enchant every moment of life. Suppressing paradoxes, actual or potential, and trying to regiment everything into a consistent order disenchanted modern existence and rendered the modern experience unidimensional. Such suppression and regimentation were not able to eliminate paradoxes anyway—since paradox is (re)created by just another way of looking at, interpreting, or de(re)constructing the order or the system. Instead, paradox or even paradoxical juxtapositions of opposites, according to postmodernist thinking, can be employed to look at things from different perspectives, thus contributing to a multiplicity, multi-dimensionality and, ultimately, a (re)enchantment of life.

Tolerance

In postmodernist discourse, then, the idea is to have tolerance for difference. Since there is no absolute foundation or an essential(ist) base from which one can begin arguments to prove, or try to prove, the *truth* of one's perspective or position, the only possibility of universal agreement on anything is through conversation among the positions. Modern science endorsed this same concept in the idea that nothing can be known with certainty, that we only have degrees of confidence in what we know. This means that even when we feel "sure" of something, we have to allow a probability, even if a minute one, that we may be mistaken. In the strictest sense of the word, we cannot be sure or "certain" of any knowledge we have. Without going into a deeper explanation of the concepts involved, we note that this idea arises from the realization, among modern scientists, that any *representation* of things—material objects or events, for example—or of the relationships among things, is bound to have the possibility, therefore a probability, of having errors in it. Thus, the modern scientific idea follows the adage: "Everything must be taken with a grain of salt." This means, then, that even when we have a very high confidence in what we know—perhaps as a result of having performed scientific research to arrive at this knowledge—we must tolerate the possibility that we do not know perfectly. Therefore, someone else's opposing or incompatible knowledge must also be tolerated. Now, if we have very high confidence in what we know, we will allot a very small probability to knowledge that disagrees with ours. Nevertheless, true scientists must tolerate the possibility that they may be wrong and others may be right; even if very unlikely.

A powerful example of where intolerance leads us was presented in Jacob Bronowski's television series based on his book *The Ascent of Man*.[43] He walks into a puddle at Auschwitz, dips his hands in mud that possibly contains the ashes of the bodies burnt at the concentration camp, stressing in a visually impressive and shocking manner the results of idea systems that are intolerant, that never question themselves critically. Postmodernists have often called Auschwitz the end of modernity. In the Holocaust they see the *end* of the totalizing, universalizing, therefore, intolerant modern metanarratives. How did modern thought become so intolerant and universalizing even when (and as) science clearly preached tolerance? How does science that is a, if not *the*, cornerstone of modern discourse become a silent partner of totalizing inhumanity? The postmodernist response to this question would be that it is not because only ill-directed strands in modern discourses or idea systems are intolerant; indeed, all modern thought is totalizing, universalizing and intolerant. Even science, the foundational pillar of modernity, is tolerant of alternative discourses only to the extent such alternatives fit the criteria of being "scientific," as defined by scientists. Of course, even such tolerance is only an ideal type. The history of science is full of examples of intolerant scientists and of paradigms intolerant of alternative scientific perspectives. After all, to be intolerant while preaching tolerance, the only thing one needs to do is to declare the opponents to be *unscientific*. The idea is to be tolerant as long as the rival theories are deemed scientific. And who decides if any method, theory, idea or knowledge is scientific? A group of scientists, of course! The recognition of this circularity of logic is what made Kuhn's ideas popular in the 1960s and Feyerabend's ideas admissible in the 1970s.[44] These periods overlapped with the growth of movements that (re)launched postmodernity.[45] These movements suggested that there were, and urged that there be, different ways of looking at the world, culture, life in general. Many such movements rejected the dominant culture, which they identified as overly materialistic, individualistic, capitalistic, commercial, and totalizing, representing *the way* or the *only* way of life. Heroes of these alternative movements surfaced around the world. At first, established institutions, politicians, and leaders of modern society turned a cold shoulder to them, trying to discredit, belittle or ignore them. In most cases, marketing organizations shied away from these exponents of counterculture. Once the postmodernist ideas started to catch on, however, and the width and depth of their impacts became evident, hippies and the flower children, and other counterculture proponents came to be accepted, initially as a twisted fact of life, and later as a market and, more importantly, as a source of marketable concepts.[46] The micro-economies built around the defining consumption items of each movement—clothing, music and musical groups, special diets, etc.—were drawn into the mainstream economy through culmination of the commodification and commercialization processes that had already started within the communities associated with the movements.

This postmodern approach has created greater acceptance of fragmented consumption. The necessity to (re)present a continual, consistent, authentic, and unique self in all life situations of the consumer is no longer pressing. In most cases, what was earlier achieved in the arts and intellectual discourse— a greater allowance for different ways of knowing[47]—percolated into consumption. In other cases, diversity in consumption led to diversity in discourse. The same trend is observable in the arts, architecture, literature, and in management. In the arts, the overwhelming dominance of (representational) painting and sculpture has waned, allowing the entry of other art forms into high culture. In architecture the dominance of modern form— one that is functionalist and universalist—gave way to regionalism and eclectic, aesthetic forms.[48] In management, the Fordist, hierarchical structure of organization has been successfully questioned and transformed to more varied, participatory and different forms.[49]

Fragmentations

At the threshold of postmodernity, fragmentations in every-day experience abound. They persist in the media, the most important and dominating mode of exposure to our universe in contemporary society. Fragmentation is in advertisements on television, for example, where we have the 30-second spots, each further fragmented into many fleeting moments of spectacular visuals which rarely link with each other.[50] The purpose of these fleeting scenes and visuals that are exciting to the senses is not to connect or to (re)present a centered, unified meaning. In much of televisual marketing communication, the necessity for continuity or complementarity is transcended, allowing for a free play of visual images. Such images are only meant to leave the audience with a heightened sense of excitement about the product being marketed, an image montage that grabs the emotions and imprints the cognition of the targeted individual. While television is the major medium in contemporary society, it is by no means the only medium of fragmentation. Spots on the radio, blurbs and quotes interspersed in magazine articles, newspapers with condensed TV-style reporting, highlighted brand names that flash by on billboards on a highway—all these constitute fragmentation in media experiences along with television.

Furthermore, advertising is not the only form which presents fragmentation in the media. News programs on radio and television, news items in magazines and newspapers, situation comedies, soap operas and other programs on television, all exhibit similar fragmentation. One form of this fragmentation is the partition of the programs into short, disconnected moments and items, presenting each with great sophistication in technique and style, as successive spectacles, to keep the interest, attention, and excitement levels high in the audience. Lacking a unifying content, and unable to hold audience attention for too long with their exciting but disconnected and fragmentary moments, television programs (and other programs such as video games) have to "move along" at a brisk pace, onto other spectacles. Even news programs attain (or at least attempt) the intensity of commercial ones, playing the spectacle and the spectacular in each item of news, moving from one item to the next, each a spectacle, often framed (verbally and visually) for maximum impact.[51] This is no different from the form of a situation comedy, for example, which moves at a fast pace from one scene to another, one funny "incident" to another. The trick in all programming for the mass audience seems to be one of allowing the audience to come in or leave the "scene" without feeling awkward, disoriented, or as if something is missing. Each moment, each item, each spectacle has to stand on its own. The gauche modernist requirements of inception, narrative, and conclusion must give way to exciting, fragmentary, intense, momentary, and spectacular presents/presence.

Juxtapositions

This new requirement and, at the same time, strength of the spectacle is related to the second form of fragmentation. The disconnected moments, items, and scenes are also fragmented and disjointed from any context. As Gitlin, a sociologist and observer of postmodern culture, articulates, each moment, each spectacle is decontextualized. No longer do things belong within a context or a historical process. "Anything can be juxtaposed to anything else. Everything takes place in the present, 'here,' that is, nowhere in particular."[52] It becomes possible, even preferable, to represent historical events on an even surface, without depth or a sense of the historical process, as bricolage,[53] in ways that are spectacular, maximize the excitement, and result in an emotional high. Events, scenes, and personalities from completely independent and disconnected contexts are often superimposed and juxtaposed onto each other in television news programs, newspaper reportage, news items in magazines, radio news announcements, and elsewhere. In the (post)modern, this is not absurd or improper journalism. Rather, the visual sensation of the bricolage is greatly enjoyed.

Along with this continual fragmentation and decontextualization in our media surrounding and informing us, there is a fragmentation of our thoughts, desires, and behaviors from our own contexts. The postmodern generation, the contemporary youth, especially, often sever themselves from the worldly events around them. To the modern mind this is a state of being uninformed or ignorant. To the postmodern mentality this is an alternative form of being; one that liberates from the conformities or impositions of a single "regime of truth."

Fluid signification and decontextualization

The postmodern existence is characterized by another set of fragmentations; that of the signifier from the signified, the object from the function, and the product from the need. That all signifiers are only arbitrarily linked to the signified (and the referent) has been well recognized by semioticians at least since Saussure.[54] The link is only pragmatic, that is, culturally, linguistically (semiotically) imposed. In the postmodern, the modernist assumption of a natural link is ended and the freedom of the signifier is both declared and celebrated. As in marketing campaigns, in all aspects of life, "free-floating" signifiers are playfully and gainfully employed in (re)signification. They are constantly imbued with novel or nostalgic or reinforced meanings to represent a multiplicity of ideas, things, and positions.

Along with the fissure between the signifier and the signified, there is also a fissure between the object and its function. All objects, even if specifically produced for a particular function, are nonetheless only arbitrarily connected to that function. At the moment of its origination, the object attains its independence from its culturally signified function. Imagine, for example, the number of different uses a child or even an adult not acculturated to a western kitchen could find for a hand-held electric mixer commonly found in such kitchens. It would be very unlikely that they could correctly guess the use of such a mixer in western civilization. This liberation of the object from its intended use (freedom of objects from their functions) was well recognized by surrealist and other artists such as Duchamp, Dalí, Rauschenberg, and Warhol, who turned utilitarian objects (urinals, meat grinders, clocks, Coca-Cola bottles, Campbell's soup cans) into icons and art pieces in their own right.[55]

Finally, the product acquired in the market is breaking free of the need(s) for which the consumer initially sought it and the producer provided it. This, of course, is just an extension of the separation of the object from its original function. In effect, the consumer acquires the product for the image that it represents, and this image is only partially, if at all, constructed on the basis of the need perceived by the consumer. Furthermore, a single product is capable of representing multiple images, as signified by culture and by the marketing effort. This culminates in the disconnection of images and products from each other, from their original contents, and from their contexts.

The market and marketing practices accelerate the fragmentation of the product. In contemporary markets, given the competitive conditions, it is a practical necessity to concentrate on the singular product or a narrowly defined product group. Both in earlier representations of products by commercial artists in catalogues and in more contemporary forms of advertising, the focus is the product. The product is the figure that has to stand out from the cluttered, competitive ground. The product has to focus the consumer's attention on it. Such isolation of the product (or more accurately, its iconic representation, the brand) from its context, as in the case of "Just do it" Nike advertisements, reinforces the fragmentation that the consumer experiences in consuming the products. Such decontextualization often enhances the marketability of a product by making it a canvas for spectacles. An example is the Navajo sand painting, which originally was

part of a medicinal ceremony and was destroyed at the end of that ceremony. As a commodity, it becomes merely an object of desire, an art object,
to be viewed and admired, to be bought and sold. Such decontextualization
is by no means original to marketing, however, as evidenced in the sacraliza-
tion of products through attributing values and meanings to them
independent of their original function or status.[56]

Images and selves

Fragmentations are reflected in the everyday life and being of the consumer.
With the growing, almost complete, domination of life by products bought
in the market, the consumer's life experiences also become fragmented. In
consuming each product, the consumer is involved in an independent, separate task that is only connected with other tasks in the culture's imaginary.
These connections occur in narratives of purpose regarding a healthy life, a
long life, an enjoyable life, etc. Otherwise, there are no connections as the
consumer eats a frozen dinner, watches television, feeds the cat, washes dirty
clothes in the washing machine. The narratives struggle to seek a central,
unified meaning and purpose for a life in settings that are increasingly fragmented into moments dominated by tasks required by products consumed.
The impulse to seek connections, unite and universalize goals for humanity,
and forge unity in human experience is, indeed, inherent to modernist narratives and a product of the modern imaginary.

The consumers of (post)modernity seem to be transcending these narratives, no longer seeking centered, unified purposes, but increasingly seeking
meaning and to "feel good" in separate, different moments by immersing
themselves in a variety of experiences and partaking of the associated
images. In a market system this is achieved by (re)producing self-images that
are marketable, likable, and/or desirable in each moment. There is, indeed, a
growing disillusionment with committing oneself to long-term consistent
goals or characters. Such commitment, it is felt, never delivers the promises
of the narrative that required it. As a result, we observe a growing playful-
ness with the game of simulating and switching images to make the best of
each situation the consumers find themselves in.

Thus occurs the fragmentation of the self. In postmodern culture, there is
no insistence on making the self consistent, authentic, or centered.
Postmodernists will argue that the self never was, in its core, or in tendency,
centered or authentic, but that in modernity the illusion of such a self was
sanctified and, therefore, sought by the consumer. The postmodern generation has transcended this quest and neither seeks the centered self nor feels
guilty about not seeking it. On the contrary, the growing ability to switch
images and represent different selves is perceived as liberating. By trying
products that represent various images, allowing themselves to lay claim to
powerful or successful images, postmodern consumers experience freedom
from monotony, boredom, and the necessity to conform. Perhaps ironically,

postmodernism, which vehemently opposes any commitment to the modern project of emancipation of the modern subject (from the impositions of nature and the exploitation by others), proposes a new project: emancipation from the projects of emancipation.

The fragmented body and the market

This fragmenting of self into self-images also partitions the body into body parts. The media, advertisements, music videos, artistic representations, abound with such fragmentation.[57] This reinforces the objectification and commodification of self—through signification of (fragmented) self-images, marketable in different situations. Each body part—the lips, the hips, the thighs, the abdomen, the chest—is considered separately, each as a means of enhancing a required or desired image. In the process of (re)shaping or (re)dressing each body part, with marketability in mind in each situation, there is a decontextualization of body parts and their perception as distanced from the individual's own being. The individual's gaze, very much a part of the self and mostly directed at the other in modernity, becomes disembodied and turns on its own body. There is, in this process of perceiving each body part as a marketable item (as in the case of models whose hands or feet only are "rented" for use in advertisements), a process of distancing—a standing away from one's body and looking on as the other, testing and scrutinizing oneself from the vantage point of a distanced gaze, the gaze of the other. While this may invoke the Cartesian separation of the mind and the body, it is in fact quite different. That which is detached from one's own body is not the *mind* but the *gaze*. Specifically, this is not one's own and independent gaze (as the Cartesian mind is) but the gaze of the *other*. The scrutiny is done from the perspective of the *other*, this "other" proxying for the expectations and requirements of the culture for which one's image must be rendered marketable and to which the body (representing the self-image) will be marketed.

For help in partitioning the body and perceiving each part as an object to be dressed or customized[58] for marketability, the consumer turns to the market. The market is a cornucopia of products s/he can acquire to craft the images s/he wants or needs to represent. The market not only provides products that can be attached to, draped over, or embellish the body but it increasingly provides the means to customize body parts in terms of plastic surgery, implants, etc. While the general perception is that women have such surgical customization of body parts, the number of men who acquire biceps, calves, and get their faces lifted is also growing very fast. The separation of categories of gender (feminine–masculine) from categories of sex (female–male), in tune with fragmentations in the signifier–signified relationships, has allowed increasing possibilities for males to express themselves as consumers.[59] These possibilities and the break in the traditional (modern) connections between sex and gender are increasingly represented in advertisements such as those for the perfume Charlie, where women are represented in traditionally masculine roles and men are represented in traditionally feminine roles, and in Calvin Klein's CK-1, the unisex perfume that can appeal to a melange of gender roles.

Some observers of postmodernity have chosen to call the fragmentations in self-representations and the switching of self-images the schizophrenic self.[60] There is a distinction, however, between this postmodernist fragmentation of the self and the modernist definitions of schizophrenia in terms of an estrangement from oneself and from society.[61] While there is an estrangement from *a* self in the postmodern fragmentation of self-images, one cannot really talk of an estrangement from society. The multiple self-images are the results of consumers' reading of social and cultural expectations about *any* self. In a culture that expects multiple self-images, *not* being schizophrenic, in the sense discussed, may come to be categorized as pathological.

A new metanarrative

In a market exchange economy, these multiple self-images are represented through the products acquired in the market. The market becomes the locus of realizing the fragmented self, the fragmented moments of finding meaning in the present and "feeling good." The market, however, is itself fragmented. It has no central, unified agenda, and is composed of many consumers and products. All relationships in the market are truly momentary, no transaction requiring deep commitment on the part of the consumer. As long as they have the buying power, consumers can be true dilettantes. They can buy and try various products, drop favored brands, and use products momentarily or sporadically depending on the image requirements of a situation, then flit to another situation, experimenting with other products. The market and its fragmentation become the *center* of all activity, *the medium* through which all is signified and represented without the appearance of any unified purpose, ideology, or narrative. Thus, contrary to the claims of the postmodernists for an end of metanarratives, there appears to exist, at least at this juncture of the (post)modern, a new metanarrative that lies outside the modernist categories. Fragmentation itself, and its medium—the market—constitute, in fact, this new metanarrative.

Postmodern culture, as many of its philosophers would argue, is not a break from modern culture, but largely a recognition and acceptance of the above listed conditions accentuated by modernity. While modernity either created or reinforced these conditions, taking them to heights not experienced in earlier cultures, modern culture repressed or denied the existence of these conditions in its *metanarratives* in order to hold on to the central modernist idea of the *modern project*, and to (re)inforce an order that would make this futuristic ideal possible. Postmodernism, on the other hand, is a call to playfully, artfully, critically, and unabashedly practice these conditions to re-enchant human lives, rather than sacrifice them through commitments to what postmodernists regard as dead-end projects.

7 Postmodern consumption

When the conditions that created the modern consumption pattern, one that is individual-private-passive-alienated, are dissolved through the transitional processes into postmodern conditions, it is logical to expect that consumption patterns will also change. In earlier chapters we discussed the historical development of the modern consumption pattern as well as the central characteristics of modernism that constructed the meanings and nature of consumption in modernity. As modernity wanes, understandably, the meanings attached to consumption will also transform, as will its whole disposition in society. We are presently at the cusp of such substantial qualitative transformations. While it may not be possible to precisely foresee what the outcomes will be, some principal aspects of postmodern consumption may be envisioned, based on an understanding of emergent postmodern conditions.

Let us begin by exploring the changes that can be expected, particularly those that are already observable in consumption patterns during the transitional period, and the paradoxes that characterize the transformations.

CONSUMPTION PATTERN CHANGES IN THE TRANSITION PERIOD

Modern society was one where the proper and the improper were very much identified in all spheres of life. Proper attire for different functions, for example, was decided and enforced through political and social sanctions. In many cases, people were not allowed to enter certain premises without proper attire, and if legally allowed, they were ostracized. Having set such rules, the modern impulse was to try and repress or suppress any subversion of the rules, again using political and social sanctions. Thus, if a woman wore trousers, properly a male item, this was immediately taken as a sign of rebellion. Women authors, such as George Sand and George Eliot used such rebellion, paradoxically, to gain acceptance in a very masculine literary community. Women, as well as other underprivileged groups in modern society, often used subversive consumption to signal rebellion and trigger rebellious movements.[1] For such improper consumption activities they were put in jail or excluded from their communities through other social means. Instead of co-opting these rebellions, or absorbing them into the norms which defined the proper, attempts were made to suppress them and to rehabilitate or incarcerate those involved in subversion.

Much of this still goes on in this transitional stage we seem to be in, from the modern to the postmodern. We can observe many attempts to suppress, deem illegal or unhealthy or socially uncouth, quite a number of subversive consumption attempts. Consider, for example, the public reaction to the use of certain language in rap music. Several musical groups have been taken to court for their "consumption" of language. There are drugs which are subversively used for non-medicinal purposes, and such consumption has also been banned. Control is attempted through the social prescription practices and policing actions.

Marketable subversions

Subversions considered to be less "harmful," however, have begun to be handled differently. We see this with many of the youth movements that have attempted to reject and subvert what they perceive to be a materialist and money status, privilege-oriented, discriminatory mainstream culture. Take the punk movement, for example. Originally it developed as a countercultural movement, rejecting the values and the materialism of capitalist western culture. The members of the movement indicated their displeasure and disappointments with mainstream culture by subverting consumption, by using clothing items in "improper" ways, by using hair dyes in unintended manners on unintended parts of the body, by using conventional musical instruments to create unusual, unconventional music. They developed many expressions of rejection of popular culture through subverting regular consumption items. By now, however, almost all of these expressions, the music, the attire, and the hairdos, are part of the fashion industry, both popular and high fashion, of the mainstream, and of every-day markets (the music market, the clothing and accessories market, etc.). The expressions have been emptied of their original rebellious countercultural contents and meanings and have become successful market items selling in the millions and consumed by millions, many of whom have little or no idea of what these items once stood for or meant, or if they do know, they do not care. Once the market recognizes the marketing and, therefore, commercial potentials of these expressions, it transforms them into marketable commodities, imbuing them with commercially attractive and seductive meanings.

In the transition to postmodern consumption, therefore, we find an increasing multiplicity or plurality of consumption patterns. The consistent and insistent movement toward the individual-private-alienated-passive ends of the dimensions, which defined the major tendencies in modern consumption relationships, continues in some consumption instances, but changes direction in others. Modern consumption increasingly pushed consumers into the private domain, towards home and recreational activities, to expand market transactions. Increasing moments of life in the private domain became dependent on products bought in the market. The more the consumer households withdrew into the private domain, the more they referred to and depended on the market. Yet the realization in the transition to postmodern consumption is that once the consumer culture is established, commodification of the private domain is not antithetical to the commodification of the public domain. In fact, the two domains are not separate as envisioned or depicted in modernist thought. Consumption does not occur only in the private domain but also in the public domain; just as production is not only in the public domain as modern theories insisted. Production and consumption are concomitant processes that continually overlap and inter-merge. In every moment of production there is consumption (the consumption of energy—human and otherwise, and of raw materials) and in every moment of consumption there is production (the production of the human being—physically and mentally—biological cells, rejuvenation of mental energy, encoding of world views, creation and solidification of values). Postmodernist insights recognize that any separation of consumption and production is purely cultural and arbitrary, useful solely for the purpose of development of modernist theoretical and philosophical concepts, frameworks that shore up the modern idealization of economy and society. Rather than being seen as means for developing insights, or as the imaginary of a sociohistorical context, if these frameworks are taken or claimed to be representative of "reality," then we begin to construct prison walls around our own abilities to act freely.

Since consumption occurs at every moment of human activity, the extension and expansion of the market simply requires the commodification and commercialization of various aspects and elements of each consumptive moment. Examples of this can be provided in different spheres of (post)modern life. The punk countercultural movement takes used, out-of-fashion clothing items and re-employs them through wearing them in cut, retailored and unusual forms, and in unusual places. The reaction of the market is not to make the members of this movement outcasts from the marketplace, but to provide for them even more exciting or spectacular specimens of the subverted clothing items to buy. Then, using these members of an originally outlandish group as examples of daring images, there are efforts to expand the marketing of these accessories and wearables for use by others who are looking for moments of daring yet acceptable rebellion—not to be adopted as a constant or complete life style, but for fragmented instances or as singular additions to usual attires. If an ecological countercultural movement comes along, the market provides commodities to interject into the processes required by this new consciousness—such as green products, low-waste packaging, and containers to hold recyclable items. If people begin to get concerned about passive life styles resulting from excessive television viewing habits, or use of private automobiles, there are opportunities to launch a fitness movement, suffused with marketable commodities as part of this activity—treadmills, athletic shoes, active-wear garments. All rebellions and rejections can be rendered marketable by resignifying them as acts of market-served consumption, fragmenting the moments of consumption, and commodifying and commercializing each, thereby enabling all consumers (and not just the rebels and dissidents) to participate in the fragmented moments.

Multiplicity through fragmentation

The modern capitalist consumption pattern expanded and extended the market within its own borders. Fragmenting the consumption experience attempts both to expand and cross these borders, as well as to allow other forms of consumption to be brought into the market. The consumption trend that created the individual-private-alienated-passive consumption continues to be strong, especially during certain fragmented moments, helping to expand the market. Encouraging consumers to experiment (during fragmented moments) with diverse and offbeat consumption patterns, now also commodified, necessitates the purchase of products that represent not only the modern consumption pattern, but also acquisition of products that represent other consumption patterns as well. This helps the market to grow even more. For example, contemporary consumer households, even with a modicum of affluence, tend to own multiple television sets and subscribe to multiple movie cable channels, yet, induced by well-crafted design and marketing of "the movie-going experience," members of these households also wish to participate in movie-going at other moments of their lives. The purpose is not to substitute the more public consumption of going to the movies by the more private consumption of having movies at home, or vice versa, but to make the consumer acknowledge that both can be done, each in its own moment, each for its own purposes. The transition to such postmodern trends regarding these entertainment forms is recorded in the recent history of the United States. The advent of television and the modern emphasis on this medium, because it fits the modern consumption pattern, as well as other modernist goals,[2] led to the demise of some movie theaters. The subsequent repositioning of the two media not as competitive but different—each having its place in fragmented moments of life—has resulted in the successful growth of both markets.[3]

Thus, the change in this period of transition from modern to postmodern is not a change in the dominant consumption pattern, but a transformation from the dominance of a singular consumption pattern to a preponderance of a multiplicity of consumption patterns, enabled through fragmentation.

PARADOXES OF THE TRANSITION PERIOD

In consumption, this leniency has meant tolerance for different styles, specifically, for example, in dress. The unity of singular attire for certain functions gave way to several possible ways of dressing for functions. In settings requiring a formal attire, such as going to the opera, semi-formal attire has become acceptable. The typical business attire, while still strong, has lost its total hold on the "correct way to dress." The business uniform, the "three-piece suit" or the "suit and tie" for men, for example, is no longer a standard that cannot be broken. There is even a trend to promote a more open organizational culture through "dress-down Fridays" and such. Different business attire styles have developed, especially with the greater participation of women in management. Yet, still, the range of tolerance is not fully developed. This is a transitional era; many modernist maxims still linger even as postmodernist ideas capture a growing share of imagination. This creates an interesting circumstance already discussed. Postmodernism's discursive claims are dissolving the modern narratives, creating great doubts and skepticism about and disinterest in grand(iose) universalizing, communalizing projects and themes.

Hegemony of the market

Postmodernist tendencies are currently much stronger at the discursive end, however, than they are in practice. The postmodern practice of every-day life still has to be largely conceptualized and put into play. The different approaches to postmodernism[4] seem to be a result of this ambiguity about the practice of the postmodern. Some celebrate its ideals while others observe the current situation and criticize postmodernism based on contemporary circumstances. The question is: Will a postmodern culture, if and when instituted in practice, be similar to what we observe today or be very different? In this transition period, the void from the demise of modern metanarratives at the political and social discourse level is being filled by the mechanisms and the logic of a modern capitalist market. As a result, while the idea systems and consumption practices are becoming increasingly fragmented, capital and its control of the media[5] and the market are becoming increasingly concentrated and unified. Consequently, the establishment of postmodern practice envisioned by postmodernist discourses will require much struggle against the current mechanisms and logic of the capitalist market. That is, the market has yet to be postmodernised, and the postmodernists have to confront, attack and deconstruct the current logic and the workings of the market if a postmodern society is to be constructed. This is especially important given the fact that in current society, the market (in an essentially modern form) has become the sole locus of legitimation.

Thus, in the absence of and as a result of the disintegration of other forms of legitimation in (post)modern society, the market, which is the medium of the economy, the already centralized sphere of modernity, takes over in full force. The modern market, however, is unidimensional. It has a singular logic or rationality: that of commercial efficiency. It cannot therefore fulfill the multidimensional and multirational, multifaceted demands and needs of postmodern society. The market indeed could not function well on its own even in modern society. In repeated instances, across the history of modern society, the political apparatuses were invoked to "tame" or "organize" the market.[6] The basic rule of the market, competition, was often adjusted through laws and regulations to achieve what was termed *workable competition*. It is clear, however, from the growth of deregulation, mergers, and takeovers in the United States, that recently the market has been increasingly left to its own devices. Distrust of institutions that can organize or modify the market is much greater than the distrust of the market itself.

The benign veneer

The market does seem benign in many respects. The prevailing idea is that it is something that works almost independent of human agency. Early economists, such as Adam Smith and David Ricardo, called it the *invisible hand*. In any event, theoretically it seems that no one party can control the market, that it works on the principle of equalizing those who demand and those who supply. Such assumptions about the market have largely been questioned, as we discussed in Chapter 4, but recent historical experiences have dimmed the memory of such questioning. One such experience, of course, is the victory of the so-called free market economies against the so-called command economies. This has given greater impetus to the market to expand and work unhindered on a global scale. Another recent historical experience is the perceived failures of government actions. Inefficiencies and graft in government operations, scandals of dishonesty, theft and unfair practices, have greatly hurt the image of the state. By comparison, the market, something that is not human but inanimate, seems devoid of human weaknesses and evils and looks good. It works, many tend to think, only if those interacting with (or in) it are willing to participate. Since the market performs when everyone interacting is present at the scene, all parties seem equally empowered, and no "behind the scenes" or "under the rug" dealings appear possible.

Such images of the market, while clearly unwarranted in many respects, as the critics of the workings of the market have repeatedly illustrated,[7] nonetheless have been powerful. It is not surprising that such images have been promoted and reinforced by those who are powerful in the market and who benefit from it. The champions of "free" markets have been helped immensely by recent historical experiences.

Sooner or later, however, postmodernist discourse will abut the logic of the market head-on. While it may be difficult to discern, the market is not without its own rationale, its ideology, or metanarrative. The market and its fragmentation represent another universalizing, totalizing way of life, rationality and being. Much of what contemporary critics of the current state of life, being, and affairs criticize has to do with the market. The market, after all, is *the* medium of the central sphere of modernity (the economy), and it has been steadily gaining control of life in contemporary society. Thus, much of what we have today is the doing of the market. If we are not satisfied, therefore, we must blame the market.

From market to theater?

Could the market be modified, deconstructed and then reconstructed to allow free association as well as concerns and criteria other than commercial viability, material resource efficiency, or economic rationality? In other words, could the market be reconstructed to enlarge the fragmentation of consumptive moments, which it has already mastered, to the fragmentation of ideologies, realities, ways of life and being? Could it permit to exist and flourish choices, concerns, and patterns of life that do not satisfy the criteria of economic viability? That is, could the market stop being only an economic medium and (re)construct as the medium of cultural interaction, multidimensional, multifaceted, and multilayered? Can "culture," sundered by modernity and market into separate moments, each with its own guiding principles and logic, each seeking autonomy from the other, be resynthetized? Such a transformation will need a medium of cultural interaction that resynthetizes its moments, that allows different criteria, rationales and beings. It will need its *theater*.

Currently, moving from a singularly rational market to a multirational theater seems an almost insurmountable task. There are many ideological hurdles and material difficulties. We shall explore these at some length in the final chapter as well as make some suggestions regarding the methods of overcoming them. In the rest of this chapter, our intention is to provide some insights into the potentials of postmodern consumption when the transition is complete.

CONSUMPTION IN THE POSTMODERN ERA

Our discussions of consumption, postmodernism, and the growing hegemony of the market during a period of transition imply that there is a need to distinguish the current conditions of consumption culture from established postmodern consumption. While the success of postmodernist discourse has helped in the (trans)formation of the nature of contemporary consumption culture, it is a mistake to equate this culture with the postmodern. A valid postmodern culture can or will be established only when the hegemony of the modern market over all legitimation processes in society is dissolved. For modernity to finally end, as many philosophers are (falsely) already announcing, the dominance of all its institutions and meta-narratives must end, and a theater that allows multidimensional, multifaceted, and multilayered fusion or coexistence of multiple narratives and/or myths, must evolve.

Much of the ambiguity about or critique of the end of modernity or the postmodern today can be attributed to the confusion between what is post-modern and what is contemporary. The commercialization and marketization of all that is "successful" today leads many social and cultural critics to label the postmodern as devoid of depth and content, hedonistic, consumptive (in the modernist sense of material resource utilization or destruction-oriented), superfluous, and prone to emphasize style over substance. Some of the more prominent postmodernists are partially guilty of this (mis)perception.[8] While recognizing that the distinctions between production and consumption were mostly modernist constructions,[9] and that the modern narrative positing that value creation occurred in produc-tion was indeed a myth, postmodernists still continue to utilize the terms (consumption and production) distinctly, often in their modernist forms. This, of course, helps the modernist myths to survive.

If, indeed, value is created in consumption, it means that consumption is something different from what it used to be in its modern significations. Or it may be that the activity has not changed (such as eating food, wearing clothes, etc.), but the concept of what is (of) value is different. Let us explore this point to better understand postmodern consumption.

The entrenched economic

As we discussed in Chapter 3, under modernity products were considered to contribute to the creation of value if they afforded the producer surplus-value within the exchange-value products commanded in the market. The nourishment of the human being, her/his growth (growth of body cells, growth of knowledge, ideas, tastes, and mentalities) were not considered as activities resulting in the creation of value. Two reasons permeated this framework. One reason was that the market-value (exchange-value) of the consumer did not afford a surplus and therefore did not contribute to the growth of the economy, per se. Only what the consumer produced in the public domain, to be exchanged in the market, made such a contribution. Second, the consumer was the target for whom value was created, so to think of consumers themselves as creation of value would be absurd—it would mean that the consumer was a product. While the modern market system did indeed transform the consumer's being into a product and treated her/him as such, it would be unthinkable for the modern emancipa-tory rhetoric and ideology to admit this. After all, modern (meta)narratives and the modern project(s) were constructed on the premise that the consumer (the human being) was the subject.

While enshrining the human subject, the modern framework also paradoxically devalued human beings. In the modern framework, the growth of the human being, per se, does not contribute to the sum value in society. Only what he or she produces for the market is of value. Human beings are valuable only insofar as they contribute to the economy. That this is the prevailing idea in modern society seems to be well evidenced by the number of homeless, for example, in the United States, by all accounts the most affluent society in the world.[10] Human beings who do not or cannot directly contribute to the economy do not share in the wealth because, it seems, they do not have value merely as human beings. The modern economy is based on the production of value for market exchange and distributes its resources and remunerations only on the basis of contributions to such a system of exchange-value. The recent triumph of the market in the United States, for example, is evidenced by the attacks on entitlements: the welfare system and other programs that attempt to distribute benefits to human beings without direct ties to this economic framework of "value" creation.

The ascendant symbolic

Modernists dislike the postmodern particularly because postmodernism rejects this economic narrative of value. As such, postmodernism is radically detrimental to the continuation of modernity. Postmodernism attempts to (re)establish the symbolic order, the reign of culture, which is multidimensional and multirational as opposed to the universalism and unidimensional economism of the modern. Value is found in all aspects of life, in social relations, emotional experiences and, especially, in the aesthetic and the symbolic as opposed to the material. Postmodernists consider the universalizing and the uniform rationality-imposing elements of the modern to have disenchanted human life while claiming to improve it. By seeking multiplicity and difference, postmodernism embraces the multidimensionality of humanity and of human life, thereby hoping to re-enchant it. Since modernity sought the hegemony of reason, specifically scientific and economic reason, and postmodernism rejects this hegemony, many interpret postmodernism to be anti-reason and anti-science. This appears to be a misguided and defensive critique of postmodernism, however. The postmodernist idea is not to eliminate reason, science, or the economic, but to remove them from the central and hegemonic position they have occupied in modernity, restoring them to their (equal) place among the other dimensions of being human, without unduly privileging any.

Multiplicity of life modes

Postmodern consumption, therefore, does not privilege economic market value over other consumptive experiences. Contrary to modernism, there is no one way to define or achieve "improvement" of life in postmodern culture. Acquiring and using more and "better" material products to control nature is not a privileged idea or a path to an enchanted human life. There is greater acceptance that a human life that lacks material or economic "afflu- ence" may be just as enchanted, and an acceptance of people and communities that choose such a life style. The modern perceptions that such communities are "backward," "underdeveloped," or "primitive"—all, of course, underprivileging qualifications—do not apply in postmodern culture. In postmodernism, there is no fundamental or essential point of departure for making such judgements about life choices and, therefore, they must be accepted on an equal footing. Life mode choices must be viewed as different ways of living an enchanted life, without any assignment of superi- ority or inferiority, with consideration only of individual or community preference.

Life choices and life styles that do not fit the idea of the "proper" in modern culture are currently on the increase, indicating the gradual dissolu- tion of the modern. They also indicate the effectiveness of the postmodern cultural ideas that are more tolerant of different ways.[11] There is, for example, a growing number of people and communities that live back-to- land life styles. Many of these are people who once had high income professional careers, such as medical doctors and lawyers, but have chosen to leave their highly material consumption-oriented lives in large cities and move to parts of the country where they can have much less material, more social and nature-oriented life styles.[12] In popular culture, which earlier rejected, alienated and harassed communities such as the Amish which opted for a different life pattern, there is a growing tolerance, acceptance and respect for such communities.[13]

Yet another characteristic of the postmodern is that consumers who choose life styles different from that ordained by the modern do not have to commit themselves to only one. As there is tolerance for those who choose alternative life styles, there is tolerance for those who wish to experience not one but multiple life styles. Moving among life styles, not sticking with one but frequently revisiting each, is just as acceptable since each allows different experiences and enriches life, thereby enchanting life in different ways. This has become a highly visible occurrence in contemporary North American society, especially among high income professionals. Given the hegemony of the market, this frequenting of multiple life styles usually appears in highly marketized forms, that is, they are generally highly dependent on marketed products. Many professionals who are caught in what are considered to be stressful jobs in their every-day lives have, for example, taken to motorcy- cling at the weekends. They shed their suits and other business garb, put on leather jackets and other logo-ridden paraphernalia and take to the (moun- tain) roads on their Harley-Davidson bikes, living characters completely different from who they are during the week. Biking is not the only trend. There are hikers, mountain climbers, campers, rafters, and band players.[14] It is interesting that many express a desire to get away from the fray to find their true selves. It is interesting because this is an expression of a belief that what they do in their every-day lives is not "true" or "real." There seems to be an almost tacit recognition that what modernity built around them is not "real" but hyperreal. The modernist streak, however, still urges them to find something that can be "true." Postmodernism is the recognition that what is true in every-day human lives is that which is constructed. The emphasis shifts from trying to find something that is authentically and enduringly "real" to constructing something temporally real that is most agreeable to our sensibilities. Nevertheless, were it not for the new found tolerance, these people who live fragmented life styles and present multiple selves would have been considered "out-of-touch," pathologically schizophrenic, perhaps even criminal.

Contemporary market culture immediately catches on to these life styles. It channels the desire these people have for experiencing difference toward marketable products, such as motorcycles, "in" clothing for each life style, and other paraphernalia. Yet, for the postmodern consumer, marketization is not necessary or even important. Given the current hegemony of the market, and the difficulties of going outside the market system (as we explored in Chapter 5), individual consumers can do little but get caught up in the market. The society is organized in such a way that unless, like the Amish, one isolates oneself from it, the market does not provide alternative forms or institutions providing for life styles and needs. You are either in it or isolated from it. This is a logical outcome of the totalizing nature of modernity; it requires total commitment and conformity.

Experiences, images, meanings

For the postmodern consumer, consumption is not a mere act of devouring, destroying, or using things. It is also not the end process of the (central) economic cycle, but an act of production of experiences and selves or self-images. In effect, it is the process of producing one's life, not mere sustenance or maintenance of life.[15] In postmodern culture, life is conceived to be multidimensional, not to be spent in search of a single goal or purpose and not to be committed to a single project. The way to enhance and enchant life is to allow multiple experiences, to be sensed emotionally as well as through reason, utilizing all the aspects of being human. Anything that attempts to totalize, universalize or render uniform the meaning and experience of life, such as the modernist metanarratives or the market logic, therefore, is to be kept at bay or rejected. Life is to be produced and created, in effect, *constructed* through multiple experiences in which the consumer immerses, as opposed to being *led* via the detached and objective perspective of the modern *subject*. The postmodern consumer (re)unites consumption and production, which were ripped apart in modernity, (re)synthesizing the process to make all activity experiential and immersible instead of separated and detached. In modernity, the subject (the consumer being) encounters the objects (products) as distinct and distanced from her/himself. In postmodern consumption, the consumer renders products part of her/himself, becoming part of the experience of being with products. As the consumer defines the products, products define the consumer. The issue for consumers is not to utilize the products for a personal purpose but to immerse themselves into a context co-determined by the consumers and the products. Through such immersion and the experiences it produces are constructed the meanings and values, the selves and self-images for all involved. For the postmodern consumer these experiences are possible with or without the mediation of the market, with or without material products. A social gathering with great austerity and mere human interaction—discussions—is just as valid and exciting a consumption experience, a production of life, as is a party with strobe lights, electronic games, recorded music, bottled drinks, and other marketed products. The questions that remain pertain to which consumption experiences are preferred, how often, and when; and not how products are bought and financed. The point is that the need for market-mediated consumption is transcended in the postmodern sensibility.

Examples of consumptive experiences that simulate postmodern consumption abound in contemporary society. The reason for the success of thematized environments we mentioned earlier—theme parks, thematized city centers, and Las Vegas[16]—is this willingness and attraction on the part of postmodern consumers to immerse themselves into experiences. These consumption experiences are particularly interesting to consumers because they represent experiences that are different from the "everyday" experiences in a transforming, yet still very much modern, job world. Therefore, they give consumers a chance to experience different life styles that provide excursions into production or "customizing" of alternative selves and self-images, experiences that allow playful experimentation, and the fulfillment of various human dimensions.

Limits of market-mediated experiences

In a transitional period where consumption experiences have to be mediated through marketized and/or commercialized contexts and products, such as Las Vegas or Disney World, the postmodern consumer encounters paradoxes in trying to synthesize consumption and production, and in what is experienced. Consider, for example, the urban dwellers who, finding their everyday career lives in the city burdensome and "unreal," decide to take rafting trips in "nature" to get in touch with their true selves. Many sign up for rafting trips organized by rafting outfitters who provide them with a group, equipment, and a guide. The catch is that the trip is indeed organized to make sure that the consumer finds what she or he is looking for. The day of the rafting adventure is planned and programmed so that every stage of the trip contains the elements of an adventure. Through this "packaged" experience, consumers set out to find their true selves. These are, indeed, exciting and touching experiences; they have been planned to create situations which provide the rafters with feelings of accomplishment, risk, adventure, and bonding (with nature and others), and for many it does become a time of self-discovery. Even for those for whom such a trip "works," in the self-discovery sense, only one of the possible selves is discovered. Furthermore, the production of the experience and of the finding of self is as much outside the control of the consumer as her/his life in the city. This is largely because in our contemporary transitional culture almost all experience is mediated by market interactions, and into every interaction, even the most intimate ones, are interjected the products of the market.[17] Postmodern consumers who seek emancipation from the impositions of the modern project are, nevertheless, caught in the metanarrative of the market.

Other, usually younger, consumers play at different experiences and selves in other ways, by customizing themselves, again largely through marketed products, for various environments and situations. Michael Jackson look-alike contests, for example, where the contestants "have to look like Michael, and think like Michael,"[18] are increasingly popular. Often, there is no need to be in a contest. For different occasions, consumers assume different personalities, to experience life as another self, to test and recognize their preferences, to find which ones and how frequently they wish to live them to enchant their lives.[19]

The look-alike experiences are, of course, programmed by the market culture, in that the people who are simulated and modeled after, are the ones that the market has popularized. Not surprisingly, the paraphernalia needed to look like these models are also available and accessible in the market. The process reminds one of the masked balls of the rich and famous, which were, of course, mostly organized to allow the same kind of experience: the assumption of other selves. They were also highly integrated with the fashion industry. In this sense, fashion is indeed the metaphor for contemporary consumption.[20] It allows change and difference, it organizes content (the true experience) through style and form, and it is fragmented. The consumer can be her/his cool and serene self by wearing Armani, and lively and exuberant self by wearing Versace. Yet each attempt by the consumer to produce an individual self is planned and the spontaneity and naturalness of each experience is programmed by the fashion system.[21]

Regaining the theater

Under such circumstances postmodern consumption cannot flourish. The contemporary market system does not allow crossing the boundaries of the commercial, and thereby severely limits the possibilities. The market moves with alacrity to encompass many rebellious and offbeat forms. The modern system of privileging market-based consumption experiences while de-privileging—and assigning to an inferior status—non-market consumption experiences continues at the present juncture. Postmodern consumption implies that consumers are free to choose patterns or styles of consumption that are less or not at all material resource-intensive, and not conducive to market exchange. Given that postmodernism moves the emphasis from the economic to the cultural and the symbolic, postmodern consumption will promote less market and more theater-based narratives. Such narratives may spell disaster for modern "production" and "consumption" systems, and the market, unless the market adapts itself as an integral part of the theater. The theater itself, as the locus of multidimensional human interaction, needs some rediscovery. Modernity, in its impulse to commodify things by extracting them from their original (con)texts and (re)presenting them in objectified forms—to be observed from a detached position—turned theater, the medium of culture, into a "staged" spectacle or a "show." In postmodernity, the theater has to be regained and developed into its participatory forms.

Tolerance and negotiation

Movements such as the ecology movement will find postmodern consumption to be friendly because postmodernism dissolves the ideological superiority of material resource-intensive consumption patterns. Of course, since postmodernism promotes tolerance, there is likely to persist some preference for market-driven, resource-intensive "consumptive" life styles, but such styles will not overwhelm the rest. In postmodernity, for any consumption style to be preferred, tried and experienced, it must be rendered attractive in the cultural and symbolic arena, the theater.

A postmodern community is one with tolerance for varying realities of its members. Consider, for example, a member whose reality is that she or he has been harassed, and who truly believes that harassment has occurred. A modern community would struggle to establish whether the perceived harassment is "true," if it "really" happened in the sense of an "objective" truth. A postmodern community, once it recognizes that the member in question is certain in her or his own mind that the harassment has occurred, would try to understand that person's definition of it and tolerate/respect this definition in interactions—instead of trying to force her or him to adhere to another (universal/uniform) definition. If there is sufficient common ground, the member will remain in the community; if not, she or he may choose another community that has common ground. In this situation the idea is: rather than contesting/rejecting each other's realities, negotiate/tolerate them. This clearly allows for constructive and persuasive communication and change/transformation of realities.

MODERN AND POSTMODERN CONSUMPTION EXPERIENCES

To summarize, then, postmodern consumption is when consumers become producers in constructing selves, self-images, and meaningful experiences by immersing themselves into simulated processes. Consumption is not an end but just another moment in the continuous cycle of (re)production. Perhaps most important in this process is the signification and representation activities in which subjects and objects—subjects as objects, not in the modern sense of commercialization and commodification where the object is presented to the market, but rather in the sense of constructed/produced selves—collaborate and conspire to enchant lives through the creation of experiential moments. In modernity, the eyes were turned to the future and life was a concatenation of moments of continual anticipation. That is, every moment was lived in anticipation of a promised arrival; arrival into the bright future. As we drive our cars we seek to arrive at our destination. Each time we arrive at our destination, there is the preparation for departure towards another arrival. While this is basically due to modern ideologies, partially it is due to the technologies of speed and organization of space. When one flies from New York to Los Angeles, for example, one is unlikely to enjoy the flight as an experience on its own: it is in cramped quarters, it will end soon, and the purpose of the flight is not itself, but the arrival in Los Angeles. Modernity organizes its moments of consumption not as experiences in their own rights but as means for arrival in the future. This is a never ending quest. Rather than being lived well now, life is about the future.

The radical present

Postmodernism, while not forgetting the future, turns its eyes to the present. It requires that meaning be found in each present moment lived, not just in moments to come. This tendency in postmodernism often leads to charges of shallow hedonism. Such charges, however, occur only because in contemporary society, with the hegemony of the market, meanings sought almost always require the presence of marketed products and depletion of resources. Therefore, the implications arise of no concern for tomorrow, only for "immediate gratification" and reckless hedonism.

The rejuvenated intellectual

Consumption in the present has increasingly moved away from the intellectual, social, and the political to the material. This is of course paradoxical. Modernism has privileged the mind and reason, therefore the intellectual over the body, in its rhetoric. Yet, because of the requirements of an economically sound market, at every turn that cultural movements have sought to emphasize the intellectual, modernity and its technologies have found ways of marketizing the movements, pulling them into the realm of material consumption. A good example of this is television, which always holds the promise of becoming a great educational tool, but unfailingly delivers entertainment.

Modernity separated the idea of the intellectual from the idea of entertainment and polarized them as opposites. If one was being entertained, then one could not be involved in intellectual activity. If someone was involved in intellectual activity, it could not be entertaining. Such separation is not necessary. Intellectual activity and entertainment can be—and are—one and the same. In modernity, however, such separation led to the waning of the intellectual. Entertainment was signified as exciting and fun. It also allowed immersion into the experience without fears of loss of objectivity, since entertainment was a subjective affair. The intellectual was dull and difficult. Furthermore, it also required the detached, distanced, objective—an altogether onerous—stance. It is interesting that with the postmodern may come the rejuvenation of the intellectual in consumption.[22]

Ending separations

Finally, as postmodern consumption is the (re)synthesis of production and consumption, and consumption is immersion into experiential moments of enchanted, multifaceted, spectacular encounters with life, it can be expected that all consumption/production will develop as simulated and thematized processes. Work and play will (re)merge, and the separation between moments and sites of "production" and "consumption" will gradually disappear.[23] With the advent of new information and communication technologies, and reorganizations of the workplace (and home) to make "work" more seductive, this trend is already visible.[24]

The implications of postmodern consumption for culture, society and humanity in general are varied and substantial. We will explore these in the final chapter. First, however, we wish to discuss the effects of (post)modernity, the transitional period we have been exploring, at the international level.

8 Global consumption

The *citizen*, whose rights and privileges were identified and preserved through political institutions, and who constituted the modern *subject* of the nation state and represented the central entity of modern political economy, is losing significance and her/his privileged position. As Stuart Ewen proclaimed in the television program, *The Public Mind*,[1] it is no longer the citizen but the *consumer* who constitutes the unit of analysis, the central entity, or the locus of social discourse in the contemporary world of globalization and globalism. In the world of global markets, the only rights and privileges that transcend all boundaries without the necessity of treaties and accords—such as human rights accords, which may or may not be signed or heeded by arrogant nation states—are those of the consumer in the global marketplace. When consumers speak, especially in unison, even the most powerful corporate and governmental entities listen.

THE CONSUMPTION CONNECTION

Cultures are increasingly, and in many cases solely, linked by the products (television programs, athletic shoes, brand name(d) T-shirts, beverage brands, fast food restaurants, automobiles, etc.) of a market that is indeed global. In countries and regions where even ideas, political systems and rights, and people (tourists, among others) cannot reach, one now encounters popular global brands. In a small, native bar in Puño, Peru, for example, where a tourist is rarely seen, you can find the walls covered with posters of Madonna and Michael Jackson, and people clad in T-shirts bearing their names. As you ride in a tuk-tuk, the native Bangkok taxi, the taxi driver, finding out that you are American, may ask you to tell Michael Jackson to do a concert in Bangkok. "Tell him we love him," he will say, imagining that being from America, you must know this artist who is so much "in the public." Then he proudly displays his prized possession, a photograph of "Michael." Wherever these brands and products are, they connect their consumers through their images and conditions of usage (warranties, for example).

From citizen to consumer

Consumption, therefore, may be the most important force that unites the contemporary world. As the utility of the term citizen wanes, that of the consumer waxes.[2] Not only are the many significant citizenship roles and responsibilities on a decline—as observed in the declining proportions of eligible voters who cast their ballots in elections in the United States, for example—but to the extent citizenship is now performed, it is performed in a consumer mode. We are not called to carry out our citizenship rights and duties, such as voting, sitting on juries and performing civil acts, but are cajoled, seduced and sold into doing so. We have to be marketed the idea that it might be fun or in our interest to do it. As in the case of the silent majority in Baudrillard's *In the Shadow of the Silent Majorities*,[3] we are too tired to act or speak out, we need to be surveyed, polled, urged and represented, and we barely provide a semblance that citizenship is alive and well.

On the other hand, citizens around the world are eagerly poised to be consumers. We all seem to revel in the act. Instead of being reminded of responsibilities and obligations as citizens, as consumers we are sought out, pampered, and wooed. Furthermore, of all the rights we have, possibly the rights that are most consistent and equal around the globe are our rights as consumers. Two people in Pakistan and France may not have the same citizenship rights, but if their Sony Walkman breaks down, they have the same warranty rights, as consumers of this product. Being a consumer may be creating more linkages around the world—in terms of belonging to same consumer segments, for example—than anything else in history. It is also creating a deeper understanding, at the level of emotions and dreams, among groups of consumers who have nothing else in common than, for example, being fans of alternative music. This is such a strong bond that young people who come to the United States or Canada or Denmark for higher education from cultures thoroughly foreign to each other can immediately recognize and entertain each other.

Globalization and marketization

Many look at this global cultural proximity that has developed and argue that we have globalization; that the whole world is becoming one and the same. We hear of terms such as the "global village"[4] and the "global customer."[5] Often, linked to this, are the implications of westernization, Americanization[6] or imperialism, implications which are understandably received with much cynicism, anger, negativity and concern, not only in the Third World but also in Europe when it comes to influences from the United States of America.[7]

There is, indeed, some truth to these implications. The implications, however, are somewhat different from what immediately comes to mind when terms such as westernization or Americanization are mentioned. It is not so much that the products from the west or America are diffusing around the world, or that the television programs and films that dominate in practically all societies are American.[8] Yes, there are many American products that dominate many markets, from television programs to cigarettes. But the television sets are often Japanese, Korean, or European. The major music genre that dominates is, indeed, in English and mostly from the United States and the United Kingdom, but there are other major successes such as Pavarotti and his classical music renditions mostly in Italian,[9] as well as minor successes such as the Urdu lyrics of Nusrat Fateh Ali Khan of Pakistan providing background music for Hollywood movies such as *Dead Man Walking*. The phenomenon of globalization is not westernization or Americanization in terms of their products, industrial or cultural, but in terms of *marketization* and, of course, along with it, of the market ideology of the west or America. In this sense, there is indeed an imperialism.

This is not a development without paradox. For example, there is an entrenchment and growth of the rhetoric of peace and democracy around the world. These concepts are considered to be attractive to audiences around the world to whom politicians and other leaders seek to justify their actions. At the same time, one observes an increasing number of regional, ethnic, and national wars and local armed conflicts. The power of the markets is such that even groups and countries in conflict trade with each other in the global market, often using clandestine means, and through secretive intermediaries. Common markets serve seemingly incompatible enemies and combatants.

Globalization of development and underdevelopment

Along with the growth of world developmental agencies and increased funding for development projects, especially projects deemed pro-market, one also observes growing differences developing between the wealthy and the poor. Enclaves of poor and rich are appearing in both the economically developed and economically underdeveloped countries and regions of the world. It is becoming increasingly difficult to apply the labels economically developed or underdeveloped at the level of a country, given that extremes of poverty and riches can now be found in practically every country. The United States, for example, a country which controls a large proportion of the world's resources with only a small proportion of the world's population, clearly one of the most affluent countries in the world, has a growing segment of the homeless and the poor.[10] As we walk along the touristic and so-nicely organized Third Street of Santa Monica, California, we observe many well dressed, wealthy looking people, occasionally a film star or two, lounging in the sidewalk cafés, shopping in high-fashion stores, and visiting trendy theaters. Yet, walking two blocks to the park on the cliffs overlooking the famous Santa Monica beach, where once upscale hotels flourished, or on to the beach itself, we encounter the hundreds of homeless. They also huddle around the Santa Monica City Hall where meals are occasionally distributed. Although the geographical location of the two is the same, there is an almost invisible shield separating these rich and poor areas from each other. One seldom sees the wealthy in the areas that the poor occupy, and vice versa. On the other hand, we find enclaves of substantial riches in countries generally considered to be economically underdeveloped. These rich enclaves are often guarded by armed security personnel and separated by high walls from the rest of society. Within the walls, we find incredibly wealthy life styles complete with clubs, tennis courts, swimming pools, all the frills of a luxurious life pattern. Of course, in the United States we also find these exclusive "gated communities," grounds that one can enter only if invited, as an owner or a potential buyer, and perhaps by looking sufficiently respectful and driving an upscale car. In many respects, the so-called developed and underdeveloped countries reproduce each other's experiences.

GLOBAL GLUE OF CONSUMPTION

The reproduction of these experiences is on a platform of *consumption*. Consumption experiences tend to be the ones that are most easily transferable. Almost anywhere in the world, one can have a bottle of Coca-Cola and eat a McDonald's hamburger, rent a Toyota, listen to Madonna and Sting tunes, enjoy a croissant for breakfast, and follow one's favorite soap opera on a Panasonic, RCA, Sony, LG, or Philips television set . On the one hand, such diffusion of brands, programs, and products continuously feed the fears, especially among observers of these trends from the Third World countries, that many cultures are being overtaken by others, that many a culture is now endangered.[11] On the other hand, globalization of information is (re)creating a touristic, voyeuristic interest in different cultures as well as in experiencing them. It might be this interest which results in the establishment or celebration of Little Tokyo, Little Italy, Little India, or Chinatown sections in major cities around the world. One can find a slice of simulated, upscale Rome on a section of the Rodeo Drive (aptly named Via Rodeo) in Beverly Hills, California, or the "American Experience" complete with its KFC, McDonald's, skating rink, and many other brand names and stores at the Galeria shopping mall in İstanbul.

Borderless world

The brand names and images are increasingly becoming the spectacles for the global tourist. They can now be found all around the world, signaling the same or similar meanings and experiences, their familiar surroundings reassuring the exploring tourist as well as the returning native. All this is facilitated and accelerated by global communications, specifically in terms of visual images, delivered via television, films, music videos, and advertising spots. As many international marketing organizations are well aware,[12] market segments transcend national boundaries, forming global communities of consumers or brand-specific "image tribes." Even those who cannot decipher each other's languages are able to decipher the images, the meanings of each other's consumption and, based on observing consumption patterns, can place each other on social maps that cross cultural boundaries.[13] The images of consumption are already well globalized. Markets are globalizing rapidly,[14] as are the symbols—the brand names and advertising images—which signify the meanings of each moment in life. There are growing pressures to unify economies, currencies, and markets (as apparent in the European Union) in order to keep up with trade and finance which have already globalized. The rapid diffusion of information technologies, exponential growth in mobility, and the ability to communicate across national boundaries has rendered all borders nominal and almost superficial, especially for those in possession of powerful passports and brands.

Cultural fragmentation

Along with such gathering globalizing tendencies, there is also a paradoxical growth in fragmentation in different respects around the world. On the one hand, independence or autonomy sought by different ethnic groups often creates conditions of intense political struggle or even civil war. On the other hand, there are increasing calls to recognize different life styles, family formations, sexual orientations, religious beliefs, and social organizations. There is a weakening of uniformity and universality in approaches to living and being in general. In the United States, for example, the idea of a "melting pot" is gradually giving ground to the idea of a (cultural) "mosaic." Under conditions of prosperity, the tendency to recognize and respect different ethnic, religious, social, and ideological cultures and allow them to exist in their own ways seems to gain strength,[15] signaling a reversal of the modernist quest for a universal, single, rational order of progress.

GLOBALIZATION OF FRAGMENTATION

At first glance, the two trends of globalization and fragmentation seem contradictory and paradoxical. Yet what seems to be occurring is a *globalization of fragmentation*. That is, all images, products, brand names, and life styles which create excitement, sensation, attraction and interest, and have the potential to be globally marketable, can and do find such markets. Consumers, regardless of their nationalities or countries, are willing to experience and sample varying styles and cultural artifacts, often at distinct times and for varying purposes. Globalization in the contemporary world, therefore, is no longer a process wherein one form or style dominates and eliminates all others. Rather, it is the diffusion of all different forms and styles across the world. Since the postmodern consumer experience is not one of committing to a single way of being or a single form of existence, the same consumers are willing to sample the different, fragmented artifacts. The consumer is ready to have Italian for lunch and Chinese for dinner, to wear Levi's 501 blue jeans for the outdoor party in the afternoon and try the Gucci suit at night, not only changing diets and clothes, but also the personas and selves (self-images) to be (re)presented at each function s/he participates in. The possibilities of such representational consumption—in terms of life styles and behaviors "originating" from a variety of countries and cultures—are opening up all across the world.

Themes and enclaves

Thus, we have a globalization of fragmentation in all respects. We can find poverty everywhere, wealth and riches everywhere, America in every country, and every country in America. The epitome of this phenomenon is the World Showcase at the EPCOT Center in Walt Disney World, Florida, where tourists can visit France, England, China, Japan, Morocco, or Norway, experiencing their sights, sounds and tastes. Yet, this is only the intensified, theme park version of what takes place in everyday places, in our cities and shopping malls.[16] Themes, the simulated experiences of different cultures, life styles and existences are increasingly becoming everyday experiences.[17] We see this in the (re)created and renovated sections of our cities, the wharf areas, the city centers and shopping centers. The simulated theme areas attract so much interest and traffic that they are then replicated and become the *norm* for our (sub)urban existence, constituting our (sub)urban "reality."[18] Furthermore, the contemporary consumer seems to want to sample and experience different themes rather than a single theme. The (sub)urban experience is increasingly manifested as fragmented sets of themes, none of them unique, because once successful in finding a consuming audience, a theme reappears across cities, regions and continents.

For fragmentation of such consumption experiences to be successful, what may be called *enclavization* is necessary, or at least helpful. In Chapter 7, we alluded to the tendency and willingness of postmodern consumers to immerse themselves in experiences, instead of standing aloof and observing the "reality out there" from a distanced, detached, and allegedly objective position. Enclavization of fragmented consumption experiences enhances this immersion. This is evident in the experiences of consumers in thematized enclaves—be they in Disney World's EPCOT Center, where national cultures are represented in enclaves as spectacles,[19] or in Las Vegas where many a hotel on the Strip represents extravagantly spectacularized themes.[20] When the fragmented sets of themes are enclavized, it becomes possible to really immerse oneself in the experience of each theme. The enclave limits the intrusion of elements that do not belong to the theme and, thereby, enhances the intensity of the experience.

As (sub)urban centers suffused with (post)modern culture have grown and increased their population, thereby increasing the numbers of consumers exposed and attuned to postmodern themes, enclavization of consumer environments has also increased. For example, rather than just having many restaurants dispersed around town, each representing food from a different culture, it is sometimes lucrative to develop sections or districts that provide more than the food and represent some semblance of the total atmosphere of being in that culture. We are talking, of course, of sections of towns such as Chinatown and Little Italy. There are good reasons why, when we talk of thematized sections of (sub)urban centers, it is these cultural districts that easily come to mind. One reason is that in the contemporary culture of consumption, culture itself has become a consumable. Culture is now just another marketable product. Second, among all products for consumption, culture is, by its very nature, most conducive to immersion. Culture is a way of life, a set of values, it constitutes a total environment. When culture is offered as a product, it is easy for consumers to immerse themselves in a total experience.

CULTURE CONSUMED

Modernity had taken major steps toward commodifying culture. For one thing, modernity created a culture that caused its members to be extremely proud of the achievements of modern society. Modernity was highly associated with domineering outcomes that were industrial, military, medical, and, above all, technological. These outcomes were domineering in the sense that the material power they afforded to early modernizing societies enabled them to exert control over other societies. This control took political, social, economic, and, in its narrow sense, cultural forms. To the modernists, who had gained much hegemony over the ideological and political apparatuses in western cultures by the nineteenth century, this power and the ability to control other nations were proofs of the superiority of modernization. If the industrialized, technologically advanced, modernized west was not superior, how could it have had such influence over the rest of the world? The ethnocentrism and the enthusiasm fueled by the success in overpowering the rest of the world further provided the bases for beliefs that the west was indeed superior; that the rest of the world realized and believed in this superiority, and therefore wanted to imitate the west.[21] The west was being good and benevolent in transporting its ways to the rest of the world, and modernization, proven by its unprecedented success and universal power, was the only way to progress.

Thus, modern culture created leaders, industrialists, technicians and other professionals who wanted to exhibit the success and power of modern society. They wanted to showcase what modernity could and did achieve: its victories over nature, its technological strength to overcome physical and engineering difficulties, its agricultural feats, and medical breakthroughs. Each modern nation, and even further, each region, each modern city, wanted to produce monumental, spectacular manifestations of the greatness of its culture and its achievements. Often, world fairs and other global events provided the contexts for such showcasing. They allowed each culture (nation, city, region) to (re)present itself in terms of spectacular structures and landscapes, in terms of superior products, which became the symbols that promoted the culture (for example, the Eiffel Tower in Paris). The spectacular, material products and structures representing the modern cultures and their greatness were most exciting and meaningful to a visual, voyeuristic culture: a culture of tourism. Many of the spectacles were, indeed, monumental proofs of the achievements of the industrial modern society. Seeing (observing) them left little doubt about what modern society could accomplish. These spectacles, extracted and abstracted from local culture, became the representations of that culture. They translated and were translations of culture; and they fulfilled the visual needs of the culture.[22] Each modern culture asserted its existence and established its "originality" through these spectacles (spectacular products, structures, etc.) that translated its qualities into cultural meanings. For a visually oriented modern world this was the best if not the only claim to existence.[23] Each culture that found ways of translating its qualities into marketable experiences (be it croissants or hamburgers) extended its reach and power beyond its original borders.[24]

As cultures increasingly asserted their existence through their elements translated into spectacles to be seen, experienced and consumed, these spectacles in turn came to be the only means through which a culture could establish and maintain itself. The modern consumer culture that has installed the market as the sole locus of legitimation, thereby forcing the marketization of everything, has, paradoxically, transformed culture itself into a consumable. All around the world today, especially in western societies, culture is no longer so much what people belong to, as increasingly something that they consume.

Marketability and cultural survival

The fragmentation generally experienced in contemporary, (post)modern market culture is conducive to the fragmentation of cultures into their discrete elements such as food, attire, music, art, dance, shopping environments and popular media. Those discrete cultural elements that can be translated into *marketable* commodities represent the vitality and ensure the continuity of a culture. The isolation of these discrete elements, from the culture they were originally embedded in, has an interesting side effect. It provides these elements with a relative autonomy from the culture from which they emerged. It becomes possible to resignify each element, to invest it with some new meanings that make it more alluring, seductive and marketable to various touristic and consumer markets. In effect, each element so commodified begins to create its own hyperreal. This process, while allowing the culture to sustain itself, also provides the seeds for its transformation into something different, specifically, into a more commercial entity. It is through this commercial identity of a culture's elements that the global consumer comes into contact with it. Seeking to find an immersed experience of the culture, s/he consumes and becomes absorbed in its commercialized elements. Such an experience can be repeated with multiple cultures.

Cultures of all kinds—ethnic, national, regional—that are able to translate their qualities into marketable commodities and spectacles find themselves maintained, experienced and globalized by the touristic consumer of the contemporary world. Cultures which cannot or do not (re)present themselves in terms of marketable elements, simulated instances, experiences, and products find themselves divested of members. Traditional cultures, atrophying under the encroachment of the market, find (quite paradoxically) that the way to keep their members, especially the young, interested in maintaining their culture is to involve the youth in the marketization of the culture, most particularly as touristic spectacle, through their music, dances, food, clothing and ornamental items. This allows the youth to have incomes and, thereby, the ability to participate in the larger global market. Whether a Native American culture in the southwestern United States, or one in Kashmir, India, or an aboriginal culture in Hokkaido, Japan, traditional cultures are either fading away or finding ways to make themselves marketable. Cultures that cannot succeed in translating some of their qualities into spectacles or commodities seem to vanish, leaving only traces as museum relics.

Thus, contemporary global consumption is a testament to the re-culturation of social existence. Consumption is (the) culture and culture is the most preferred consumption. Images most sought, even when communicated through high-powered brand names such as Benetton, Nike and Disney, are the ones that provide the consumer with intense cultural experiences.[25] These are experiences of belonging, even if momentarily, to a culture; experiences of producing diverse self-image(s) and meaningful life moments. Each brand name, each movie or television program, each popular song, each shopping mall and each food item, that is, every consumption experience with a product, is imbued with the representations of a culture from which it arose. It is this cultural theme that enables the consumer to experience an immersion into the simulation and the spectacle. In the global marketization of all such experience is the marketization of culture through and in its artifacts. The way to experience any culture away from its original site, or by those who did not originally belong to it, is through its artifacts. In the (post)modern global marketplace, artifacts begin to represent the culture even in its original site and to its original members. Even for their own members, those cultures that have successfully translated their products, styles, qualities into marketable commodities, signal survival and thriving. The cultures that cannot achieve such translation lose touch not just with their touristic audiences and global consumers, but with their own members as well. This is why the consumption culture, having marketized all (consumption) experience has, paradoxically, transformed culture itself into a consumable. This is true for traditional cultures rooted in ethnic, national, regional, or religious histories, and even more so for the new cultures (such as American, pan-European, pan-Asian, yuppie, punk, green, techie) that transcend these boundaries. In the global marketplace, establishing a new culture means making it appealing in the market. Furthermore, as already mentioned, culture is likely to become the most popular commodity sought because it gives meaning to the rest, not only spectacularizing the experience through such meaning, but also allowing total immersion in the experience.

Cultural multiplicity

As a result of the globalization of fragmentation, the marketization of cultures through their artifacts, and growing postmodern influences around the world, the experiences of many, including international marketing organizations, are likely to change. These organizations are going to encounter markets that are qualitatively different from modern international markets, especially in terms of the cultural environments. Any marketing organization that goes into a new market expecting to find the consumers to be influenced by a singular culture (such as Spanish, Italian or Japanese) is bound to encounter failure. Instead, the culture(s) they encounter will be multilayered and highly related to the cultural meanings of the products and brands in question. Success or failure in the international marketplace will depend on the complex interactions of multilayed cultures of place and product. This is an area where even firms with superior cultural abilities may stumble—as happened to Disney in Europe in the early 1990s.

The international (or global) experience for consumers will also change. In fact, it has already changed. A consumer going to Paris, for example, with the expectations of experiencing that which is uniquely French may be rather disappointed, for now Paris is not just French but international. At every turn one will encounter artifacts of other cultures; their music, restaurants, language and behavioral mannerisms as well as attires. In the theaters, on television, on the streets, and even in private homes, are the products of and, consequently, the ways and experiences of a multiplicity of cultures. This experience of multiplicity is not, of course, just in Paris, but around the world: in Singapore, Athens, Mumbai, Buenos Aires, or Tokyo.

One of the major effects of the postmodern influences and trends discussed earlier is the decreasing interest among consumers in consuming for consumption's sake. In other words, material resource-intensive consumption is likely to decline among economically affluent consumers as they increasingly seek experiences instead of products. This does not necessarily mean that the consumers will consume less, but the forms of consumption, as well as the reasons behind their consumption, will change. A major reason for this trend is the decreasing commitment to the modern project which linked (equated) the levels of material consumption to success, achievement, development, and improvement of (human) life. Successful countercultural movements, such as the ecological movement, have, indeed, eroded the belief that more is necessarily better. Also, the general disillusionment with the products of modern technologies, mass-production systems and life styles has caused more and more consumers to seek meaning in what they consume. This results in changes in what they consume, although not necessarily in how much they consume. Such transformation reinforces the links between culture(s) and the product(s) that people consume, since meaning is usually derived from imbuing the product with cultural themes. In consuming a product, postmodern consumers are not just seeking and receiving the satisfaction of utilitarian needs (nutrition, shelter, mobility, etc.), but also the meaningfulness of having immersed themselves in a cultural experience. This is why thematic consumption offerings, including theme parks (e.g. Disney World, Universal Studios), eateries (e.g. McDonald's, Planet Hollywood, Hard Rock Café), and shopping environments (e.g. Rodeo Drive, Mall of America), have become successful with contemporary consumers. The variability and differentiation of the postmodern condition, however, implies that no entity, brand, theme, or environment will sustain itself without cultural renovation.

CONSUMPTION, GLOBALIZATION, AND DEVELOPMENT

Market hegemony in the global culture of fragmentation

When the market system and its logic are hegemonic and invade practically all aspects of human life and culture, especially at a time of globalization of fragmentation and the commodification of culture, interesting results ensue—interesting especially in their seeming contradictions and/or paradoxes. Consider, for example, visiting the Hopi reservation in northeastern Arizona, in the United States. This reservation, or Hopi Land, is left as an island in the midst of the larger Navaho (or Dinne, as the nation calls itself) Land. The historical conflicts between the clans of the two nations over land claims are well known. In the end, however, the Hopis, who consider themselves the descendants of the Anasazi (the ancient people of this area of North America who mysteriously disappeared around the fourteenth or fifteenth century, according to several theories) have been circled by two nations: the Dinne and the United States. Over the centuries, this has meant that many revered ways of life had to change for the Hopis, or become dependent on others. In acquiring the cottonwood, which is traditionally used in carving the kachina dolls, for example, they have to trade with the Dinne, since the Dinne now control the lands where the cottonwood trees are. As a result of the agricultural and animal husbandry practices of the nations that surround them, as well as a result of their being settled in a reservation by the treaties and tricks of the United States government, the

Hopis have also had to change their diets. Specifically, for example, their ceremonial dishes that traditionally used rabbit meat are now cooked using lamb, bred and sold to them mostly by the Dinne and other breeders. As their history and their letters to the United States government by their leaders—now displayed at the reservation museum—attest, they feel cheated, used and defeated, overall they feel extremely skeptical, hurt and resentful. Many of their traditions, symbols and cultural artifacts, such as the kachina dolls, have been appropriated and commercialized by other tribes and nations. Consequently, the contemporary reaction of the Hopi nation to this history is isolationist. The Hopis no longer allow outsiders to observe their ceremonies or even their kivas (ceremonial halls) and private homes. They do not want much to do with outsiders in general.

One immediate thing that strikes the tourist who interacts with the Hopi in their land is that this isolationist feeling has not completely worked. While the windows and doors to their homes are well sealed and curtained to prevent anyone (tourist) from seeing the interiors, the television antennas on their roofs are highly visible. Also visible are the brand name clothing items (mostly shorts and T-shirts when one of the authors visited Hopi Land) and brand name shoes (typically athletic shoes) worn by the Hopis of all ages. Clearly, therefore, while largely diminishing the trade and tourism for their cultural artifacts, to stop them from becoming commercial market items and thus desecrated,[26] their purchasing of the products of the larger market has not stopped. A paradoxical consequence of this demarketizing of their own cultural artifacts while still engaging in buying the products of the larger market may be the easily observed poverty in the villages in the reservation and the lack of public services and infrastructure. The villages indeed resemble the poorest villages in countries considered to be economically underdeveloped. These observations regarding the living conditions in Hopi Land bear witness to how the hegemony of the market leads to the impoverishment of those who wish not to belong to the market completely. In the contemporary world, indigenous cultures have a stark choice: live (mostly) without the market in poverty or live with the market and lose authenticity.

Similar conclusions arise from observations of other cultures that have peripheral links to the market system around the world. Consider two examples, one from the Altiplano in Peru and another from Jogjakarta, Indonesia. The people of the Altiplano, the 13,000-ft high plateau in the Andes mountains in Peru, are a major supplier of the alpaca sweaters much sought in North American markets. These sweaters are clearly a product of the many conditions—climatic, historical, natural and otherwise—in the Altiplano, and they must originally have been knitted to meet the necessities of keeping warm on such a high plateau. They fit the climate and they use the natural resources (alpaca wool, for example) of the region. In many of the other places where these sweaters are now sold and worn, they do not fit the climate too well: they are basically used as a stylish clothing item. In becoming such a touristic product and a successful marketable item, it seems, their value and prices have gone above what the locals of the Altiplano can afford. When one visits Puño, for example, at the edge of the plateau and next to Lake Titicaca, one generally sees only the tourists wearing the sweaters while the locals are clad in attire made from industrial, synthetic materials that are cheap in the market, but not as fitting for the conditions of the Altiplano climate. The sweaters have also become valuable to the locals as cash products, and since producing them at the rate demanded by the tourist trade is not easy, they are usually sold in order that the local people can buy other products of the market now available in this part of the world: from television sets and transistor radios to music albums by western artists. With the market success of the sweaters, the prices of the ingredients required in knitting them (specifically, alpaca wool) have also gone up, making the sweaters and the ingredients too valuable to be bought or kept by the locals. In the end, therefore, many of the local people of the Altiplano do not or cannot consume these products that would best fit their needs in their part of the world. Furthermore, they become increasingly dependent on the market products for their living.

When one visits Jogjakarta, Indonesia, the ancient capital on the Java Island, one encounters similar circumstances but reflected in different conditions. The new products of the market have displaced many income-earning trades of the past. One of these trades was the bicycle-driven taxis (pedicabs), which, from the numbers that were still by the sides of the roads in Yogjakarta in 1985, had clearly constituted one of the basic public transportation modes until recently. The arrival of motorized vehicles, especially the minibuses (mostly from Japan), put the pedicab drivers out of work without creating new means of employment for them. Consequently, for tourists coming out of a hotel to explore the city, one major experience was these pedicab drivers crowding around to propose competitive prices for "driving" them round the city. In the course of this drive one impressive sight was the rows and rows of idle pedicabs, with their drivers usually occupying themselves by playing sidewalk gambling games. The poverty of these drivers was obvious from their attire and easily observed failing health conditions (as well as the measly number of fares they could get even from the tourists). The market allows few alternatives to the dominant modes and indeed impoverishes those who cannot integrate themselves into its ways.

There are many such examples around the world of the power of the market, as the hegemonic system, to outcast, disadvantage and displace all non-market forms, even in economically affluent societies, as in the case of the Hopi, or the homeless in the United States. Another affected group are the indigenous peoples of the Appalachian region in the United States. The advance of market relations in this region through mining opportunities and tourism (for example, Floridians and Georgians buying real estate in the region to escape the summer heat in their home states, or skiers in the winter, sightseers in the spring and fall) have caused land prices and real estate taxes to appreciate substantially, causing the locals to lose their land ownership, and to find themselves in working conditions which can only produce poor living conditions.[27]

The triple economy

In many cases, especially in regions of economic underdevelopment, a triple economy emerges with the growth of the market. One sector of this economy is the market sector where consumers are well equipped not only in terms of market skills, but mostly in terms of purchasing power. These consumers are usually from the relatively privileged segments of society, such as the wealthy owners of capital and land, high level managers, politicians and professionals, and media celebrities. While the consumers in this segment control most of the discretionary incomes, and therefore buying power, in the economy, they constitute a minority in numbers. A rather large segment of the population is constituted of consumers at the fringes of the market economy, subservient to the market sector, but not in a position, in terms of either market skills or purchasing power, to have any control over resources. Lacking good purchasing power and the market skills, this segment of consumers is not able to integrate fully into the market economy, and sometimes deals in degenerated and/or irrational markets.[28] Finally, the third segment of consumers indirectly serves the market economy, and at times purchases insignificant (amounts of) market products, but is generally isolated from the market. These consumers are usually living in subsistence conditions. While they may be producing agricultural and other products that end up in the market sector, their relationships to those who control the land, capital, inputs and the trade for these products disallow them from earning sufficient cash incomes to participate in the market directly as consumers.[29]

In most Third World economies there are consumers who straddle these three sectors, moving in and out of them seasonally or occasionally. The conditions they encounter as the market develops and extends its dominance depend mostly on which sector they are generally associated with. As can be surmised, the growth of the market has major impacts on all three sectors, but the impacts are generally undesirable ones, as we discussed in the above examples, for the fringe and isolated sectors.

While it is the economy of the market that induces these impacts, the most important undesirable effects on the fringe and isolated sectors are rarely economic, since these sectors are minimally involved in the economics of the market. The wider impacts of market growth are generally social, cultural, political, psychological and ecological. Because it is the market sector, the consumers with the purchasing power, that can sustain the economics of the market, the market fashions itself to accommodate the needs of this segment of consumers. The priorities and needs of this sector, however, are greatly different from those of the fringe and isolated sectors. As a result, as the market takes over, and the many social, political and ecological systems that historically supported life in the non-market systems degenerate or are destroyed[30] without being replaced by new systems workable for the members of these sectors, the living conditions and standards deteriorate for these sectors.

Fragmentation and enclavization foster this paradoxical development; one sector flourishing economically while others deteriorate in terms of all life dimensions. Enclavization and fragmentation render the poor sectors "invisible" to those economically benefiting from the growth of the market. All kinds of interesting cultural effects develop. For example, the poor enclaves, which have not been able to integrate into the "modern" way of life, may be considered and showcased as examples of the "authentic culture" of the region or country, at times becoming foci of pride. The members of such enclaves, then, have to endure both the impoverization and the spectacularization of their living conditions.

There are many such paradoxical results of market hegemony in an era of the globalization of fragmentation and the commodification of culture. Let us turn to one more of these. In the fragmentation and enclavization of life styles and patterns, the economic achievements of the market sectors in both economically underdeveloped and developed countries are clear, and constantly vaunted by the modern elite. The achievements of such "development" in terms of life dimensions other than economic, however, are questionable even in the market sectors. We are all very familiar with ecological problems, even in affluent market economies. As addressed earlier, issues of psychological health and, relatedly, crime in cultures that emphasize the economic are increasingly becoming major concerns. In general, while the economic *quantities* are successfully enriched, more and more people are beginning to wonder about the *qualities* of life.

A simple example of this may be observed in food. In most parts of the United States we can find apples, bananas, and tomatoes throughout the year and in large quantities, but it is difficult to find any with the quality of taste that once was available (and is still available in "underdeveloped" regions where these items are sold only seasonally). In ensuring the provision of the quantity desired by the market on a continuous basis, the modern production and distribution systems disallow natural ripening, greatly sacrificing quality of taste—and, maybe, even of nutrition.[31]

Another example is the loss of quality in terms of variety of species of food. For example, in the case of grains, marketization has resulted in fewer kinds of wheat, rice, and other grains: focusing on varieties conducive to high-yield cultivation for productivity. These "cash crops" have taken over, because they are marketable, virtually wiping out many other kinds of wheat, rice, etc., some of which are more nutritious or have different qualities that may make them more viable should there be substantive climatic changes. The encroachment of the market, therefore, often reduces variety and quality in many respects, even for the economically affluent.

Postmodernity and global development

The conditions we have discussed are presenting circumstances and experiences that humanity has not known before. In premodern and modern times, for example, identities of clans, tribes, or nations had paramount signification in terms of representation and knowledge of self and community. In premodern society identity was marked or constructed ascriptively through one's connections to the past, whereas in modernity identity came to be shaped through achievement and promise for the future. The typical example of modern identity was produced in North America. Immigrants who came to the United States in the late nineteenth and early twentieth century were provided with symbols of the promise—the Statue of Liberty, for example—that becoming an American meant. Identity in America, the model of modern society for the twentieth century, was one that was not inherited from one's ancestors, but earned, assumed or obtained. The immigrants were asked to denounce or forget—and many were quite ready to do so—their past identities and be proud of, feel a complete belonging to, the promise of America—to become part of the melting pot that was America. The idea was, whoever you were, wherever you came from, you now became an American, a member of the land of promise and a grand future.

It is clear from many literary works, personal diaries, films and other kinds of documentation that, indeed, for at least a century, most immigrants truly believed this promise of a bright future. They came to North America in great numbers and seem to have accepted the rhetoric of and for (the assimilation of) immigrants. This rhetoric is still alive and well. Many immigrants, however, are now considered "illegal," "undesired," and "nuisances" by substantial segments of the United States population. The paradoxes that signal the end of modern America are increasingly more blatant. Furthermore, there is the growing awareness of inconsistencies between the rhetoric of promise, of the future, for the European immigrants, and the forced migration of slaves and the near obliteration of Native Americans. As the "other" face of modernity becomes more and more visible, indicating that modern society was not, after all, the harmonious, orderly, united and uniform model of progress it was professed to be, the attempts of the ideological right to salvage the image become more furious and desperate, attesting to the inevitability of a tarnished image of modernity.

Rather surprising, therefore, may be the apparent efforts in the Third World to replicate the modern "miracle" of North America. It should not be so surprising, however. When development is defined solely in terms of economics and, consequently, market growth, there is no example more stellar than that of America. The "other" dimensions, or the other face(s) of modernity are hidden from view by the barrage of positive images and forceful rhetoric of what America is. Its glowing economic façade, (re)presented through media mostly controlled by the economically affluent in America and the elites in the Third World countries who follow and aspire to the wealth and the life styles of the "rich and the famous,"[32] masks the other facets of America.

It is unlikely, however, that the "unpleasant" facets of modern development can forever be suppressed. In America, increasing numbers of people are beginning to feel the effects of the negative side of modern development—pollution, crime, poverty, etc.—and the same is likely to occur in the rest of the world once the honeymoon with expectations of economic growth is over. It will become evident that there are discrepancies between the promises of modern, industrial, material, market-based growth and the policies and politics required to sustain such growth.[33] For some, these discrepancies are already evident.

The quest for alternatives

The ideology that embraces the idea that there are no viable alternatives to market growth has been very successfully marketed. Such success often produces the denial of the familiar or the repression of suspicion, a condition that some have called "double-think."[34] Under the hegemony of the ideology of market growth, it becomes difficult to voice doubts about its inconsistencies, or question the idea that viable alternatives do not exist, or experiment with alternatives. Instead, energies are channeled to reforming the dominant model of development, further entrenching its hegemony. Often, any attempt at alternative models is, therefore, immediately tainted with the image of being "inferior."

Why should development that is not solely based on economic growth not be attainable? This critical question gathers strength when the hyper-real[35] character of social reality is understood. With this understanding it also becomes clear that the impediments for alternative models of growth lie in the denial of multiplicity and difference. Instead, all models are charged with classifications in terms of their superiority or inferiority. In such a framing of development, of course, there must then be one alternative that is superior to all else. This system of ranking undermines the multiplicity of visions, imaginaries, and preferences that different communities have regarding the reality sought or the living conditions desired. "Oh, no," we end up saying, "how can the way those people choose to live be equal to ours? They don't even have automobiles and television!"

When alternative modes of life sought by some are not compatible with that which is dominant, it is no longer possible to produce a development that harmonizes with the hegemonic rhetoric. Yet, even within the dominant system, the rhetoric is rarely supported by the semiotics of the cultural theater. The reason for the rift is that hype—as producer of reality—is not solely constructed on the basis of the public rhetoric (in the sense of political and social messages that dominate the media and political discourse). Many other signs in the culture equally communicate what is or could be "real." When the visions, promises, and dreams that are promoted in the speeches, teachings, and authoritative discourses are contradicted by other signs, the hype is not uniform but polemical. It will thus not produce a "reality" that corresponds to the dominant rhetoric. For example, there may be state policies enacted into law, business practices that reward or disadvantage some, or social privileges that result from political actions that are contrary to those revered or promoted in the public rhetoric. A good example of such hype is found in the historical conditions of women in modernity. As we discussed in Chapter 4, at the same time that they were put on pedestals and afforded much respect in the public rhetoric as mothers and sisters, they were denigrated and devalued by legal and economic practices. Consequently, their realities did not match their images in the public rhetoric.

Postmodern culture is likely to bring a greater acceptance of the multiplicity and, thus, of the differences in the conceptions of global development(s). One potential outcome is that development will be defined as a multidimensional process, and not as solely an economic one. A singular model of development—one path that others ought to follow—would become unsustainable, perhaps even unmarketable.[36] No one model would be able to sustain the claim that it is more "developed" than others. Even "successful" models would have to admit that only in some respects (dimensions) they may have produced more desirable (preferable) outcomes than others, while less desirable outcomes may characterize other dimensions. Moreover, evaluations of what is desirable or preferable along each dimension may differ for different groups, as may the number and definitions of dimensions along which development is evaluated. It is this multiplicity and allowance for such difference that will largely define the postmodern orientation(s) to development.

The discursive result of all this multiplicity is that making a distinction between the *developed* and the *underdeveloped* (or *less developed*, *developing* and similar concepts used in "kinder" or "more polite" literature) will become impossible, and all global activity will have to be considered in the context of development. That is, all countries, nations, societies, communities will have to be considered as *developing*. The perspectives which signify some as developed, and therefore superior, and others as underdeveloped, and therefore inferior, become untenable in a postmodern world. This is of course threatening to those who have enjoyed the status of being superior, and they will fight the postmodern culture vehemently, as they are already doing.[37]

Globalization of markets and consumption modes

While postmodern influences are shaping the current trends in globalization of markets and modes of consumption, globalization itself is very much a modern phenomenon. Human history is replete with global movements and relations, thanks to pioneering explorers and merchants, but it is modern technology and the necessities of modern economies that paved the way for global society. We had knowledge of distant lands and cultures, as well as their more exotic products and artifacts, but never experienced the day-to-day connections with them until the rise of modernity. Thanks to modernity, all parts of our globe are in daily contact. The quest for materials, labor, and markets has pushed modern economies into a frenzied rush to expand right across the globe. This expansion has taken many forms, from colonialism to trade agreements. As a result, the nexus of interests that span the globe has ballooned and increasing numbers of people are beginning to recognize these interests. People realize that what happens in what used to be considered "remote" areas of the world impacts upon their daily existence. Some people become interested in the affairs across the globe because fellow human beings are involved. For reasons of self-interest or altruism, increasing numbers of people care about events around the world. Modern global linkages spawned and sustain this trend.

Consider, for example, the recent reactions to the use of child labor and low wages in Third World countries by United States corporations. When the new Nike Town store opened in San Francisco, the opening ceremonies inside were accompanied by groups of protesters who demonstrated outside the store criticizing Nike's wage and child labor policies in Indonesia and elsewhere. Such events are relatively recent, beginning in some force with the boycotts of the products of companies in the 1960s, companies that were deemed to use "unethical" practices in marketing their goods in the Third World. As modern capitalism globalizes its activities, organizations are finding out that they have to deal with all issues on a global platform. The world has become a stage for organizations, and the audience is global.

Novel communications technologies are speeding up this trend. Electronic, virtual communities are forming through the Internet and electronic mail. Practically every day we get messages informing us of events taking place in different locations, help that is needed, actions that can be initiated or taken. A radio station in Bosnia is under attack from the government and immediately an electronic community forms to take action and send messages to the Bosnian government to stop; a child in the Middle East has a dying wish and virtual communities across the world form to help; political oppression in South America results in similar communities which form and take action; and the practices of a multinational company that violate people's sense of fairness are confronted by a global community.

Globalization and postmodernization are trends that reinforce each other, specifically because globalization has taken the form of globalization of fragmentation. Instead of a unitary and universal culture or life mode dominating the world, we are witnessing the simultaneous appearance of varied modes in different parts of the world. This is, indeed, a postmodern trend, save for the persistence of the condition that all such diffusion of difference is singularly mediated by the market. In the instant and intense global linkages, however, lie the possibilities of creating new life mode communities that will transcend the hegemony of the market. We turn to these possibilities, and the conditions impeding or aiding such possibilities, in the following two chapters.

9   Consuming people

We come, then, to the crux of the issue. We have studied and analyzed the history of consumption as it evolved in modernity, and we have explored the ongoing transformations in consumption, both in the construction of the meanings of consumption in (post)modern[1] times and in the practices of consumption. At this juncture, then, where do we stand—we the people, consuming people? Is consumption consuming us, the people? Or can we turn things around so that we consume *for* ourselves, so that consumption is *for* us? Is it possible to have *consumption of the people, by the people, for the people* rather than *consumption of people, qua consuming people*? These are some of the central political, cultural, and philosophical questions of our time. Unlike modernity's quest for the democratic rights of the individual subject—a quest that postmodernity transcends by taking these rights as given—the challenge for the postmodern era is to create or find (consumption?) processes that are liberating rather than repressing, diversifying rather than totalizing, connecting rather than alienating. While modernity waged its struggles at the barricades and ballot boxes, postmodernity carries on its discourse in an electronic sea of symbols, a sea of symbols that is technologically dynamic and culturally volatile. In modernity, production—its relations, its value, its control—was the contested terrain. In postmodernity, consumption—its relations, its significations, its liberation—is the issue to grapple with.

MODERNITY'S LEGACY

Our investigations leave us with a long list of problems that face humanity today, all immediately related to consumption. Many of these problems are perceived as threats to major advances humanity has made throughout its existence on Earth, especially since the Enlightenment: democracy, freedom(s), civil society, science and rationality, civilization and civility, intellectual maturity, and, in general, the degree of knowledge of and about ourselves that gives us control over our own lives. To many observers, the current developments and transformations portend a readiness to jettison all of this away as a result of deepening resentments, doubts, skepticism, and distrust. There is fear that we are about to lose too much. It seems we had made major strides towards the humane society, but with the loss of our commitments to its progress and the general deterioration of an awareness of history, we may lose it all.

Most observers of our time, unless they are in the "business" of creating excitement for economic activity and business, find an unstoppable erosion of our material and intellectual resources. Increasingly people are seen to act without thinking, following herd mentalities. Interest in intellectual matters and world affairs, affairs that matter to the future of our lives, appears to be waning. There tends to be a loss of commitment to projects of humanity, for the general interests of humanity, while an increased concern is observed for matters of money and commerce. Many people seem to be turning away from altruistic interests and toward self-interests. There appears to be an erosion in the ethical and moral, as well as the intellectual fiber of society. Too many people seem to be turning to protection of narrow interests or causes to the detriment of the broader interests of humanity as a whole. The burning issue has become one of finding political solutions under the prevailing politically uninterested and divided conditions, especially at a time when politics is being supplanted by the market.

Many observers of our times who are nostalgic for a past when causes could muster thousands and millions to march and to react, to take a stand and challenge authority, and to sacrifice their whole lives to a grand and noble cause, are dismayed that commitment to such grand projects and causes appears to be dying. Could a civil rights movement ever take place now, at the end of the twentieth century? The answer seems to be "No." People just don't trust anyone—including themselves—to represent situations and conditions in earnest, and trust even less their ability to propose solutions. Such distrust manifests itself in the lack of interest in political processes in the United States, and in the high level of cynicism about (political) leaders and their motives in Europe and elsewhere. What we observe instead are small numbers of people vehemently trying to advance narrow causes, such as the anti-abortionists in the United States. For growing majorities of people, interest in grand causes is sporadic and short-lived. Belonging to or supporting a cause is increasingly "a thing to do," a consumption experience, rather than something to be completely and unwaveringly committed to. With the rise of "consumption," there appears to be a rise in singular, temporal, micro causes; or, at least, a rise in the media coverage of such causes.

A modernist inclination

There is, in the above observations and interpretations of the conditions of our day, a modernist inclination. The distrust in the ability of the masses to recognize their condition(s), as well as the belief that the masses are unaware and uninformed, is very much a modernist tendency, despite the fact that modernity insisted on the primacy and centrality of the human subject. It was the *knowing* subject, however, that modernism exalted, and the majority of the human subjects in modern times have not been sufficiently educated. The modernist thinkers therefore do not generally trust the majority's ability to judge and make "rational" choices. As a result, much of modern society is structured to "help" or "guide" the people, to protect them from the follies they may get themselves into, to keep them from making the wrong, "irrational" choices. There has always been a high level of interest in controlling the behaviors of human beings in modernity, as evident in the organization and structuring of production sites (offices, plants, factories, plantations) to assure rational behaviors from the workers. It is ironic that modern society continually generated ways of making sure that the human being was "controlled" in order not to stray from a "rational" course, given that modernity was founded on the premise of giving the human subject control over her/his destiny.

Why did the modernists develop such distrust of the human being, and why is this distrust at an all time high among the intellectuals of our time? Originally, it seems, the reason was that the educational efforts had not reached sufficiently large proportions of the world's population. This is understandable since modern thought privileged the *knowing* subject, one who was aware of the scientific discoveries. Such knowledge was primarily related or diffused to people through modern educational institutions. To achieve a community of knowing subjects it was important to extend and expand education to all. The failure to achieve this goal in most societies of the world resulted in distrust in the ability of the masses to act as knowing subjects.

Yet, even in the countries of the First World, where major educational successes have occurred, this distrust persists, especially among the literate and the intellectuals. The lack of trust in the masses appears to have increased in the last few decades. As a result, there is an attack on educational institutions in the United States, and in Europe there is an attack on institutions such as the media, which are seen as competitors to educational institutions. In the United States, educational institutions are said to fall short in providing good education. In Europe, the media competing with education is blamed for misleading youth and thwarting educational goals. Of course, there is also a similar attack on the media, especially television, in the United States by some intellectuals.[2]

In 1989, the ABC television network broadcast a program looking into the failures of education. The program was called "America's Kids: Why They Flunk." It represented the mainstream's interpretation of the condition of today's youth. The program exposed the general lack of knowledge of today's youth in subjects deemed important, such as mathematics, geography, biology, and history. Students in their junior and senior years of high school across the United States displayed an appalling ignorance of even recent historical events, such as the Vietnam War, along with a nonchalant attitude toward their unawareness. Instead, their interests clearly centered around clothes, movies, and partying. The program blamed a lack of values, goals, and discipline among youth for this "failure." The burden of responsibility was placed on the young people themselves, their parents, and their teachers. It was indeed telling that a major television network's program did not mention the role of television and the contemporary culture at all—very much a televisual culture[3]—in this analysis of the state of education in the United States.

While the conclusions of the program are likely to be disputed by many sociologists and by those in cultural studies, the concerns about the failures of society in delivering good education and creating a community of informed, intellectual members are widespread. Modernity has to carry much of the blame for this state of affairs. On the one hand, it is modern technologies and modern economic activities that have inundated our lives with images, interests, and distractions that pull us away from intellectual pursuits and rob us of the time to reflect on issues. Modern culture has privileged the visual over all other senses and over all other forms of information,[4] and spawned the visual media that are more alluring and seductive—partially due to their multidimensionality[5]—than the written media. On the other hand, modern intellectual discourse has privileged the written word. The ability to construct logical arguments that progress in linear fashion by using words as the medium of informed, scientific, rational knowledge generation and dissemination has been deemed paramount in realizing the modern project.[6] Therefore, when visual media such as films and television became so dominant in modern society, they came to be seen as oppositional to intellectual activity. The commercial interests controlling these media have found it profitable to position them almost purely as entertainment media. Due to their historical disdain of these media, intellectuals have readily relinquished control of such media to commercial interests. In general, the intellectuals have largely bought into the idea that television and films are entertainment media, and have consigned such media to an inferior position vis-à-vis written media.

The modern separation between "education" and "entertainment" has played an important role in this oppositional juxtaposition of written and visual media. Related to the separations between home and workplace, and public and private domains, the separation between "serious" and "consequential" (intellectual) versus "light" and "frivolous" (entertaining) activities has influenced our dispositions toward books—especially intellectual books—and television. Given the belief that intellectual endeavors, such as education, learning, and reflection, cannot be or should not be entertain(ment)ing, the element of fun has been drained out of education, reading intellectual/academic books, and having intellectual discussions. By the same token, given the idea that what is entertaining cannot be intellectual, "entertainment" media have largely been emptied of substantive content. Thus for our youth as well as adults, education, learning, and intellectual discourse have become largely boring and a chore, while activities such as watching television, going to the movies, listening to popular music, and having parties are fun and enjoyable.

Of course, the separation between entertainment and education or intellectual activity is mythical. As our youth expose themselves to entertaining media, learning does take place.[7] What is being learned, however, is not what modernist intellectuals and educators think is important. Furthermore, the form of learning is different, due to the characteristics of the new communications technologies that first find their applications in and as the entertainment media. Rather than the linear logic-based learning privileged in modern education, a multifaceted, nonlinear form of learning is taking place. After all, when one watches television, informative/communicative signs (visual images, sounds, and words) are not encountered in a linear, sequential, linked form. Instead, the viewer encounters a barrage of signs (visual and other) that are multilayered and often disjointed. Learning and literacy, therefore, are changing, and a new synergy has to be found between intellectual endeavor and entertainment that takes the changing form of literacy into account. Rather than give up or struggle to regress to a modernist form of intellectual discourse, which clearly has failed against the new communication technologies and has not worked in producing an intellectually armed world population in (post)modern times, we can and need to develop ways of interjecting reflection and substance into the forms of postmodern literacy.[8]

The pessimism about our youth and, therefore, the future of human society, is also linked to their seeming lack of interest in and lack of knowledge of general world affairs and public discourse. Of course, this is related to the "failures" in education and learning. In effect, many educators and intellectuals tend to dislike the way that contemporary human energies are channeled; the priorities seem all wrong: too little interest in general and in-depth knowledge and in substantive matters, too much interest in and time spent on frivolous things. People so "educated" are easily manipulable and ready to conform to dominating ways and ideologies. Here, again, a modernist tendency that induces pessimism and elitism in interpretation can be discerned, instead of a postmodern recognition of transformations, potentials and possibilities.[9] However, given the momentous changes occurring in our cultures, and the powerful developments in technologies, it is highly improbable either that the modernist goals can be realized as envisioned, or the revered modernist means towards these goals can be maintained. Instead, there is a need, and indeed the potential, to redefine humanity's goals and construct exciting new means. To realize these potential(s) and to construct new cultures of living and learning, there is first the need to change our attitudes and our orientation from one of holding on to the old to one of critical yet playful engagement with the new conditions.

We shall discuss the potentials that await us in the next chapter. To gain a comprehensive understanding of the new potentials, other major concerns, which arise when contemporary culture, society, and conditions are studied, need to be articulated.

The culture of consumption

A set of problems that worry the socially concerned and the intellectuals pertain to the culture of consumption and its implications for contemporary society. Increased material consumption and, therefore, increased production of objects to be consumed create problems, not all of which are related to ecology and the environment. It is clear, indeed, that pollution and ecological decline are contemporary ills associated with a culture that marks the ability to consume an ever-swelling stream of material goods and services as the sign of prosperity, achievement, success, and a better life. As yet, no alternative goals exist to replace this goal of ever increasing material consumption. Therefore, despite recognition of the problems produced by this culture, it continues to reign in full force. If at any time production or consumption tend to falter, so does the economy, going into recession or depression. The nexus of economic health and an ever-growing cycle of production and consumption further fuels the ideology of material consumption. Thus, it becomes a vicious (virtuous, for the market) cycle that is difficult to break out of.

When development, better life, success, and the like come to be defined in terms of material consumption, it is unlikely that major discrepancies in the world between the rich and the poor, the haves and have-nots, would dissipate. The financial and technological advantages that the economically rich countries have over poor countries are very unlikely to change in the foreseeable future.[10] While small relative gains in favor of poorer regions, countries, and populations may occur, due to relatively higher (but, of course, with diminishing differences) growth rates for the poorer countries, they are never likely to catch up economically in any foreseeable future, barring the occurrence of some catastrophic event in economically richer countries.[11] This is a problem because, especially with global communications, inhabitants of poorer countries are unlikely to accept the everlasting discrepancy in well-being and life styles. The bright possibility in this respect is that the definitions of achievement and meaningful life could change, and the energies of human beings around the world (including those in rich countries) could be directed to goals that do not require high levels of technological and material consumption. Already, especially in the western cultures, which have tasted the economic and technological leaps dreamt of in modernity, there is growing disenchantment with this never-ending quest. As we discussed earlier, recognition that such advancement does not necessarily bring greater meaning and happiness to life, and perhaps breeds many ills (including greater abilities for destruction), is causing many segments of society to seek different or alternative ways to live and reasons to live for.

This is one of the major forces behind the growing influence of postmodernist ideas and culture.

When ideas for alternative modes of life are proposed to poorer nations by representatives of these segments or by official agencies, there is understandable resistance, resentment, and skepticism. Proposals and advice to curb the national hunger for the kind of affluence that is constantly displayed in media productions from the United States and other economically richer countries sound too imperialistic, self-serving, or didactic: "I have tried it, I have enjoyed it, but I know that it is bad, I am telling you that you should not try it, it is not good for you!" This is the message that tends to come across to members of poorer nations. At the same time, the old modernist propaganda about how superior the United States (or United Kingdom, or other western countries) are thanks to their great economical and technological achievements, supported by the great capitalist system and western democracy, continues unabated in the global media. Calls coming from the west for moderating high levels of material consumption, therefore, generally fall on deaf or very skeptical ears. Observers of developments in poorer countries of the world are well aware that the engine of more and more material consumption still surges ahead across the world.

How can these contradictions between what we say and what we do, between what we can afford and what we aim for, be resolved under the constant barrage of an ideology that seeks and requires growing material consumption to satisfy its dream of well-being and happiness? We shall discuss the potential responses to this question in the next chapter, based on the (hi)story of consumption and consuming people we have studied in previous chapters.

CONSUMPTION AND IDENTITY

Forces other than the ideology of the consumer culture contribute to the impetus for increasing material consumption. One major force is that identity construction, or construction of selfhood, is increasingly dependent on consumption. In the contemporary world, in order to define oneself to others, even to one's self, requires greater and greater use of products and consumption experiences. Increasingly, we are what we consume. People assure themselves of who they are and how much they have achieved through what they consume. Others judge them and their identities by the same criteria. This is an ironic state of affairs from a modern perspective that regarded consumption as mere appendage to production, a necessity to replenish energies in order to get on with the important, higher-order purposes of life, those of creativity and production. According to modern values, one's identity and worth were reflected in what one produced and created, and how one contributed to the betterment of society and humanity. Instead of this, we now see increasing numbers of consumers defining their identities through what they consume.

Consumption and self-image

Ironic as it may be, this turn of events is not difficult to understand or explain. As more and more productive activity has been absorbed into the public domain, greater and greater numbers of people in production have lost their ability to control what and how they produce. Other than a very small proportion made up of top-level executives and their creative staff, time in production (in offices, workshops, and production lines) has largely become routinized and a chore for most.

In the quest to rationalize production processes to achieve the highest efficiency towards maximum material outcomes (and consumption), not much discretion has been left for people to be creative or influential in their jobs. For 99 percent of people in production—the activity deemed to be the higher purpose of life where one is self-actualized through being creative and contributing something of worth—it is "just a job" they have to do, a necessity to make ends meet. As production in the public sphere has become increasingly predetermined and fixed, people have turned their creative and individual energies to consumption in the private sphere. While consumption had always offered a platform for the disenfranchised and the poor to register rebellion and disaffection[12] as well as to establish presence, it was nonetheless strongly manipulated by the actions taken in and through the public domain. Thus, the construction of identity or selfhood is a highly paradoxical process in contemporary culture. On the whole, however, individuals find *relatively* greater freedom and control in the sphere of consumption. Therefore, they opt to construct meaning in their lives in and through "consumption" experiences. This has interesting potential consequences. As the rigid separations between production and consumption dissolve,[13] and the productive outcomes of consumption in terms of life meanings, human body and mind, and self-images are increasingly recognized and valued, the cultural calculus of valuation and signification enters a state of flux.

The power to signify

Because a large proportion of the global population has little ability to "consume," in the modern sense, and with the continuing hegemony of the market, the issue of the poor and the disenfranchised still looms. As we assign greater and greater importance to consumption, what is to become of those who have very little ability to consume? This, indeed, may be the most difficult philosophical and pragmatic problem in the construction of the new world, through postmodernity or otherwise. On the one hand, if the importance of material consumption were to decrease—as we argued would happen when and if the hegemony of the market is broken—then the assessment of poverty and being disadvantaged would change to the benefit of those who are *currently* poor and disenfranchised. Instead of an emphasis on how much material resource is missing from their lives, the emphasis would be on the meaning(fullness) of life. Consequently, "poverty" would at once become less prevalent and more diffused. There would be a growing recognition that life can be meaningful without riches, at the same time that the meaninglessness of the lives of many who possessed riches would become transparent.[14] On the other hand, the ability to assert the meanings sought and preferred in the life experiences will depend on communicative prowess, and on the power to participate in the signification and representation processes. Having such ability, prowess, and power will depend on an ability to consume, not necessarily in terms of material resources, but in terms of resources that improve communication, and communication will require (multi)signefficacy (see Note 8).

FROM GRAND PROJECTS TO INCREMENTAL ACTION

Today, many complain that people are no longer willing to unite for a cause, and that it is impossible to mobilize people for social change. People seem to be too caught up in every-day life and to have lost hope in the possibility of change. As a result, many who perceive the need for significant social change keep looking for things that will energize the engines of change again. They yearn for yesteryear when masses or massive movements could be mobilized.[15] Often what is blamed is the drugging or immobilizing effects of the media, or the move to "consumption," or the indifference induced by the dominant ideology. It could be argued that the methods and results of *modern* mass movements for social change are also to blame. While those from within the change movements may dispute this, the inescapable conclusion is that all modern projects vying for social change and promising grand futures have been failures, or are regarded as failures, including ultimately the project based on the capitalist market economy, although for the time being it seems to have come out as the victor among projects.[16] Even those of us who still believe in the goals of any of these projects have to agree, if we are not oblivious to conditions on Earth, that in the final analysis modern projects are failures in practice or implementation if not in theory. Their goals and intentions may have been honorable and good, but the insistence on each one's superiority over others and the requirement for total commitment have resulted in wars, poverty, and misery.

Doing it

It is not surprising therefore that the great majority of people today no longer trust in promises of social change for or through grand projects to better human life, and that they are not willing to commit themselves to such projects, or to become mobilized. Instead, for many who have not been drugged by the media or by "consumption," it is better to commit to small, "do-able" projects that can bring small but observable and controllable, therefore "testable" and modifiable changes. As already discussed, the forms of action and agency for social change seem to be changing. The "revolutionaries" are not seeking confrontational strategies to create mass movements to challenge and overthrow the systems or social formations they face and disapprove of. The contemporary and paradoxical tendency for social change is one of *indifference* towards the powers and authorities that rule, in effect, opting to ignore them, and trying to live in ways that seem meaningful, to construct life styles that make sense, "do one's own thing," independent of the dominant ways of living. Such movements confront authority only when they are confronted by it. The inclination in such movements seems to be "let me be and I'll let you be." We see examples of this "strategy" in gay and lesbian communities and back-to-the-earth communities, among others, but also among the general population in the United States. This is one reason for the withdrawal of many from the political process, except in their local communities.

The potential success of such agency, revolting by *doing* instead of *confronting*, is open to question. We shall discuss the potentials and threats in the next chapter, but here it may be necessary to say that this is a relatively recent social change strategy. Partly, it has grown out of the frustration and failures of modernist confrontational strategies, but partly it must be attributed to the contemporary culture. With the fragmentation and the barrage of market ideology in the media, it seems impossible to unite people behind singular articulations of envisioned, promising futures or ways of life. In the past century, socialism was the idea that moved people with the greatest effect and excitement—that is, people who were willing to commit to a vision. For reasons that may be forever argued, this vision's practical applications seem to have failed. Both those who vehemently believe in the necessity of social change towards a more compassionate, fair, nurturing, equitable society and world, and those who just want to live a meaningful life for themselves, have come to doubt the promises of totalizing, grand visions. They have become skeptical and afraid to commit. Rather, there is a growing need to see results, not just visions. But how is such social experimentation with alternative systems and life modes possible? Whole societies cannot switch systems to try one for a while then another, when the differences require total demolition of one set of relationships, the division of resources, and the construction of another set. Since the modern forms of universalizing, totalizing social change through confrontational strategies seem to be less and less possible, the methods of social change have to be reconsidered. This is important if the agency for social change is to remain vested in the actions of human beings, hopefully in a participatory fashion, informed by conscious philosophies and well-considered ideas. Social change, of course, is occurring all the time, but what or who is in control? Is it deliberate or haphazard? Is it based on human reflection or guided by the necessities and the rationale of technologies and institutions that come about? These are some issues we wish to address in the next chapter.

The more successful methods of social change, however, if change is to be controlled by human reflection and actions, have to consider all the conditions we have been discussing throughout this book. In the end, our current culture is one of "show me, don't tell me." This was well articulated by a young Swedish student one of us met in Paris about three years ago. He said,

> we [today's youth] are bored with people telling us what is right and good, and what should be done, how to live. We see the failure of what is done and has been done by those who tell us what to do. So we say, do it and show us, don't talk about it or tell us.

This might be one reason why rock music has had such success in defining a life style for generations.[17] Rock stars, the leaders of the movement, and other rockers do not *preach* to others. They just *present* a mode of life by what they do and how they live. To many others this life mode happens to be attractive.

Rock has had the ability to do and present by example, instead of proposing a vision, because it is so much part of the commercial market economy. For visionaries wishing to present alternatives other than modernized, marketized versions of life modes, this economy is the most important hurdle to cross. What is to be done? How can those who are outside the market system maintain their life modes and make them sufficiently visible for others to notice and consider? Are we restricted to being able to maintain and present only marketized and marketable versions of alternative life modes? That seems to be the case in contemporary society where the market has become hegemonic. What are the options and possibilities for (re)constructing the theater and multidimensionalizing and (re)enchanting life? How do we break out of the stronghold of the singular metanarrative of the market?

The culture of marketing

All the effort and desire for diversity expressed verbally and behaviorally in contemporary society seems to be absorbed and co-opted by the commercial market. The only way to express diversity is through marketable forms. This ends up giving the power to (re)present not to those who are diverse but to those who have the resources to communicate the marketable aspects of that which is diverse. It is these powerful (re)presenters who choose the types of diversity to celebrate and promote. We end up organizing our images and discourses of diversity based on the media's representations of those elements that sell. For example, to be an African-American of notice in the United States is to model the black athletic star selling sports shoes, or the rap artist in the music videos. In the end, not only others, but also the character which is represented (the self) gets to know who s/he is through these presentations.

Marketing, thus, is indeed the culture of our time. We only know what is marketed and marketable. Furthermore, we are producing people who tend to think of themselves as marketable products. People are not fools. They realize that those who have the skills to "sell" themselves in different situations are the ones that "get ahead." The marketing media control the meanings of "getting ahead," favoring those who make lots of money and can consume luxuriously, that is, become full participants in the market.

As marketing becomes the culture, culture becomes the most successful marketable. It is textured and textual, allowing contemporary consumers who are seeking to immerse themselves in meaningful experiences to have fully sensational moments. Culture is multidimensional and has depth, providing the texture and the (con)text that address all senses. Thus, it gives density and body to the experience. For any consumption experience to have such quality, the marketing enterprise increasingly links all products to *a* cultural context, thereby enchanting the experience with the product. Products are imbued with deeper and denser meaning through being immersed in cultural representations. There are however, millions of products and relatively few cultures. Therefore, marketing fosters the construction of new cultures, whether they have countercultural origins (such as punk and grunge cultures) or life style origins (such as gay and lesbian cultures) or technological origins (such as the techie or nerd culture) or artistic origins (such as rock and alternative music cultures) or business origins (such as the modern organizational culture that is now encountered all over the world). The market does not need to create these cultures. It just appropriates them by commercializing their expressions—whether they be music or clothing—and emptying them of their original (anti-market or non-market) contents. Along with the products that represent the cultural experiences, the cultures themselves are made marketable items. Now, consumers can consume cultures, including all the deeper and embedded meanings.

In the meantime, as cultures multiply, consumers can move among and "belong to" multiple cultures instead of one. In effect, as we discussed earlier, all consumers now encounter and experience multilayered, multifaceted culture-scapes. It is no longer possible to say that someone is from a French culture, or an Italian culture, or an African-American culture. None of these cultures are as homogeneous as they used to be—if they ever were—and no one can have membership of one culture alone. On the one hand, this development enables consumers to have greater understanding of each other—since there is greater possibility that many will share at least one culture with others instead of being separated by cultures. On the other hand, such understandings are always embedded in and negotiated through the commercial. The construction of human identity, of selfhood, in contemporary society is thus made even more paradoxical. Even as consumers seek independent and varied experiences that give meaning(s) to their lives by being different and "individual," they end up having to conform to the market culture, and the marketed forms of cultural experiences. Even as they seek to rebel, they conform. Consider, for example, the consumers who have feelings of greater control over their lives by modifying their bodies (through plastic surgery), as well as feelings of having rebelled (through, say, exotic forms of body piercing) against the mainstream or older generational culture that emphasizes the sanctity of the body. Yet, simultaneously, they recognize and voice their desire to conform to the popular standards of beauty, to be more "marketable." In effect, in these consumers' actions we see rebellion through conformity and conformity through rebellion. This is but one example of the paradoxical nature of the construction of identity and selfhood in contemporary life.

If the conditions explored in this chapter define contemporary consumption experience, at the very juncture that consumption has taken center stage, what happens to human agency for social change? Is it at all possible to recover human agency in social change? What positive potentials do we see in the future? The next—and last—chapter will explore these issues.

CONSUMPTION POLITICS

Changes in the workplace and the marketplace had corresponding echoes in the sphere of politics. As consumption moved from the periphery towards the center of society and economy, the levers of political power had to be recalibrated and realigned. Consumption, consumers, consuming people have become the invisible source of political power. Whatever other ideological position he or she may espouse, no politician in the America of the 1990s can appear to be anti-consumer. Politics and policies have taken on a quasi-Pareto character.[18] That is, policies must have the *appearance of* diminishing the welfare of *no one* while enhancing the welfare of some/many. Policies as different as cuts in entitlement programs (resulting in the poor being hurt) and cuts in capital gains taxes (benefiting the rich) are presented in Pareto-forms: hurting no one, benefiting some/many. In the context of the United States, the "some/many" distinction usually corresponds to the Republican/Democratic distinction: Republicans favor policies that favor a narrow "some," Democrats favor policies that favor a more plural "many." Whatever or whoever wins, the consumer never loses. In fact, when consumers feel they are losing ground, there is a ballot-box rebellion and it is "time to throw the bums out."

The politics of consumption has brought about policy making by polls. Like proposed new flavors for a soft drink or advertising slogans for a car, new policies are constantly subjected to consumers' opinion polls.[19] As with consumer tastes in other areas, the resultant "poll-icies" in some political domains are often fickle. Fashions change, something new and exciting comes along, or quite simply tedium and boredom set in—and policies have to change. In other political domains, like well-entrenched brands weighty with "brand equity" and consumer loyalty, long-established policies are unshakable—no matter who is in power or what ideological climate prevails.

Politics has become the art of winning political market share—in terms of votes, hearts, and minds. The consumer is the source of political power, but consumers are not kings and queens. Consumerism rules through the market, not the consumer. At the threshold of postmodernity, all other "-isms" lie prostrate before consumerism.

CONSUMERS AS GRASSROOTS POLITICAL FORCE

The marketization of politics is a response to what had started emerging earlier in the twentieth century—the consumer as a grassroots political force. The most potent form of such force is de-patterning of consumption, a holistic rejection of an established pattern of consumption. A famous example of this occurred during India's independence struggle against the British, when Gandhi launched the *Swadeshi* movement. Decades of British rule had nearly destroyed the fabled handloom "cottage industry" of India and machine-made textiles from the mills of Manchester were flooding the Indian market. To put economic pressure on the British, Gandhi launched the self-reliance or Swadeshi movement. He urged Indians to boycott mill-made clothes, buy cotton and hand-spin coarse yarn at home, send it to handloom weavers for conversion into cloth, and then wear garments made from this hand-spun, hand-woven cloth. Fired by the patriotic fervor of the Swadeshi movement, Indians responded in the millions, making bonfires of mill-made garments and turning to self-produced cloth. Even after five decades of independence, and with a vast domestic textile industry of its own, in order to be credible India's politicians still find it necessary to wear the hand-spun, hand-woven garments, at least when campaigning or touring in villages. The symbolic power of Swadeshi persists nearly a century after this consumption de-patterning movement was launched.

Hippies and the countercultural movement in the United States, with echoes and parallels in Europe and elsewhere, represented another de-patterning force. The torn jeans, the beads, headbands, and interest in things spiritual-holistic as well as in hallucinogens represented a major rejection of modern industrial capitalism's "organization man."

Unlike the organized de-patterning represented by Gandhi's Swadeshi movement, the counterculture movement was not organized and orchestrated by any central authority figure. The counterculture movement was decentered, spontaneous, fluid, diverse, multi-hued, and fragmented—a quintessentially postmodern movement. Like the Swadeshi movement, the countercultural movement initially brought about a confrontation between those in power and those struggling for change, but this was swiftly followed by co-optation of the symbols of hippie-dom by business and government. The potency of this countercultural movement can be judged from the fact that even after three decades, its symbols keep reappearing in powerful marketized forms.

Consumer resistance has also been used as a political force in boycotts of various types. Unlike a de-patterning movement that challenges an entire consumption pattern, a boycott is limited in its scope, usually in the form of refusal to buy specific products until certain demands are met. The boycott and resistance against Nestlé for propagating infant formula in Third World countries is a significant example.[20]

While some consumer boycotts have been successful in achieving their objectives, by and large it is possible for targets of such boycotts to sidestep the economic hostility of the boycott. In a globalized economy, it is difficult for the boycott leaders to reach all the relevant consumers and it is easy for the boycott targets to find alternative markets to replace the sales lost from the boycotters. In the 1960s, however, consumer advocates found a more potent weapon than boycotts for pressing the consumerist agenda. Instead of targeting footloose business firms that could escape to far corners of global markets, why not target power-holders whose base of power is confined to specific jurisdictions—politicians and their administrative appointees? The consumer movement in the United States, led principally by Ralph Nader, was spectacularly successful in pressing the consumerist agenda in government policy circles and corporate boardrooms.[21] After initial hostility towards the movement, big corporations eventually accepted consumer activists as quasi-allies—as safety valves for venting out the pressures of consumer dissatisfaction, and as sticks to beat weaker or stubborn competitors with, competitors who could not afford or chose not to incur the costs of meeting all consumer demands.[22]

From the success of the consumer movement to the consumerist form of politics was an easy step. The satisfaction of consumerist demands, as articulated by the movement's advocates, became a primary means of achieving success in the marketplace, commercial or political. If the consumerist demands could not be met, other strategic options could be considered— find and support an advocacy group that is ideologically aligned with your position, and tell the world that this group speaks for the vast "silent majority" rather than for the irksome vocal minority represented by the "so-called consumer advocates." Consumerism in politics, thus, paved the way for cynicism.

As political devices *for* the consumer, consumer activism and the consumer advocacy of the Naderist type are of relatively smaller value today than in their heyday of the 1960s. Politics and business have co-opted consumerism. In fact, under postmodern conditions, the cycle of co-optation has speeded up tremendously—that which took years to co-opt now takes only months, weeks, or days.

10 The new theater of consumption

We have followed the (hi)story of consumption in modern society and addressed the forms it has acquired more recently. This is a story of a radical reorganization of society, especially in western society following the Enlightenment, a saga of the rise of science and capitalism. From a society that had as its basic principle the abandonment of fates to forces beyond and above the human subject, modern society developed on the basis of the principle that the human subject held the key to and the power for shaping her/his fate through scientific knowledge of the surrounding material realities. This was indeed a revolutionary turn that required an almost complete reconstruction of concepts, norms and perspectives about life and the universe that guided human society.

THE ASCENT OF CONSUMPTION

In the previous chapters we discussed how the constructs of consumption and production, specifically their separation and oppositional positioning to each other, played key roles in this radical reconceptualization and reconstruction of human society, redefining its purpose and the rationale for its existence. The conceptualizations of consumption and production were linked closely to other key norms and constructs that also helped formulate modernity, such as the mind and body, masculine and feminine, public and private. These modern constructions are presently going through transformations, often producing paradoxical conditions. While itself undergoing transformation, consumption is increasingly taking center stage in society and the economy. Specifically, consumption no longer constitutes solely an activity of appropriating and devouring value for the purposes of necessary replenishment of human energies to be directed at "productive" work. It is re(de)constructed as inseparable from production, as the human action in and through which life experiences and meaning as well as the human being—the self(-images)—are produced. That is, it has become impossible to conceptualize and construct consumption and production as two separate and opposing phenomena, two distinct moments. We have come to realize that they are one and the same, except when we choose to signify them as different on the basis of our constructions of the concept of value.

Human agency

As explored in our earlier chapters, increasing numbers of people are no longer behaving in the ways that reify and reinforce the modern constructions of who they are supposed to be, how they are to act as producers and consumers. There are radical transformations and these create crises and confusion in many respects. For so long, we thought that we knew where humanity was heading, how and why. At least we were confident about where, how, and why we should be headed. This vision of the future that gave us so much confidence and direction is exactly what is in crisis. We are also confused about who we are, what we are capable of, and what our goals are or should be. What kind of a life and society do we want and how do we get there? In effect, the confusion has put into question the issue of human agency, the belief that human beings could choose and act with a level of autonomy and independence to shape their lives and existence—their fates—that was so central to the modern way of being.

A major reason for the confusion regarding human agency is that in modernity agency was so much linked to the "productive" and "creative" actions of individuals, performed in the public sphere. As consumption increasingly takes center stage and individuals act as consumers and are treated as consumers in most of their relations, including the political and social domains, their ability to act as agents (for themselves) comes into question. Consumption was constituted, as already discussed, as that moment of life where individuals appropriated and devoured value in order to satisfy needs and replenish energy spent in production. In the domain of consumption, the private domain, they acted largely on the basis of given needs and chose among alternatives available for satisfying these needs. These alternatives were developed and provided by organizations that were to decipher and identify our needs for the purpose of serving them. Thus, consumption was, indeed, a rather passive activity, aimed at maintaining life, not determining, controlling or deciding its direction in terms of the higher purposes of human existence. People did not determine the fate of humanity or human society in consumption. It was not the sphere of life where the contours of our futures were sketched. Human agency occurred in the public sphere, the domain of political action and production. This was the domain where creative determination of choices and the shape of human experience took place.

Many critics of popular culture (especially television) and consumption argue that from childhood onward we create consumers whose only interest is to watch (in the sense of passive exposure) and consume to be entertained.[1] This charge may have much truth to it. Indeed, as we have also argued earlier, many influences are resulting in people acting as consumers.

Of course, here we are talking of consuming in the old (modern) sense of the word. Yet, if the critics' point is that if people were not consumers, they would be active participants in the determination of their own and society's fate, that is, be human agents, this may not be the case. Our public and production systems have been so thoroughly "rationalized" and "profession-alized" that, except for very few among us, there is no possibility of being active participants in or determining the system.

Rather, for most of the world's population, "creative" life in the public sphere is one of filling in on production lines, or following professional rules of conduct to play a role in realizing the rationally planned and programmed outcomes. This is the reason for so much dissatisfaction and lack of interest in work, why work has basically become a chore to perform just to earn a living. The rationalization of the public sphere has played an important part in people's turn to consumption as the only domain left where they can decide and act for themselves. Our discussion of the development of modern consumption patterns indicates that this control over one's consumption has mostly been fantasy. There is, nonetheless, a residual element of autonomy left in consumption. When mature people behave in rebellious or "irrational" ways in their consumption, they cannot be penalized directly by an authority such as they would encounter if such behavior was performed in production or at work, in the public sphere. This presents both the impression and a relative possibility that the individual does have control over her/his consumption. The increasing recognition of the insepa-rability of consumption and production and the growing orientation among consumers to approach even the "productive" activities as consumers presents the possibility of recapturing agency that was largely lost for majorities of people.

At first glance, without a re(de)construction of our significations and categories (such as, consumer/producer, public/private, feminine/masculine, rational/emotional, and intellectual/entertaining), the possibility of human agency in and through acting as consumers seems contradictory. After all, it has been clear to many sociologists and social critics for some time that consumers are generally powerless and often lacking sufficient information and resources to take meaningful action.[2] In effect, building a theory of human agency through consumership requires rethinking many of our generally held ideas about value and rationality, reality and freedom.

MODERN SOCIAL FORMATION

The principles of the organization of modern society may be listed as:

1 the centrality of the human individual as the agent and actor;
2 democracy as the principal system through which human agency of each individual is insured;

3 freedom and inalienable rights of citizenship to allow democratic participation and independence of each individual;
4 the nation state as the guardian and mechanism of democracy and civil
   liberties;
5 the rule of law to insure that individual freedoms and rights cannot be
   usurped by the state or by others.

The principle of the nation state depended on the idea of the nation, constituted by freely associating citizens who had common interest(s) based on a
common history, language, ethnicity or, as in the case of the United States,
common vision or purpose. It is exactly this idea of common interest within
given historical national borders that is challenged by the developments of
at least the last century. Today, there are alliances of common interest across
national borders based on class, life style, cultural preferences, professional
ties, and ecological interests that are often stronger than common interests
within national borders. Equally significant is the condition that interests
have evolved to be multidimensional and therefore, an individual who has a
common interest along one dimension with one group may have common
interests along other dimensions with other groups. Consequently, the idea
that a nation of people will consistently have the same interests or even the
idea that when all interests do not match, nationhood will provide them with
one overarching interest to bond them together, is increasingly proving to be
illusory. Of course, civil wars, political and other kinds of internal strife have
always challenged the idea of nationhood and the nation state that protects
the interests of all citizens equally. Globalization, especially the globalization of fragmentation as we have discussed in earlier chapters, has weakened
the possibilities of maintaining the organization of contemporary and
future society in the form of the nation state. Other forces, beyond the globalization of fragmentation, also contribute to the waning of the nation state,
forces which we shall discuss shortly.

Within the modern nation state(s) the modern pattern of consumption
was very much a result of the separation between production and consumption. When the economy took center stage as the locomotive of modern
society, and all measures of achievement rested on the increased levels of
material production—as well as the consumption of what was produced—
culture provided the significations that made such "achievement"
discernible. The rationale of an ever increasing production/consumption was
singular, and it required a singular (individual-private-passive-alienated)
consumption pattern. Furthermore, to ensure that there were no diversions
from the rational, the production system was separated from the diverse
control of individual households and planned in the public domain, relent-
lessly shrinking "productive" activities in the private domain by drawing
them into the public domain.[3] This aided in the dominance of a singular
rationale in production—the public interest was common and one, and so
was the rationale that realized this common interest. This confirmed the

organization of the modern (re)public within the form of nation states. As a public with one common interest within the framework of the nation state, modern society could seek consensus, the recognition of a common reality, and a common perception and understanding of this reality for the common good. The modern impulse was, thus, towards unification, universalization, and unity of interests and goals.

More than anything else, contemporary transformational trends in modern societies may be indicative of the impossibility of such universalization and unity. We are constantly reminded of the many incompatibilities among the visions and interests of segments of society. Each time the modern institutions and apparatuses try to forge unifying themes and policies, some group or segment of society seems to present a challenge, resistance, or subversion. The modernist impulse still tends to be to seek a modicum of consensus, some common understanding and recognition of attainable goals. What usually happens, however, is a silencing of certain elements in modern society through the force of laws, morals, and/or policing, rather than a true consensus.[4] Whenever the legal, moral, and/or military force of the "majority" or the powerful wanes, these dissident elements float to the surface. The perceived absence of alternatives that provide better or trusted forms of living is another force that keeps in the union many who are disaffected. In this, modern politics and modern media pay a crucial role.

EROSION OF THE NATION STATE

At the present juncture, we are witnessing a general erosion in the ability of the nation states to forge national unity. Practically everywhere around the world we observe the weakening and/or breakdown of established nation states. These may take the form of ethnic strife or irreconcilable differences in modes of life and goals sought (that also often surface as ethnic disagreements). One reason why discontent surfaces often as ethnic strife is, of course, the difference in cultures that have ethnic histories. In the formation of modern nation states, a dominant ethnicity usually prevailed, often resulting in discrimination against other ethnicities in the nation. Therefore, many discontents and ideological differences, indeed sometimes consumption differences, can find strength in feelings of being discriminated against and solidarity with "discriminated" ethnic segments.

Furthermore, modern nation states have often used the historical and cultural differences among ethnic groups as a basis of divide-and-rule political strategies, in effect strengthening ethnic feelings and solidarity. It is understandable, therefore, that many issues of contention in nation states can find ethnic bases. Yet, there are other bases on which disagreements and disputes occur within nation states. In the United States, for example, there is a strong religious division in visions of life that often results in fatal confrontations. The activities of the militia groups could easily be construed as, and could easily have progressed into, a form of civil war, were they in a nation state with an authority structure weaker than that of the United States. In Algeria, the 1990s civil war was not ethnic but religion based. For years in Italy and West Germany there were groups that waged political wars against the authorities of the capitalist states. In Albania there was civil unrest during 1997 in response to a large proportion of the population losing money they invested in fraudulent pyramid schemes. Military takeovers occur often around the world in modern nation states for reasons of political or economic interests. All these indicate the failure of finding a consensus that is satisfactory to all in modern nation states.

Consumption and identity

Much of postmodern reaction is due to a recognition of this failure. It is a reaction to the modernist insistence on making everyone adhere to the same reality, the same goals, the same modes of life. Often this modern insistence turns into imposition. There is a call, therefore, to find social organizations that tolerate differences in goals, realities, and modes of life. The modern nation state does not seem equipped to provide this tolerance.

There are other reasons for what some have called the end of the nation state. Many of these are related to the developments in consumption we have discussed in this book. As we pointed out in Chapter 8, consumption is becoming a global experience through globalization of brand names, products, and fashion trends. National boundaries or identities matter little to the younger generations that have access to these consumption items. When engaging in consumption, they can connect across such boundaries and identities. The cultures that these consumption experiences represent are truly international, even if interpreted with cultural nuances in different parts of the world. Interest in purchasing and consuming brand names such as Nike, Coca-Cola, Levi's, Benetton, for example, has much to do with the tastes, values and behaviors, in effect, the cultural meaning and experiences they promise. Whether in the United States, in Sweden, or in Japan, when young people put on their Levi's and Nikes, they expect and obtain certain experiences, of a level of self-assurance and rebellion, of asserting their generational values, as well as a feeling of being "cool." A similar kind of shared experience occurs when young men and women who are fans of a musical genre such as heavy metal rock put on their wide-legged jeans. Whether American, Argentinean, or Turkish, when they meet they know and share meanings that transcend national or regional borders.

It was always known that national feelings did not spawn instinctively, that they had to be nurtured through national celebrations, teachings in school, and through media programs. That is why every young child goes through a healthy dose of indoctrination into national feelings. The contemporary world is making this indoctrination more difficult, simply due to the fact that the media—the institution that has become the most dominant in "schooling" young people into values, goals, and desires for life—is increasingly global and globalist, rather than nationalist. We find that children increasingly express global sentiments when interviewed or asked to do art work. Through global television and other media, they get exposed to seductive and desirable elements from around the world. Paradoxically, at the same time that ethnic feelings are gaining some strength, national feelings seem to be on the decline. The reason for this is clear from our earlier studies of global trends. Increasing numbers of people are trying to find "closer" identities, immersion in varied and textured, textual, touchable, palpable experiences of being and belonging, rather than distant universalizing and communalizing ones. They seek a multiplicity of immediately experienceable cultures instead of unity within broader national borders. To increasing numbers of consumers, it is more important to have and experience multiplicity than to adhere to a singular, national identity. This tendency is most apparent among contemporary younger generations who have not yet had the national feelings thoroughly instilled. This is one reason why young school children tend to be first in starting or subscribing to campaigns to recognize and aid disadvantaged and distressed populations around the globe, to protect endangered species, and to save the environment.

Other forces

Business elite circles constitute another force toward globalization and the weakening of nation states. Their motives are different from those of our youth. They are seeking free reign for the capital they control, without interference from governments, and in all markets. Rather than national governments creating blocks to free flow of commodities and capital, they are in favor of international bodies that try to facilitate global economic activity. Generally, corporate elites support less economic decision-making by nation states coupled with greater provision of security for the assets and managers of the corporations. Large corporations are increasingly able to influence and guide state policies and politics around the world. As they become more powerful they play an increasing role in the erosion of the significance of nation states. Consequently, arguments, books, discussions, and theses about the end of the nation state have flourished.[5] Much of this literature is coming from the corporate world or from scholars with close ties to the business world. They expect the erosion of the nation state in favor of regional states, corporate governance, or a global unity.

Another force and sentiment that erodes the organization of society in terms of nation states comes from deep, value-based opposition to the hegemony of nation states or the ideologies and interests they represent. Countercultural movements play an important rôle in this opposition, as do cyberspace communities, ecological movements, professionals, and current trends in arts and literature. Countercultural movements often ignore the authority of the nation states. Consider movements such as Rainbow

Gathering, where participants travel from around North America to meet at a locale communicated through word of mouth to minimize interference by state authorities. The purpose of such gatherings is to exchange information on experiences of modes of life, as well as present alternative modes to each other through exhibiting them during the gathering. Many consider this as a way of exploring and information gathering about alternatives in living and consuming that cannot otherwise be heard or found in the media. Some modes of life include what state authorities consider illegal,[6] hence the need the participants feel for some secrecy. Rainbow Gatherings occur about once a year; however, other more permanent life mode cultures, such as punk or grunge, especially in their non-commercialized forms, have similar goals and difficulties with authority(ies). They generally tend to ignore the mainstream culture's norms and values which are upheld by the nation state's regulations and laws, and experiment with variations of alternative life styles. Confrontations are rare, since these movements do not believe in confrontational challenges to the nation state's authority. Nevertheless, they work to erode the nation state's power.

Consumption as practice, consumers as signifiers

In some ways, these countercultural groups present some of the prototypical characteristics of postmodern social change. Instead of preaching modes of life to others, they practice them, experiment with variations, and in certain ways make these modes visible—mostly through music, art forms, fashion (clothing and grooming styles), or presence in public spaces. Also, the members of these counterculture groups often navigate among culture-scapes. That is, instead of constantly remaining within their singularly preferred countercultural domain, they participate in mainstream life, behave and dress differently and work in mainstream jobs, they participate as students, staff or faculty in educational institutions. They also occasionally cross over and participate in other counterculture-scapes. That is, punks may hang out with and within grunge groups (as grunge participants), or they may participate in the activities of New Age groups. For some counterculture members, specific preference for one or more life modes and life styles does not mean that they cannot experiment with and experience others.

A most important characteristic of these countercultural groups is that by practicing (therefore, presenting) rather than simply articulating or "preaching" alternative life modes, they are not simple "consumers" in the modern sense of selecting and using or devouring consumption items and experiences. They construct and signify new and alternative forms of being in and through their consumption. Thus, their consumption is, indeed, production. These countercultures (re)present a move from the citizen to the signifier—the "consumer" of the postmodern era. We argued that the late-modern marketization of society had transformed the citizen into a consumer. The further transformation of the consumer as the producer of things and life modes within the symbolic system freed by postmodern culture constructs the signifying subject—the signifier. Countercultural movements of our time are important prototypes that signal this transfor- mation.

Other cross-national communities

Cyberspace communities and ecological movements challenge the authority of nation states by eroding the significance of national borders. While this is similar to the challenge coming from the business elites and multinational corporations, the aims of these challenges are based not on economic but on non-economic values. Ecological movements recognize that in terms of ecological systems national borders are meaningless. Such movements continually work toward cross-national co-operation and alliances. Their purpose is to bring nation state governments in line with global or interna- tional policies. Their efforts continually bring interests that cross national boundaries into the limelight and unite people across the world who find closer ties to ideologically similar communities in other nations than to many communities within their own countries. Such movements, therefore, erode one of the basic foundations of nation states: national interest. These movements also propose life modes that are friendlier to the ecological systems for international populations, often overlapping with countercul- tural movements. The basic difference, however, between countercultural movements and ecological movements is that the latter are presently closer to modern social change ideologies in tending to insist on uniform and universal life modes that they believe are for the common good. Countercultural movements on the other hand usually do not have such universal claims. Consequently, members of ecological movements, while trying to put proposed life modes into practice as experiments, also adopt more "preaching" strategies to talk others into joining a necessarily universal system.

Cyberspace communities are also global communities. People in such communities link across national boundaries, crossing physical as well as other borders. Their allegiances, therefore, also cross borders and erode the significance of nation states. The access to computers around the world, and access to Internet and other means of electronic communication and space, however, are limited to a few.[7] This limited access lessens the impact of such communities in world affairs. Those who have access and are active in cyberspace, however, are trend-setting, technology-savvy, and influential consumers. Their impact, therefore, is proportionately greater than their numbers. Many of these communities construct ideas and practice, even languages, that they sample, experience, and develop preferences for. Somewhat similar to countercultural groups, the members of these commu- nities are adept at navigating among actual and virtual communities, participating in the construction of various identities and life modes. Borders, limits, and boundaries of nation states have little, if any, significance in cyberspace.

Professionals are also playing a role in the erosion of nation states by positioning themselves and acting as players in fast growing, global networks. Academic disciplines, for example, are global, as are the standards and benchmarks of architecture, medicine, engineering, and the like. Even the legal profession is growing rapidly in its international aspects. Laws that were the domain of nation states and nationally constructed legal systems are increasingly coming under attack and stress due to a globalizing world, having to recognize and adjust to global conditions. Leading professionals who set the trends in their fields—academics, engineers, architects, and medical doctors—operate on an international canvas. Such leading players are sought around the world, and they seek to be recognized beyond national boundaries. They are often on the move across international borders, participating in different gatherings and communities in varying roles.

Arts and literature exhibit similar patterns. Artists and the members of literary communities, especially leading ones, play the international scene. They correspond globally, gather, get invited to and participate in exchanges across the globe. Like the professionals, artists and literary figures travel to different places and gatherings and encounter varying cultural and/or style experiences. They participate in the construction of these experiences, and adapt to and learn to be comfortable in varied experiential modes.

FLUID IDENTITY

Many of the above forms of erosion of the nation state are, therefore, signaling more than an end of the nation state. They are also providing glimpses into changes in the formation of identity and self-images. It is understandable that celebrities, starting with actors, have become the role models and idols for so many. Celebrities represent the possibility of changing roles, and more than just roles, entire identities. As different scenarios, circumstances, and experiences require, celebrities adjust their identities. They signal the possibility that living and experiencing, sampling and testing different modes of being or life are indeed possible. Artists, professionals, counterculture participants, and cyberspace community members largely follow this possibility, enjoying the initiation of new experiences, of immersing in different cultures, rather than proselytizing for a singular way. As these communities and their members interact, as they experiment with and experience modes of being, new cultures arise, further enabling immersion in different textured and textual (culture) scapes.

Succession of identities

Sociologists have recognized the changing trends in identity formation in contemporary society. While in high modern society the purpose was to discover one's singular identity, to know oneself and be known to/by others, in the late-modern period this has been changing. Bauman, a leading sociologist of contemporary trends, observes a progression from singular identity quest to seeking of multiple identities (multiphrenic selves[8]) and provides imaginative metaphors to express the transformations in the quest for such identities. As modern society develops, the identity seeker first simulates the pilgrim, then the stroller, the vagabond, the tourist, and finally, in post-modern culture, the player.[9] As in the progression from citizen to consumer to signifier in the construction of the human subject, the progression presented by Bauman represents a transformation from an individual who seeks to find her/his identity to one who looks and "shops" for different available pre-produced identities—gazing at and experiencing and taking on for satisfactory periods of time—and then on to one who is interested in constructing different identities in which to immerse and live. While for the citizen and the pilgrim the different roles one plays is to affirm the one identity one has (and finds)—an identity of active (productive) contribution to the bright future of society—for the signifier and the player the roles can be (and are preferred to be) complete, in the sense of not complementing or affirming a singular identity but allowing immersion in different identities.

Another sociologist expresses this idea in terms of the (re)emergence of tribes.[10] Maffesoli describes the roles played by individuals in modern culture as "functions," since these roles are played to serve purposes of a singularly driven society—driven for the common good towards a bright future for humanity, organized as political economies and in contractual groups (namely, nation states). In postmodernity, he sees roles played by people as true roles, rather than functions. The society is organized as a mass that is fluid in terms of fluctuating and ever (re)forming affectual tribes. The participation of people in these tribes, and their playing the respective roles, is temporary and based on affective (more so than rational) involvement. As Grossberg puts it in discussing contemporary political and social change possibilities:

> Individuals are always simultaneously located in a number of fluid, temporary and competing positions. It is no longer possible to speak of a singular group identity or an authentic grounding experience, politics has to confront the increasing power of such multiple identities in the contemporary world.[11]

The disappointments with singular grand projects and the erosion of the belief that there is or can be a singular "best" mode of living aid or abet this tendency among contemporary consumers to seek, experience, and construct different life modes through temporary and fluid identities. In effect, what is sought by an increasing number of consumers is to participate fully in different culture-scapes, constituted around the different and regenerating life modes and life styles, through construction of identities that allow immersion in and, therefore, total experiencing of these cultures. Such behavior is both consistent with and aids in the development of the multilayered cultures. The constitution of these cultures and their relations to each other are also in transformation. Unlike the culture–subcultures structuring of modern nation states, postmodern cultures increasingly stand on their own. In the United States, this is transforming the "melting pot" into the "cultural mosaic." American culture, therefore, is becoming one of the many cultures found in the United States, rather than the "umbrella" under which many subcultures were contained.[12] People are becoming increasingly comfortable in *navigating* among cultures, which exhibit greater speed of change and fluidity within themselves, rather than *belonging* to a culture. This development is, in itself, also diffusing the existence of national interests, and contributing to further erosion of the nation state.

REDEFINITIONS OF FREEDOM

One of the major obligations, and perhaps the key reason for the existence of the modern nation states was to secure and protect the freedom(s) of its citizens. In modern culture, freedom is primarily understood as the ability to define and pursue goals actively. Freedom is viewed as an active power. It is the power to develop and fulfill potentials. It is having choice and ability to determine one's own actions. In modern definitions of freedom or liberty, the emphasis is on the ability to do and determine. While personal freedom is to determine one's own goals and act to realize these, the freedom of the citizen is the ability to determine and act upon the goals the enfranchised majority chooses for the society, or the nation. Since everyone's freedom is secured by the nation state, this means the ability to participate equally in the determination of the nation's goals and the actions towards realization of these goals. Through this determination, the citizen participates actively in building the life s/he chooses.

With the erosion of the nation state, and the difficulties that arise in both securing equal participation in social choices and arriving at consensus about what life ought to be or what goals the nation should have, the definition of freedom is being challenged and transformed. In this need for a (re)definition of freedom the reversal of production and consumption in contemporary culture may be even more important than the erosion of the nation state. Production in the public domain, the focal site of modern human agency—the locus where freedom was most significantly practiced—is no longer where agency is possible, as we discussed. Therefore, if freedom is to exist, it has to occur where people exercise or seek to exercise choice and construction of life modes in contemporary society, that is, in consumption. While in (post)modern culture consumption is production, it is not production of material items for consumption as in modernity, but production of present life experiences and meaning. That is, in consumption the meanings for which products are put to use are produced, imbuing products with value; sign-value, as Baudrillard called it.[13] The nature of freedom is thus further transformed with the reversal of consumption and production.

Balancing of freedoms

To the chagrin of many intellectuals, in contemporary settings people seem willing to forfeit the freedoms that were so central and significant to being a citizen, even being a human, in modern discourse. This is evidenced in the ever increasing lack of interest in public affairs and in diminishing civic commitments. Instead of using civic rights to become involved in the determination of social directions, people often opt for indifference or disentanglement. They are opting, in effect, to free themselves from taking part in the determination of their common fates.

This option is often deplorable to the modern observer. As we just discussed, in modern culture freedom is the *freedom to*: take action, take part, determine directions that society and one's own life take. The contemporary trend, on the other hand, is a *freedom from*. To the modernist observer, "freedom from" is not freedom but a "flight from freedom," surrendering or abandoning freedom. Our experimentation with modernity, however, may be indicating that complete freedom requires a balancing or integration of both freedom to and freedom from.

Freedom from is brought into focus by the practices of youth movements, countercultural movements, and the like. In abandoning interest in what the larger society is doing or in surrendering their rights to influence decisions taken by the state, however, members of these groups are taking stands. By doing "their own thing," they are deciding how to live. By ignoring authority, they are choosing to formulate their own modes of consumption. That is, as long as there is no confrontation between the life modes they select and the social authority that disapproves of such choices, the *freedom from* participating in the affairs of the larger society is a *freedom to* construct a life mode at a local level. The danger in this is, of course, that uncontrollable events may occur that affect people's lives.

This is a major paradoxical circumstance of our time. The paradox is intensified by globalization because actions taken in one part of the world can affect another part of the world, or humanity as a whole. If we choose not to get involved in decisions made for society—or the global community—how do we prevent a community from, for example, improving the forces of destruction to an extent that they cannot be controlled, and destroying life for all of us?

It is this recognition that led modern society, which believed in a common good and a common future for all humanity, to formulations of nation states and the conceptualization of freedom as "freedom to."

Through every citizen's use of her/his *freedom to*, people would reach a *consensus* and discover a *common good*. In a world where everybody's future was so inexorably linked, this seemed to be the only solution. Everyone had to come to some degree of agreement and commit themselves to it for the common good.

The end of modernity is, in one sense, the dawning of the recognition that this is not possible. That is why there is crisis and confusion. Despite the paradoxical problems it introduces, there is a trend by so many towards opting for *freedom from*. The issue, however, is not one of stark choice between "freedom to" and "freedom from." A complete adherence to "freedom to" in its extreme form breeds *entrapment*. A thoughtless pursuit of "freedom from" in its extreme form breeds *escape*. In modern thought freedom to was revered so much because it was the means for determining the production of our future. The emphasis was on determination, conclusive signification and control of the meanings of things around us, through their conclusive representation. Today, we observe greater doubt about the possibility of such singular and fixed determination, as well as a disenchantment with fixation and the many horrors that such determination for fixing meanings and fates has brought, even when so well-intentioned, for the betterment of humankind.

Freedoms and meanings

In modern culture, increasing production, more technologies that enabled greater production, meant that the share of products we created ourselves would be greater. By deciding why and what we produced, our say would be greater regarding our destiny. Production, specifically socially organized production, not only improved our share in deciding our destiny, it also produced greater consistency in the significations, the meanings that humanity utilized to make sense of this destiny and life in general. The system of production was also the system of production of meaning, enabling humanity to get a handle on the mystery of existence, giving it some sense, determining fixed entities in an otherwise indeterminate and fluid mass (semantic mud). In the great quest to know, to determine, it was understandable that the system of production would be revered and sanctified.

Those with a postmodern orientation, such as Bataille and Baudrillard, provide us with a different perspective on the production system. When the production system begins to take over and determine too much, we encounter death. In the conclusive determination of meanings, in fixing significations conclusively, is their conclusion. Life, at least the excitement of life, is in the *excess* for Bataille, and in the *meaningless* (the meaning of which has not yet been determined) for Baudrillard.[14]

Bataille's and Baudrillard's cautions merit a hearing. Determination, or experiencing that which has been determined or fixed, may provide us with some sense of security and continuity. At the same time, it also represents entrapment—once determined, we can no longer play a role in its construction, we even lose our *freedom to*, and get trapped. We observed this in the modern evolution of the individual-private-passive-alienated consumption pattern, which emerged through the confluence of free choices and later entrenched and entrapped people, consuming people. That is the paradox of *freedom to*. The more we use our freedom to determine our destiny, our reality and our way of life, the more we may get entrapped. That is why complete freedom requires the *freedom from*. Yet, the paradox of *freedom from*, when it is taken to its extreme, is escapism. What is needed, therefore, is a balancing of the two. In fact, this balancing act may not just be a desirable condition for complete freedom but an imperative. Consider Bataille's excess and Baudrillard's meaningless. For either to exist, the presence of that which is produced (determined, "normal" and/or signified) is necessary. Excess cannot exist without the circumscribed; and without meaning, there is no meaninglessness.

What we have in modernity is the impulse to overemphasize determination through production, even to the extent of taking enchantment out of life and making death larger than life. In their rush to warn us of this failure of modernity, however, Bataille and Baudrillard overemphasized the antagonism against determination, to the extent of forgetting the social necessity of it. What we must do is perform a balancing act, recognizing fully that there is not a single measure or point of balance.

Fluid signification

What forms of social organization can best accommodate this balancing of freedom to and freedom from? It is clearly not the nation state that emphasizes consensus and common reality(ies), a common project, and a common future life mode that is deemed (agreed upon) to be for the betterment of all. There must be an agreement on what is better(ment), in effect what is best, for humanity. In modernity, in the effort to fix things as they were (are)—in the sense of fixing or stabilizing the "semantic mud"—there was also the belief in the possibility or existence of *stable correspondence*. A signifier corresponded to a signified in a stable, steady way. The meanings of things corresponded to their referents. This reflected itself in life styles. Specific styles—of clothing, of hair, of facial hair (mustache, beard), of cosmetics—corresponded to certain ideologies and life styles. The progressives had their styles and the conservatives had theirs, as did the fascists and the revolutionaries. In (post)modernity this principle of correspondence is no more. We cannot any longer read the ideologies or life styles of people on the basis of their styles. Two things may be playing a part in this: marketization (the commodification of all styles as consumables)—which is a transitional, not a postmodern circumstance—and the postmodern sensibility of non-commitment to any eternal style.

MODERNITY'S LAST STRAWS?

Recognizing that there is no fixed representation or stable correspondence, the thinkers of our time who still endorse the necessity and possibility of consensus and common goals for humanity, continue to seek ways for realizing them under contemporary circumstances. We can mention three efforts towards this end: Habermas' project of communicative action, Foucault's proposals of discursive power, and efforts for theorizing reflexive modernization by Giddens and Beck, in which Lash also joined.[15]

The difficulties with Habermas' theory of communicative action have been explored by others, including those who sympathize with the project, such as, McCarthy and Apel. As McCarthy elaborates,[16] Habermas sees capitalism as having an "indissoluble tension" with democracy. Democracy, in Habermas' view, is truly possible if a community of rational actors communicates under conditions of equal legitimizing power to arrive at consensus that is persuasive for all. Such true consensus can only be achieved when rational communication based on certain codes of conduct and criteria occurs. Habermas' project has been, then, to explore these codes and criteria for the success of rational communicative interaction among the parties involved.

The assumptions underlying the realizability of such communicative action constitute the greatest difficulty with Habermas' theory. Namely, it is assumed that people involved in free communication with equal participation (equal legitimizing power) about needs and goals will rationally arrive at the same interpretations of reality, social goals, and the common good. Yet, as Apel expresses, the paradox of modern life is that for such consensus on values, goals, and interpretations of reality "a universal, i.e., intersubjectively valid ethics of collective responsibility . . . seems both necessary and impossible."[17] Because such a universal has been repeatedly found to be impossible, we encounter oppressive means of inducing consensus throughout history. Foucault studied these and posed them as a challenge to Habermas' project, also leading to his critique of rationalism, which was similar to Nietzsche's.[18]

The theory of reflexive modernization, proposed separately by Giddens and Beck, does not rely so much on rationality to be achieved through communicative action. It is based on the premise that with greater modernization individuals become ever more free of structure, of the impositions of industrial society, for example.[19] Individuals, thereby, are more able than before to act as agents toward changing society. The issue of how change occurs when directions for change are not agreed upon by different agents is, however, left largely unexplored. Furthermore, as Giddens suggests

> In some circumstances, burgeoning reflexivity is emancipatory. In other respects, and in a diversity of contexts, it produces the contrary: an intensifying stratification. . . . Increasing freedom for some regularly goes along with, or is even the cause of, greater oppression for others.[20]

How and for whom the increased agency works, or could (not) work, and under which circumstances, is thus largely unknown.

Foucault's analysis has some similarities to reflexive modernization, especially the aesthetic reflexivity version advanced by Lash. Foucault's emphasis, however, is on power and its distribution into the "capillaries of society" more widely and in different forms than allowed in other theories. The form of power that Foucault especially articulates is discursive power. As in the case of reflexive modernization theories, however, how and in what ways this power is likely to be used (or could possibly be used) for social change in contemporary communities is not much articulated. Instead, the emphasis is on individual self-construction and/or "the arts of individual existence."

The shared shortcoming of these alternative theories is that, even as they seek insights into human agency and social change, they tend not to explore alternatives to the current forms of organization of society, namely the nation state and representative democracy. The same tends to be true for Rorty, a pragmatist and a critic of the above theories. Rather than explore the possibilities and impossibilities of agency and social change, Rorty tends to express faith in the pragmatic logic of informed individuals to arrive at pragmatic solutions and agreements.[21] The difficulties arise in envisioning changes that are needed in order for there to be masses of informed individuals. Even in the case of Bourdieu,[22] who provides us with insights into the sociology of culture, underscoring that economic practice is not the only determinant among a set of social practices, the domain of all the practices remains, nevertheless, the modern organization of society. As such, all these attempts at developing insights leave us wondering how and whether the potentials they promise can be realized. It seems that, in the end, they all fall back on the same *assumptions*—the desire, will, and initiative of individuals to take on social change projects—*forms*—consensus, (pragmatic) reason to arrive at common conclusions—and *domains*—democracy, nation state— that constituted the backbone of modern discourse.

Given the transformations we have discussed throughout this book, to expect that human agency and social change can be revived under the set of modern assumptions, forms, and domains is highly questionable. Not surprisingly, therefore, these attempts at initiating social change do not go much beyond theoretical discourse and do not move many people into (radical) practice.

NEW POSSIBILITIES

Any new proposal for human agency and social change has to take into consideration the conditions of our time: fragmentation, globalization, the turn to consumption as the domain of social/political practice and discursive action, the imminent erosion of the nation state, decreasing commitment to grand projects, lack of interest in social change movements, the cultural turn away from an interest in the future to an interest in the present, a general distrust and disbelief in promises of visionary proposals, among others. The question, then, becomes: what do these conditions and transformations tell us about the potentials of human agency, social change, and freedom? What forms of agency are most likely to have a chance to produce the sought after results? One thing seems to be clear. For effective human agency, freedom, and meaningful social change new practices for/in new organizations of society are imperative. Modern practices within modern organizations of society are not likely to guide us to changes we currently seek on Earth.

Modern culture's impulse was to remove difference. It sought to unite people toward a common goal to improve life and their control over life. Therefore, modern political process sought consensus through reasoned discussions among disagreeing parties to arrive at commonly held values, tastes, and visions based on the common reality that humanity shared. Today, as we encounter the impossibility of these lofty ideals and the failures of attempts to implement them, there is a growing mood to accept differences and tolerate different, alternative modes of life. In effect, as we have discussed earlier, experimental and ideological life mode communities are developing around the world. Members of such communities are willing to navigate among communities, and comfortable doing so.

This presents a possible response and solution to the necessity of balancing freedom to and freedom from, two forms of freedom that seemed oppositional in modern culture, but increasingly need to be integrated or balanced to achieve complete freedom. Freedom to can be exercised when the individual participates in the construction and experience of a life mode community, but freedom from is exercised when s/he leaves this community to experience others. In a global society organized as a set of fluid and (re)constructing life mode communities, therefore, a free flow among the communities must occur to achieve complete freedom for the people.

Two major constraints impeding this development are the market and the current organization of the nation state. While the navigational life mode communities flourish in virtual space—where there are no limits to movement—and even to an extent within current national boundaries, the impediments set by nation states largely block navigation among life mode communities across national borders. The hegemony of the market similarly impedes the formation of life modes that seek to construct production of meanings through interactions that do not emphasize market exchanges.

Theater

We have to invoke the metaphor of the theater as a medium of cultural interaction that is different from the medium of economic interaction, the market. Consider that, instead of the stage, the backstage, and the audience, the theater is composed *only* of the stage. All interaction across all dimensions—economic, social, political—occur on this stage. This means that everyone is a player, an actor. On a stage, different groups of actors may be engaged in different interactions simultaneously. They all contribute to what is happening on the whole stage.

Modernity was the attempt at rationalizing what goes on the stage, an attempt to order, make effective and efficient that which is seen and constitutes the scene. In this quest, modernity partitioned the stage and "staged" the theater. The acts (scripts, scenarios) were composed in and controlled from the backstage and acted on by the actors with specially developed skills on the stage. The large mass—the audience—engaged in (largely non-participatory) observation, reacting to show appreciation through applause, or disappointment through booing and hissing.[23] Furthermore, this becomes an economic exchange because decisions have to be made about whether to buy repeated performances or not. This relationship, then, makes "being bought" the only significant purpose, in order to be able to continue to act. Thus the prominence of the economic efficiency criteria in our lives.

Reclaiming the stage

How can the stage be reclaimed for all? Maffesoli's tribes may provide an insight. Basically, the observation of the social here is that people move in and out of relationships and situations that they belong to, temporarily and affectively. In a similar vein, people are members of temporary or momentary communities. They exhibit a diminishing desire to remain in any one community or experience frame "for good" or forever. It is this movement, and, therefore, the likelihood, finally, of the creation of multiple alternative communities to the market society that will produce the alternative to the market: the society of the theater, the theater of life.

Transformation in fragments

Under contemporary conditions, a modern transformation of society in the sense of a universal, common movement with results that encompass a whole society (as in the case of the French Revolution or the Russian Revolution) toward a postmodern social change, cannot be expected. Instead, the social transformation of our day can be expected to occur through pockets of resistance, not in terms of a frontal attack or challenge, as in the case of modern political confrontations, but in terms of ignoring authority and insisting on doing "one's own thing"—living the life or lives one desires without seeking confrontation or a frontal challenge until and unless the authority(ies) at hand initiate a confrontation. It is in this sense, also, that the modern structures of authority, which concatenate into nation states, are losing and will continue to lose their relevance. Thus, the demise of the nation state is imminent.

What comes in its place? How will people organize social relations in the future, if not through the nation state? The clues lie in fragmentation and the growing tribal culture-scapes. In a "show me, don't tell me" world, it is the formation of life mode communities that will provide the seductive examples of alternative ways of being. Instead of visions that are promoted without being put into practice, such communities can be constructed, experienced, participated in or left at will. The path is to construct alternatives *outside*[24] of current society. The radical social change energies ought not to be spent in confronting current society but in constructing alternative ones by fragmenting from current society and ignoring current authority. The radical position today is not one of confrontation or one of requiring or requesting that economic (re)sources (income, wealth, capital) be equally distributed or demolished, but one of acting and developing practices that erode their importance in life. The strategy is not to accept the current status as the playground or stage, but to construct new playgrounds. When modern capitalism arose, it did not do so by modifying the distribution of pre-modern sources of power, but by enforcing its own.

The strategies to "develop" the world, in terms of the criteria of affluence modernity has imposed, will always put some ahead and leave some behind. The solution, therefore, is not to try and diffuse this form of development, but to allow alternative definitions and forms of development to coexist, and to enable free flows of players among them. The radical stance, thus, is to agitate for tolerance and for free existence of life mode communities, as well as the free flow of individuals among them. The role that an eroding nation state (and perhaps emergent global compacts) could play is to ensure this ability to construct life mode communities and the free flow among them.

We already see some of this happening. Increasing numbers of people seek to find experiences that provide meaning in their present lives without being constrained by any single experience, thus turning to consumption. We try to find meaning (and escape from it into meaninglessness), but most of the time are confronted by meanings produced by others, some of whom are equipped with many apparatuses of power or have greater access to means (media, money, etc.) that are signified and constructed as the arbiters of power. How do we know, under these circumstances, that we can have our own meanings? A more fundamental issue may be whether we all need to have our own meanings—who says we do? In the end, it is a matter of discursive preference. Rather than constructing systems that decide for us one way or another—that is, either imposing upon us that we participate in constructing our own meanings, or privileging others' meanings over ours— we need to construct systems that enable us to have the chance to be players in the construction of our own meanings if we want to, to immerse in meaning constellations constructed outside of us (without our participation) if we want to, or frolic in the excess and the meaningless if we want to.

THEATERS OF CONSUMPTION

Throughout this book, we have explored and analyzed the evolution of the market in modernity. We have witnessed the growing hegemony of the market in modernity as well as its continued—even strengthened—dominance in the contemporary, transitional, (post)modern era. We have elaborated the way in which, despite the erosion of the cultural influence of modernism, as well as of the modern social and political institutions, the market has been very resilient in maintaining, even reinforcing, its dominance over human relations. We argued, in fact, that the market has increasingly taken over as the sole locus of legitimation in (post)modern society. Almost all, if not every, social and cultural attempt at circumventing, rejecting, or rebelling against the market—including countercultural movements, ecological movements, and life style movements—have been co-opted by the market as just another marketable commodity. Given the market's resilience and its ability to co-opt originally challenging, alternative modes and cultures, how is the theater of life that integrates the market as only one of its dimensions, but is truly multidimensional, ever to emerge?

It is clear to us that the theater as an alternative to the market cannot emerge if alternatives to modern modes and cultures try to evolve within or as part of the market dominated system. To avoid co-optation by the market, alternatives have to develop within permeable but distinct enclaves that allow a free flow of people in and out, but maintain an autonomy from the mainstream market culture.

Enclaves: old and new

The possibility of such alternative and market-independent life mode communities may be questioned. After all, examples of such attempts in the past tend to present evidence to the contrary. These past examples, however, had substantive differences from the life mode communities we are beginning to see developing and that we are envisioning. Specifically, alternative modes of life that tried to construct communities outside of the mainstream market society in the past were different from the current ones in two important ways: first, they were presenting themselves as systems opposing the mainstream system—communes or kibbutzim, for example—as "permanent," totalizing modes of life; and second, they were more or less isolationist. That is, once the members belonged to these communities they were expected to stay "for good," and they were not to interact with other communities. Choosing these communities was an act of total commitment. They did not present themselves as experiences to be sampled, left, returned to, and left again. Instead, they were presented as the "best" and only alternative, to be chosen and to be committed to permanently. In effect, they were "modern" alternatives.

The difference in currently developing life mode communities is that they present themselves as experiences to be sampled, found meaning in, but not to be imprisoned in. As we have discussed in previous chapters, this kind of experience of different ways of being and seeking meaning in alternative life experiences is exactly what a growing number of trend setting consumers are looking for.[25] The availability of such alternative life mode communities—whether in cyberspace or in physical thematized settings—and the desire on the part of contemporary consumers to have and experience alternative life modes is going to expand the numbers of such communities and legitimize their existence. Because of the desire to experience truly different modes of life, consumers are likely to demand that each enclave should be unique. While desiring freedom of movement for themselves, therefore, consumers would not like the experiential enclaves contaminated by intrusions from other enclaves. That is, colonization among enclaves will not be desired or readily tolerated by consumers. Respect and tolerance for the integrity and autonomy of cultures—which develop in and through modes of life, that is, in life mode communities—is on the rise around the world. This is a trend that will help in each culture's (life mode community's) ability to sustain its own dynamic of development and change without colonization.

The emergence and multiplication of such permeable but distinct, porous but bounded, life mode cultures promises the possibility of the new theaters of consumption that can break the hegemony of the market in contemporary human life. As modes of life that do not mediate all relationships and interactions through the market are sampled and found to be meaningful, as they become experiences that are sought and preferred, therefore, repeatedly returned to, they will begin to account for growing portions of one's life space. There is no guarantee that some life mode communities or cultures will not be as unidimensional in their forms of mediation of relations as the market culture is today. Moreover, the market will remain as one arena among many. The multiplicity of life mode cultures will, however, produce many alternative theaters of consumption that are indeed multidimensional. By this we mean that these life mode communities will be shaped based on many diverse interests and considerations rather than solely on the reasons of economy or any other single purpose. That is, choices made in these communities for the kind of life experiences their members want will be informed and influenced by multiple criteria, trying to satisfy a multiplicity of purposes and goals—ecological, sexual, social, psychological, and biological, as well as economic. Interactions among the members of these life mode communities—many of whom may be temporary players in them—and their relations to each other, thus, will be guided by many considerations, not only by considerations of economic market efficiency. Furthermore, these interactions and relations will be mediated by multiple forms of intercourse, not simply through market exchange.

Consumption—in its currently developing sense of construction of meanings, life experiences, and identities—is the domain that will provide the field for these multiple forms of intercourse, or the stage for the theater(s) of life. Having lost the ability to influence the public domain of socially organized production in modernity, consumers are turning to the theaters of consumption in postmodernity. As signifying subjects, consumers are producing and will increasingly produce the varied meanings and identities they wish to play with and experience through these theaters of consumption. To understand the transformations and potentials we are facing, we have to reformulate our concept(ualization)s and categories to accommodate the new forms of consumption being manifested in every-day practice, in the developing theater(s) of life. Our new understanding may further empower consumers in their quest for reclaiming the stage.

Observations of contemporary conditions is leading scholars from different parts of the world to converge on the recognition of the growing importance of consumption, and the role that consumption will play in "new ways of being citizens"[26] or, in general, human subjects. For example, Garcia Canclini, a Latin American scholar, is trying to reformulate the "Anglo-American cultural studies approaches to cultural consumption [that] speak of 'interpretive communities' [by extending] the notion to 'local and transnational interpretive communities of consumers'."[27] Expanding on these observations by Garcia Canclini, Yúdice argues that

> Globalization has transformed the traditional sentimental-educational terrain of citizenship formation. National patrimonies, folklore, and the high arts are losing viewers and users, or their functions have shifted. Consumption, then, has to be rethought in relation to the culture industries.[28]

Radical postmodern positions

As in the case of any cultural development, there is little doubt that human agency is required for the evolution of the life mode communities. Both their emergence and their sustenance necessitates an interest and diligence on the part of their potential constituents. An organization of humanity in terms of life mode cultures to allow complete freedom—one that combines and enables varied balances of "freedom to" and "freedom from"—requires that human beings take a position in and for their lives. The fact that contemporary trends tend to support this position—one of desiring and demanding the existence of alternative life modes to sample—does not imply that sustaining this position is effortless, or that it does not require a conscious stance. To assure the development of life mode communities as the new form of sociopolitical organization of humanity, in a way that will foster complete freedom, certain radical positions have to be maintained and furthered. These are:

1 defending the formation of life mode cultures/communities;

2 protecting the (conceptual) boundaries of each community so that it is not colonized by another;
3 demanding free flow of people among life mode communities;
4 promoting tolerance of difference *qua* difference, not as superiority or inferiority, among life mode communities;
5 protecting the rights and ability of each consumer to have preferences for the cultures of any set of life mode communities.

Life mode communities so constructed in enclaves will be separate from each other, but this separation must not be understood only as separation in physical space. As we see with the development of many virtual communities, as well as with communities that overlap in physical space but are separate in practice, boundaries today are more conceptual than physical. Technologies of our day and our abilities to navigate experiential terrains while occupying the same physical space means that these separations need rarely be physical. In effect, people will be navigating among the life mode communities by using new technologies of communication and information—virtual reality, telepresence, hypermedia, and others—and by switching identities and ways of relating to each other and to things.[29] It would be in relatively few cases that people would feel the need to transport themselves physically across space to experience a different life mode community.

Construction of life mode communities will multiply the cultures of tastes, values, and realities. Our freedoms, preferences, and choices for ways of being and living can be improved most by participating in the construction of, immersing in and experiencing, experimenting with, sampling, and navigating as many cultures as we wish. This may be the only chance we have if we wish to avoid being consumed.

Notes

1 THE CONSUMING SOCIETY

1 When talking in sociocultural terms, we will deliberately employ the term America in this book rather than the United States. We are fully cognizant of the imperial appropriation the term signifies, trampling as it does over the common heritage and sensibilities of two dozen nations spread across two continents. But this expansive and hegemonic meaning is precisely what we have in mind in using the term America. As the vice president of a leading advertising agency remarked at a keynote address that one of the authors attended, "United States is the stars and the stripes, but people all over the world consume America."

2 For discussions of contemporary consuming societies, see Gary S. Cross, *Time and Money: The Making of Consumption Culture*, London: Routledge, 1993; David E. Nye and Carl Pedersen (eds.), *Consumption and American Culture*, Amsterdam: VU University Press, 1991; and John Brewer and Roy Porter (eds.), *Consumption and the World of Goods*, London: Routledge, 1993.

3 See Daniel Miller, *Material Culture and Mass Consumption*, Oxford: Blackwell, 1987; Richard Wightman Fox and T. J. Jackson Lears (eds.), *The Culture of Consumption: Critical Essays in American History*, New York: Pantheon Books, 1981; and Richard Butsch (ed.), *For Fun and Profit: The Transformation of Leisure into Consumption*, Philadelphia: Temple University Press, 1990.

4 This is forcefully presented by Stuart Ewen in the first segment ("Image and Reality in America: Consuming Images") of the television program *The Public Mind* hosted by Bill Moyers, which was broadcast on the Public Broadcasting Service on November 15, 1989.

5 There are observers of the cultural shift from the modern to the postmodern in many different fields of scholarship and research including sociology, literature, art, architecture, philosophy and history. Some of the most prominent among these include Jean Baudrillard, Zygmunt Bauman, Gill Deleuze, Umberto Eco, Jürgen Habermas, Ihab Hassan, Charles Jencks, Arthur Kroker, Jean-François Lyotard, Mark Poster, Richard Rorty, and Elisabeth Wilson.

6 See A. Fuat Fırat and Alladi Venkatesh, "Postmodernity: The Age of Marketing," *International Journal of Research in Marketing*, vol. 10, no. 3, pp. 227–249; A. Fuat Fırat and Alladi Venkatesh, "Liberatory Postmodernism and the Reenchantment of Consumption," *Journal of Consumer Research*, vol. 22, pp. 239–267; and A. Fuat Fırat, Nikhilesh Dholakia, and Alladi Venkatesh, "Marketing in a Postmodern World," *European Journal of Marketing*, vol. 29, no. 1, 1995, pp. 40–56.

7 For a discussion of simulacra, see Jean Baudrillard, *Simulations*, New York: Semiotext(e), 1983.

8 This belief is evidenced in the search of almost all major modern scientists for this order, including Einstein. See H. Butterfield, *The Origins of Modern Science*, London: G. Bell, 1949.

9 The strength of structures in modern society is evidenced by the wide acceptance of structuralist orientation and analysis in modern social sciences.

10 Jean-François Lyotard, *The Postmodern Condition: A Report on Knowledge*, Minneapolis, MN: University of Minnesota Press, 1984.

11 In 1993, the United States population was 4.6 percent of the world population. In the same year, United States consumers consumed 26.3 percent of the world's gross product (see *United Nations Conference on Trade and Development Handbook of International Trade and Development Statistics*, New York: United Nations, 1995, p. 6). In 1991, North America, which had 5.1 percent of the world's population, consumed 29.8 percent of the commercial energy in the world (see *Statistical Yearbook*, New York: United Nations, 1994, p. 26).

12 See Robert J. Samuelson, *The Good Life and Its Discontents: The American Dream in the Age of Entitlement 1945–1995*, New York: Times Books, 1995, p. 39; and Stanley Lebercott, *Pursuing Happiness: American Consumers in the Twentieth Century*, Princeton, NJ: Princeton University Press, 1993.

13 Stanley Lebercott, *Pursuing Happiness*, op. cit., p. 129.

14 These numbers are taken from a variety of sources, such as, *The World Almanac and Book of Facts, 1994*, Mahwah, NJ: Funk & Wagnalls, 1994; *The US Consumer Electronics Industry in Review*, Washington, DC: Electronic Industries Association, 1992; *Statistical Abstract of the United States 1993*, Washington, DC: US Department of Commerce, 1993; and *Statistical Yearbook 1990/91*, New York: United Nations, 1993.

15 We have wondered why the *Statistical Abstract of the United States* stopped reporting this data for some years after its 1978 edition. The data in the *Statistical Abstract* was broken down by income categories of households. Our guess is that the relatively appalling numbers for the lowest income category became politically embarrassing, especially as other affluent countries began to catch up with the United States.

16 Thomas M. Stanback, Jr. and Richard Knight, *Suburbanization of the City*, Montclair, NJ: Allanheld, Osmun & Co., 1976, pp. 56–57, Table 3.1.

17 Consider the predicament of the arts during these suburbanization years. Broadway reduced its output from over 140 productions per year in the 1930s to 63 in 1963. The number of playhouses dropped from 54 to 36 in the same span of years. The number of commercial theaters across the country shrank from 590 in 1927 to barely 200 in the mid-1960s. Expenditures on arts admissions as a percentage of the consumer's average income fell by about 25 percent between 1929 and 1963. In 1929, 15 cents of each 100 dollars disposable personal income was spent on arts admissions. This figure fell to 11 cents of each 100 dollars disposable personal income in 1963. See William J. Baumol, *Performing Arts: The Economic Dilemma*, New York: The Twentieth Century Fund, 1966, Chapter 3.

18 Average weekly movie attendance in the United States jumped from 50 million in 1926 to a high of 90 million in 1948. It began to decline thereafter because of the rapid growth of television. The number of television stations on air jumped from 6 in 1946 to 456 in 1956, 699 in 1966, 960 in 1976, and 1,106 in 1983. These data are from Harold L. Vogel, *Entertainment Industry Economics*, Cambridge, MA: Cambridge University Press, 1986, Tables S2.2 and S6.2.

19 In his book *The Good Life and Its Discontents* (New York: Times Books, 1995), Robert J. Samuelson writes: "In 1986, Consumers Union published a book called *I'll Buy That!* appraising the most significant consumer products of the

previous half century. Much of what we now take for granted dates from these early postwar years. The original modern detergent, Tide, was first marketed in 1947. National credit cards began with the Diners Club in 1950. . . . Synthetic fibers, led by nylon and polyester, boomed after 1945" (p. 40).

20 See Robert J. Samuelson (1995), op. cit.; Esmond Wright, *The American Dream: From Reconstruction to Reagan*, Cambridge, MA: Blackwell, 1996.

21 *Selling the Dream*, a video program produced by the Smithsonian Institution (Washington, DC) and aired on the Public Broadcasting Service (November 1991), provides several examples of "infomercial" type programs promoting the consuming life styles.

22 See Rosalind Williams, "The Dream World of Mass Consumption," in *Rethinking Popular Culture: Contemporary Perspectives in Cultural Studies*, Chandra Mukerji and Michael Schudson (eds.), Berkeley, CA: University of California Press, 1991, pp. 198–235.

23 See, for example, Russell Lynes, *The Tastemakers: The Shaping of American Popular Taste*, New York: Dover Publications, 1980.

2 CONSUMPTION PATTERNS

1 See Jean Baudrillard, "Consumer Society," in *Jean Baudrillard: Selected Writings*, Stanford, CA: Stanford University Press, 1988, pp. 29–56.

2 See Peter Petschauer, *The Education of Women in Eighteenth-Century Germany: New Directions from the German Female Perspective: Bending the Ivy*, Lewiston, NY: E. Mellen Press, 1989.

3 See K. N. Cameron, *Humanity and Society: A World History*, New York: Monthly Review Press, 1973; and Fernand Braudel, *Capitalism and Material Life*, New York: Harper & Row, 1973.

4 See Karl Polanyi, *The Livelihood of Man*, New York: Academic Press, 1977; and Immanuel Wallerstein, *The Modern World-System I*, New York: Academic Press, 1974.

5 Classical economists spent considerable efforts in demarcating these concepts. See John Stuart Mill, "The Principles of Political Economy," in *Collected Works*, London: Routledge & Kegan Paul, 1967 [1836]; and Jan-Baptiste Say, *A Treatise on Political Economy*, New York: A. M. Kelly, 1964 [1821].

6 See Ernest W. Flick, *Household and Automotive Cleaners and Polishes* (3rd edn.), Park Ridge, NJ: Noyes Publications, 1986; and Glenna Matthews, *Just a Housewife: The Rise and Fall of Domesticity in America*, New York: Oxford University Press, 1987.

7 See A. Fuat Fırat and Nikhilesh Dholakia, "Consumption Choices at the Macro Level," *Journal of Macromarketing*, vol. 2, 1982, pp. 6–15.

8 See C. Reuven, *The Kibbutz Settlement* (trans. by H. Statman), Tel Aviv: Hakibbutz Hameuchad, 1972.

9 Social trend-watcher Faith Popcorn has labeled the tendency "cocooning" (Faith Popcorn, *The Popcorn Report: Faith Popcorn on the Future of Your Company, Your World, Your Life*, New York: Doubleday, 1991).

10 Stanley Lebergott, *Pursuing Happiness: American Consumers in the Twentieth Century*, Princeton, NJ: Princeton University Press, 1993, p. 134.

11 See, for example, L. Neil Johnson and Samuel M. Tully, *Interactive Television: Progress and Potential*, Bloomington, IN: Phi Delta Kappa Foundation, 1989; and John Carey and Martin Elton, "Forecasting Demand for New Consumer Services: Challenges and Alternatives," in *New Infotainment Technologies in the Home*, R. R. Dholakia, N. Mundorf, and N. Dholakia (eds.), Mahwah, NJ: Lawrence Erlbaum Associates, 1966, pp. 35–57.

12 See *Who Makes Do-It-Yourself Home Improvements?* Washington, DC: United States Department of Commerce, Economics and Statistics Administration, Bureau of the Census, 1992.

13 See A. Fuat Fırat, "Towards a Deeper Understanding of Consumption Experiences: The Underlying Dimensions," in *Advances in Consumer Research*, vol. 14, M. Wallendorf and P. F. Anderson (eds.), Provo, UT: Association of Consumer Research, 1986.

14 Some of these items were hand-made clothing, community kitchens, and folklore, for the period before the middle of the nineteenth century; buses, movie theaters, stoves/ovens, radios, for the period from the middle of the nineteenth century to the Second World War; and television sets, microwave ovens, automobiles, and designer clothing, for the period after the Second World War.

3 THE MAKING OF THE CONSUMER

1 See John Stuart Mill, "The Principles of Political Economy," in *Collected Works*, London: Routledge & Kegan Paul, 1967 [1836]; and Jan-Baptiste Say, *A Treatise on Political Economy*, New York: A. M. Kelly, 1964 [1821].

2 See Karl Marx, *Grundrisse*, New York: Vintage Books, 1973. The discussion in this paragraph draws from A. Fuat Fırat, "Gender and Consumption: Transcending the Feminine?" in J. A. Costa (ed.), *Gender Issues and Consumer Behavior*, Thousand Oaks, CA: Sage, 1994, pp. 205–228.

3 Parallels to this idea of workers as economic assets occur in the literature dealing with slavery. See, for example, Eugene D. Genovese, *The Political Economy of Slavery*, New York: Pantheon Books, 1965.

4 See A. Fuat Fırat, "Gender and Consumption: Transcending the Feminine?" op. cit.

5 See, for example, Kenneth N. Cameron, *Humanity and Society: A World History*, New York: Monthly Review Press, 1973; Stanley H. Udy, Jr., *Work in Traditional and Modern Society*, Englewood Cliffs, NJ: Prentice-Hall, 1970; and Max Weber, *The Agrarian Sociology of Ancient Civilizations*, London: New Left Books, 1976.

6 See, for example, Johan Huizinga, *Homo Ludens: A Study of the Play-Element in Culture*, Boston: Beacon Press, 1966; and A. Touraine, "Leisure Activities and Social Participation," in M. R. Marrus (ed.), *The Emergence of Leisure*, New York: Harper & Row, 1974.

7 See, for example, Herbert Applebaum (ed.), *Work in Non-Market and Transitional Societies*, Albany, NY: State University of New York Press, 1984; Stanley H. Udy, Jr., *Work in Traditional and Modern Society*, op. cit.

8 See Rayna R. Reiter, "Men and Women in South of France: Public and Private Domains," in *Toward an Anthropology of Women*, R. R. Reiter (ed.), New York: Monthly Review Press, 1975, pp. 252–282; Karen Sacks, "Engels Revisited: Women, the Organization of Production, and Private Property," in *Toward an Anthropology of Women*, op. cit., pp. 211–234; and Heleieth I. B. Saffioti, *Women in Class Society*, New York: Monthly Review Press, 1978. Postmodern and postindustrial conditions, driven by advances in information technology, are starting to blur these historically established distinctions (see Howard Rheingold, *The Virtual Community: Homesteading on the Electronic Frontier*, Reading, MA: Addison-Wesley, 1994) and therefore will have major transformational impacts on consumption and production.

9 See Karl Polanyi, *The Livelihood of Man*, New York: Academic Press, 1977; and Heleieth I. B. Saffioti, *Women in Class Society*, op. cit.

10 See Patricia Draper, "Kung Women: Contrasts in Sexual Egalitarianism in

Foraging and Sedentary Contexts," in *Toward an Anthropology of Women*, op. cit., pp. 77–109; and Karen Sacks, "Engels Revisited: Women, the Organization of Production, and Private Property," op. cit.

11 See Ruby Rohrlich-Leavitt, Barbara Sykes, and Elizabeth Weatherford, "Aboriginal Woman: Male and Female Anthropological Perspectives," in *Toward an Anthropology of Women*, op. cit., pp. 110–126; and Paula Webster, "Matriarchy: A Vision of Power," in *Toward an Anthropology of Women*, op. cit., pp. 141–156.

12 See Ester Boserup, *Woman's Role in Economic Development*, New York: St Martin's Press, 1970; and Karen Sacks, "Engels Revisited: Women, the Organization of Production, and Private Property," op. cit.

13 See Jean Gardiner, "Women's Domestic Labor," in *Capitalist Patriarchy and the Case for Socialist Feminism*, Z. R. Eisenstein (ed.), New York: Monthly Review Press, 1979, pp. 173–189.

14 In contemporary writing, it is difficult to use the term "product" for things produced at home. The term product has been appropriated for business use and is now synonymous with the term commodity. This is clear in the marketing literature (see, for example, Philip Kotler, *Marketing Management* (7th edn.), Englewood Cliffs, NJ: Prentice-Hall, 1991).

15 See Caroline Davidson, *A Woman's Work is Never Done: A History of Housework in the British Isles 1650–1950*, London: Chatto & Windus, 1986; and A. H. Stromberg and S. Harkess (eds.), *Women Working*, Palo Alto, CA: Mayfield, 1978.

16 See Jean Gardiner, "Women's Domestic Labor," op. cit.; and Eli Zaretsky, "Capitalism and the Evolution of the Family," in R. C. Edwards, M. Reich, and T. E. Weisskopf (eds.), *The Capitalist System*, Englewood Cliffs, NJ: Prentice-Hall, 1978, pp. 69–73.

17 See, for example, Harry Braverman, *Labor and Monopoly Capital*, New York: Monthly Review Press, 1974; Colin Campbell, *The Romantic Ethic and the Spirit of Modern Consumerism*, Oxford: Basil Blackwell, 1987; and Lynn Y. Weiner, *From Working Girl to Working Mother: The Female Labor Force in the United States, 1820–1980*, Chapel Hill, NC: University of North Carolina, 1985.

18 See Heleieth I. B. Saffioti, *Women in Class Society*, op. cit.

19 See Nancy Chodorow, "Mothering, Male Dominance, and Capitalism," in *Capitalist Patriarchy* op. cit., pp. 83–106.

20 Studies in consumer behavior and marketing have usually employed the pronoun "she" for the generic consumer, especially when the consuming unit is an individual or a household. See Eileen Fischer and Julia Bristor, "A Feminist Poststructuralist Analysis of the Rhetoric of Marketing Relationships," *International Journal of Research in Marketing*, vol. 11, no. 4, pp. 317–331.

21 See Matilda Butler and William Paisley, *Women and the Mass Media*, New York: Human Sciences Press, 1980; and Susan Rubin Suleiman (ed.), *The Female Body in Western Culture*, Cambridge, MA: Harvard University Press, 1986.

22 All marketing textbooks, as well as textbooks in consumer behavior, claim the importance of thinking of the consumer as the "king" or the "sovereign" in order to be a successful organization. The "marketing concept," as it is known in these fields, refers to first finding out the needs, wants, and desires of the consumers before planning products, in order to best serve them. See, for example, Philip Kotler, *Marketing Management*, op. cit., pp. 16–25; and Michael R. Solomon, *Consumer Behavior* (3rd edn.), Englewood Cliffs, NJ: Prentice-Hall, 1996, p. 10.

4 CONSUMPTION IN MODERN SOCIETY

1 This is easily observed, for example, in marketing textbooks, all of which include a section on Maslow's hierarchy of needs. See Abraham Maslow, *Motivation and Personality*, New York: Harper & Row, 1934.

2 Needs are generally conceptualized in stages, starting from latent needs, where the needy have not yet perceived the need and are therefore inactive at the conscious level, to perceived needs, to felt needs. Conscious action to fulfill needs begins when the need is perceived.

3 See James Engel, *Consumer Behavior*, Chicago: Dryden, 1986.

4 See Philip Kotler, *Marketing Management* (7th edn.), Englewood Cliffs, NJ: Prentice-Hall, 1991, p. 5.

5 See E. Chamberlin, *The Theory of Monopolistic Competition*, Cambridge, MA: Harvard University Press, 1969 [1935]; Milton Friedman and Rose Friedman, *Free to Choose*, New York: Harcourt Brace Jovanovich, 1980; Joan Robinson, *Economic Philosophy*, Chicago: Aldine, 1962.

6 The pioneering work of Joseph Schumpeter and subsequent work have examined the impact of entrepreneurial innovation and technological change on markets. See Frederick M. Scherer (ed.), *Entrepreneurship, Technological Innovation, and Economic Growth: Studies in the Schumpeterian Tradition*, Ann Arbor, MI: University of Michigan Press, 1992; Arnold Heertje and Mark Perlman (eds.), *Evolving Technology and Market Structure: Studies in Schumpeterian Economics*, Ann Arbor, MI: University of Michigan Press, 1990; and David L. McKee, *Schumpeter and the Political Economy of Change*, New York: Praeger, 1991.

7 See Philip Kotler, *Marketing Management*, op. cit.

8 This is a central axiom in economics, in conceptualizing the *homo economicus*. The human consumer is one of economic reason, trying to minimize outlay of economic resources s/he has at the same time that s/he endeavors to maximize utility received. The reader can refer to any modern economics textbook for confirmation.

9 See Kenneth J. Arrow and Tibor Scitovsky (eds.), *Readings in Welfare Economics*, Hollywood, IL: Richard D. Irwin, 1969; and Andrew Bard Schmookler, *The Illusion of Choice: How the Market Economy Shapes Our Destiny*, Albany, NY: State University of New York Press, 1993.

10 Inelastic demand is a situation where increases and/or decreases in the price of a commodity do not cause a change in the amount demanded, or the ratio of change in the amount of demand is very small in relation to the price change.

11 See Allan Schnaiberg, "Social Conflicts in Environmental Decisions," presented in Environmental Impact Assessment Seminar Series, Midwestern Universities Committee on Air Pollution Education, Evanston, IL: Northwestern University, April 1973.

12 T. C. Koopmans, *Three Essays on the State of Economic Science*, New York: McGraw-Hill, 1957, p. 49.

13 See Andrew Bard Schmookler, *The Illusion of Choice*, op. cit.

14 See E. W. Gilboy, *A Primer on the Economics of Consumption*, New York: Random House, 1968.

15 The term "dominant consumption pattern" is used in this book to define that consumption pattern which is diffused, and therefore popular, as a result of being adopted (or conformed to) by a majority of consumer units in a society. Similar notions have been employed by R. P. Coleman, "The Significance of Social Stratification in Selling," in M. L. Bell (ed.), *Proceedings of the American Marketing Association*, 1960; and W. T. Tucker, *The Social Context of Economic Behavior*, New York: Holt, Rinehart & Winston, 1964.

16 For exceptions, see the works of Tibor Scitovski, including *Papers on Welfare and Growth*, Stanford, CA: Stanford University Press, 1964; *Human Desire and Economic Satisfaction: Essays on the Frontiers of Economics*, Brighton, Sussex: Wheatsheaf Books, 1986; and *The Joyless Economy: The Psychology of Human Satisfaction*, New York: Oxford University Press, 1992. Also see Michael J. Boskin (ed.), *Economics and Human Welfare: Essays in Honor of Tibor Scitovski*, New York: Academic Press, 1979.

17 For example, see Michael R. Solomon, *Consumer Behavior* (3rd edn.), Englewood Cliffs, NJ: Prentice-Hall, 1996; and J. Paul Peter and Jerry C. Olson, *Consumer Behavior and Marketing Strategy* (2nd edn.), Homewood, IL: Irwin, 1990.

18 See H. Lindhoff and F. Ölander, *The Influence of Consumers on the Development of New Products*, Berlin: Preprint Series of the International Institute of Management, 1973; J. W. Reich and C. A. Moody, "Stimulus Properties, Frequency of Exposure, and Effective Responding," *Perceptual and Motor Skills*, 1970, pp. 27–35; and R. B. Zajonc, "Attitudinal Effects of Mere Exposure," *Journal of Personality and Social Psychology*, *Monograph Supplement*, 1968, pp. 1–27.

19 See D. W. Conrath and G. B. Thompson, "Communicative Technology: A Societal Perspective," *The Journal of Communication*, vol. 23, March 1973, pp. 47–63.

20 Andrew Bard Schmookler, *The Illusion of Choice*, op. cit., especially pp. 156–172.

21 See Ralph Nader, *Unsafe at Any Speed: The Designed-In Dangers of the American Automobile*, New York: Grossman, 1972.

22 See Ralph Nader and Mark J. Green, *Corporate Power in America*, New York: Grossman, 1973; H. O. Pruden and D. S. Longman, "Race, Alienation and Consumerism," *Journal of Marketing*, vol. 36, July 1972, pp. 58–63.

23 See J. F. Engel, D. T. Kollat, and R. D. Blackwell, *Consumer Behavior* (2nd edn.), New York: Holt, Rinehart & Winston, 1973, pp. 614–642; Philip Kotler, *Marketing Management*, op. cit.; and Ralph Nader, "The Corporate Monster," in P. A. Samuelson (ed.), *Readings in Economics* (6th edn.), New York: McGraw-Hill, 1970.

24 For a review of such legislation, see Ivan L. Preston, *The Tangled Web They Weave: Truth, Falsity, and Advertisers*, Madison, WI: University of Wisconsin Press, 1994; and Michael Schulman, *Deceptive Packaging: A Close Look at the California State Department of Consumer Affairs*, San Francisco: San Francisco Consumer Action, 1974.

25 See Philip Kotler and Paul N. Bloom, "Strategies for High Market-Share Companies," *Harvard Business Review*, November–December 1975, pp. 63–72; and Paul N. Bloom and Stephen A. Greyser, *Exploring the Future of Consumerism*, Cambridge, MA: Marketing Science Institute, Research Program, 1981.

26 See, especially, Thorstein Veblen, *The Theory of the Leisure Class*, New York: Macmillan, 1899; and John Kenneth Galbraith, *The New Industrial State*, New York: Mentor, 1971.

27 See John Kenneth Galbraith, *The Affluent Society* (2nd edn.), New York: Mentor, 1969; and *The New Industrial State*, op. cit.

28 John Kenneth Galbraith, "Power and the Useful Economist," *American Economic Review*, vol. 63, 1973, p. i.

29 *The New Industrial State*, op. cit.

30 See Herbert I. Schiller, *Culture Inc.: The Corporate Takeover of Public Expression*, New York: Oxford University Press, 1989.

31 See Ben H. Bagdikian, *The Media Monopoly* (3rd edn.), Boston: Beacon Press, 1990; Eric Smoodin (ed.), *Disney Discourse: Producing the Magic Kingdom*, New York: Routledge, 1994; and Elizabeth Bell, Lynda Haas, and Laura Sells (eds.), *From Mouse to Mermaid: The Politics of Film, Gender and Culture*, Bloomington, IN: Indiana University Press, 1995.

32 Theoretical discussions of the interrelationships between the productive organization and the state can be found in J. O'Connor, *The Fiscal Crisis of the State*, New York: St Martin's Press, 1973; N. Poulantzas, *Political Power and Social Classes*, London: New Left Books, 1973; and G. Williams Domhoff, *Who Really Rules?* Santa Monica, CA: Goodyear, 1978. Shaken by the Japanese challenge to American economic prowess, some recent studies have taken a global view and focused on the influence of foreign capitalist interests on American policies. See, for example, Pat Choate, *Agents of Influence*, New York: A. A. Knopf, 1990.

33 See Vance Packard, *The Hidden Persuaders*, New York: Pocketbooks, 1958; and D. M. Potter, *People of Plenty*, Chicago: The University of Chicago Press, 1954.

34 See David Caplovitz, *The Poor Pay More*, New York: The Free Press, 1967.

35 Ibid., p. 67.

36 See James S. Duesenberry, *Income, Saving and the Theory of Consumer Behavior*, Cambridge, MA: Harvard University Press, 1949.

37 See D. S. Brady, "Family Saving in Relation to Changes in the Level and Distribution of Income," in *Studies in Income and Wealth*, vol. 15, New York: National Bureau of Economic Research, 1952.

38 See Karl Marx, *Capital: A Critique of Political Economy*, vol. 1, New York: Penguin, 1976; vol. 2, New York: Penguin, 1978; and vol. 3, New York: Vintage, 1981.

39 This argument is evident in the work of neo-classical economists such as Alfred Marshall, *Industry and Trade: A Study of Industrial Technique and Business Organization, and of their Influences on the Conditions of Various Classes and Nations*, London: Macmillan, 1919. Others have also argued the point, such as Joseph A. Schumpeter, *Capitalism, Socialism and Democracy* (6th edn.), London: Unwin, 1987; and the argument has become a standard part of mainstream economics textbooks. See, for example, Paul A. Samuelson, *Economics* (9th edn.), New York: McGraw-Hill, 1973.

40 Georg Simmel, *The Philosophy of Money* (trans. by T. Bottomore and D. Frisby), London: Routledge, 1978 [1900]. See also Donald Levine (ed.), *On Individuality and Social Forms: Selected Writings*, Chicago: University of Chicago Press, 1971 [1903].

41 Roland Barthes, *Mythologies*, London: Cape, 1972 (trans. by A. Lavers).

42 According to Bourdieu, structurations are relationships among different levels of social existence, such as the economic and the political, which afford attachment of meaning(s) to encounters that human beings have at these different levels of existence. These meanings, then, constitute a symbolic hierarchy, some considered more important and crucial than others. See Pierre Bourdieu, *Distinction: A Social Critique of the Judgement of Taste*, Cambridge, MA: Harvard University Press, 1984.

43 See the following books by Jean Baudrillard: *The Mirror of Production*, St Louis, MO: Telos, 1975; *For a Critique of the Political Economy of the Sign*, St Louis, MO: Telos, 1981; *Seduction*, New York: St Martin's Press, 1990; and *Symbolic Exchange and Death*, London: Sage, 1993.

5 THE SOCIAL CONSTRUCTION OF CONSUMPTION PATTERNS IN MODERN SOCIETY

1 The term *structure of available alternatives for consumption* is used to define all the consumables presently existing and all the relationships they have to each other, for example, in terms of cost, complementarity, attractiveness, (cultural) importance, visibility, etc.

2 Some years ago, the newspapers reported the story of a Pakistan-born American dentist who was frustrated by the lack of choices in dentifrice products available in the United States. He knew that in South Asia it was a common practice, especially in rural areas, to take an early morning walk, break off a small twig from a *babool* or *neem* tree, chew one end of the twig into a brush, and then use it to clean one's teeth. His medical training had convinced him that these were excellent natural dentifrice products, and using them was also safe for the environment. He pondered ways of making such products available to his patients, but gave up because the structure for making these alternatives available in America simply did not exist.

3 We use the term "primitive" fully aware that it is highly value laden and that in many respects our contemporary cultures may have more "primitive" aspects to them than those communities we have learned to call primitive.

4 This is a contention of many contemporary historians, philosophers, and others. The vast literature on modernity includes Chandra Mukerji, *From Graven Images: Patterns of Modern Materialism*, New York: Columbia University Press, 1983; Richard Rorty, *Philosophy and the Mirror of Nature*, Princeton, NJ: Princeton University Press, 1979; Jürgen Habermas, "Modernity—An Incomplete Project," in Hal Foster (ed.), *The Anti-Aesthetic: Essays on Postmodern Culture*, Seattle, WA: Bay Press, 1983; and Jean-François Lyotard, *The Inhuman: Reflections on Time*, op. cit., among others.

5 One of the major contributions of Bertrand Russell to the history of western philosophy is his book *A History of Western Philosophy*, New York: Touchstone, 1945.

6 Ibid., p. 492.

7 For discussions of these earlier approaches to knowledge-generation, see Hans-Georg Gadamer, *Dialogue and Dialectic*, New Haven, CT: Yale University Press, 1980; Jürgen Habermas, *Knowledge and Human Interests* (trans. by J. J. Shapiro), Boston: Beacon Press, 1968; Karl-Otto Apel, *Understanding and Explanation: A Transcendental-Pragmatic Perspective* (trans. by G. Warnke), Cambridge, MA: The MIT Press, 1984; Paul Ricoeur, *Hermeneutics and the Human Sciences* (ed. and trans. by J. B. Thompson), Cambridge: Cambridge University Press, 1981; and Paul Feyerabend, *Science in a Free Society*, London: Verso, 1978.

8 See, for example, Edward McNall Burns and Philip Lee Ralph, *World Civilizations*, vol. 1 (4th edn.), New York: W. W. Norton and Co., 1969; Immanuel Wallerstein, *The Modern World System I: Capitalist Agriculture and the Origins of the European World-Economy in the Sixteenth Century*, New York: Academic Press, 1974; and Kenneth Neill Cameron, *Humanity and Society: A World History*, New York: Monthly Review Press, 1973.

9 Bertrand Russell, *A History of Western Philosophy*, op. cit., pp. 525–540.

10 For a discussion of these developments, see Herbert Marcuse, *From Luther to Popper*, London: Verso, 1983.

11 See Bertrand Russell, *A History of Western Philosophy*, op. cit., p. 538; and Richard Rorty, *Philosophy and the Mirror of Nature*, op. cit.

12 The reasons were different, but nevertheless both sectors did preach restraint and prudence; the Church for fear of attachment to worldly goods and the

entrepreneurial sector for fear of waste of resources that could be put to "better," more productive uses.

13 See, for example, John Brewer and Roy Porter (eds.), *Consumption and the World of Goods*, London: Routledge, 1993.

14 See Chandra Mukerji, *From Graven Images*, op. cit.

15 For the linkages between consumption and ills that wasted human beings away, such as tuberculosis, see Roy Porter, "Consumption: Disease of the Consumer Society?" in *Consumption and the World of Goods*, op. cit., pp. 58–81.

16 See the section on literacy and numeracy in *Consumption and the World of Goods*, op. cit., pp. 305–377.

17 We are using the term "domestic" to differentiate between original markets in colonizing countries and "foreign" markets in colonized countries.

18 For an explanation of the role of the wars on business cycles and economic depressions, see Paul A. Baran and Paul M. Sweezy, *Monopoly Capital: An Essay on the American Economic and Social Order*, New York: Modern Reader, 1966.

19 For the impact of railroads on modern society see, for example, Gerald Berk, *Alternative Tracks: The Constitution of American Industrial Order, 1865–1917*, Baltimore, MD: Johns Hopkins University Press, 1994; and Colleen A. Dunlavy, *Politics and Industrialization: Early Railroads in the United States and Prussia*, Princeton, NJ: Princeton University Press, 1994.

20 We are using the name Soviet Union and not Russia here because of the era that is under discussion.

21 See, for example, *Monopoly Capital*, op. cit., especially Chapters 3–7; and Harry Braverman, *Labor and Monopoly Capital: The Degradation of Work in the Twentieth Century*, New York: Monthly Review Press, 1974.

22 See Thorstein Veblen, *The Theory of the Leisure Class*, New York: Macmillan, 1899.

23 See, for example, Jane Gaines and Charlotte Herzog (eds.), *Fabrications: Costume and the Female Body*, New York: Routledge, 1990; John E. O'Connor and Martin A. Jackson (eds.), *American History, American Film: Interpreting the Hollywood Image*, New York: Continuum, 1988; Robert J. Donovan and Ray Scherer, *Unsilent Revolution: Television News and American Public Life*, Cambridge: Cambridge University Press, 1992; and Philip J. Davies and Brian Neve (eds.), *Cinema, Politics, and Society in America*, New York: St Martin's Press, 1981.

24 For a history of the development of the railroads in the United States, see Leonard Everett Fisher, *Tracks Across America: The History of the American Railroad, 1825–1900*, New York: Holiday House, 1992.

25 For a good exposé of the converted developments in cities and transportation systems, see *Coming and Going*, a Public Broadcasting Service series, broadcast on June 3, 10 and 17, 1994.

26 For a discussion of the importance of the visual in modernity, see *Modernity and the Hegemony of Vision*, David Michael Levin (ed.), Berkeley, CA: University of California Press, 1993.

27 Hollywood became particularly influential after the Great Depression. "The heavenly gates swung open, and American motion pictures . . . entered their golden age: Hollywood took center stage in the culture and consciousness of the United States, making movies with a power and élan never known before or seen again. Not only did the movies amuse and entertain the nation through its most severe economic and social disorder, holding it together by their capacity to create unifying myths and dreams, but movie culture in the 1930s became a dominant culture for many Americans, providing new values and ideals to

replace shattered old traditions." From Robert Sklar, *Movie-Made America* (revised edn.), New York: Vintage Books, 1994, p. 161. Sklar is careful to point out that the "form that movie culture assumed grew out of interrelations with other social and economic institutions and with the state" (p. 161), a point we endorse by discussing Hollywood as one of several shapers of the American consumption patterns.

28 Consider, for example, that the television programs which are aspirational include ones such as *Lifestyles of the Rich and Famous*.

29 For a history of control in the media, see Ben H. Bagdikian, *The Media Monopoly* (3rd edn.), Boston: Beacon Press, 1990.

30 See, for example, Michael Munn, *The Hollywood Connection: The True Story of Organized Crime in Hollywood*, London: Robson Books, 1993.

31 If one reads the biography by Victor G. Reuther, *The Brothers Reuther and the Story of the UAW. A Memoir* (Canadian edn.), Boston: Houghton Mifflin, 1976, one may get a different view, however. For example, police and hoodlums were frequently used illegally by these companies against labor union movements.

32 For a history of the movie industry and the topics selected across the years in Hollywood films, see Richard Griffin and Arthur Mayer, *The Movies: The Sixty-Year Story of the World of Hollywood and its Effect on America, From Pre-Nickelodeon Days to the Present*, New York: Bonanza Books, 1957; and Gerald Mast and Bruce F. Kawin, *The Movies: A Short History*, Boston: Allyn and Bacon, 1996 (revised edn.).

33 Over the decades these statistics have remained surprisingly similar. See, for example, C. Morgello, "Wall Street: Who Owns What," *Newsweek*, December 23, 1974.

34 For a history of such propaganda, see Charles A. Siepmann, *Radio, Television, and Society*, New York: Oxford University Press, 1950; and Leo Bogart, *The Age of Television*, New York: Ungar, 1956.

35 Movies, television programs, and written media—books, magazines and newspapers—abound with the stories of such. See, for example, Ray B. Browne, Marshall Fishwick, and Michael T. Marsden (eds.), *Heroes of Popular Culture*, Bowling Green, OH: Bowling Green University Popular Press, 1972; Robert J. Samuelson, *The Good Life and Its Discontents*, New York: Times Books, 1995; Russell Lynes, *The Tastemakers: The Shaping of American Popular Taste*, New York: Dover, 1949; and Rosalind Williams, *Dream Worlds*, Berkeley, CA: University of California Press, 1982.

36 For a history of the middle class(es) and its (their) appetite for consumption, see Donald R. Katz, *Home Fires: An Intimate Portrait of One Middle-Class Family in Postwar America*, New York: HarperCollins, 1992; Katherine S. Newman, *Declining Fortunes: The Withering of the American Dream*, New York: Basic Books, 1993; and Elaine S. Abelson, *When Ladies Go A-Thieving: Middle Class Shoplifters in the Victorian Department Store*, New York: Oxford University Press, 1989.

37 For an exposé of middle-class values throughout American history, see Lawrence Chenoweth, *The American Dream of Success: The Search for the Self in the Twentieth Century*, North Scituate, MA: Duxbury Press, 1974; and Michele Lamont, *Money, Morals, and Manners: The Culture of the French and American Upper-Middle Class*, Chicago: University of Chicago Press, 1992.

38 Most of the examples in this respect came from the film industry in California which had a settlement structure based heavily on cars and highways, which became the model for suburban living. See *Coming and Going*, op. cit.; and

Stephen B. Goddard, *Getting There: The Epic Struggle Between Road and Rail in the American Century*, New York: Basic Books, 1994.

39 See, for example, the Public Broadcasting Service program *Selling the Dream*, a production of the Smithsonian Institution, where the informational segment on suburban living run by General Motors is reproduced.

40 For a history of television in the United States, see Richard Marschall, *The History of Television*, New York: Gallery Books, 1986; Jeff Greenfield, *Television: The First Fifty Years*, New York: Harry N. Abrams, 1977; Eric Barnouw, *Tube of Plenty: The Evolution of American Television*, New York: Oxford University Press, 1990; and J. Fred MacDonald, *One Nation Under Television: The Rise and Decline of Network TV*, New York: Pantheon, 1990.

41 Any economics dictionary or textbook can be referred to if the reader wishes to get more detailed information on economies of scale.

42 The marketing literature is replete with gender specific descriptors, as are all business disciplines. For critiques of such terminology, see Eileen Fischer and Julia Bristor, "A Feminist Poststructuralist Analysis of the Rhetoric of Marketing Relationships," *International Journal of Research in Marketing*, vol. 11, no. 4, 1994, pp. 317–331; and Martha Cálas and Linda Smircich, "Voicing Seduction to Silence Leadership," *Organizational Studies*, vol. 12, 1992, pp. 567–601.

43 See John Brooks, *Showing off in America: From Conspicuous Consumption to Parody Display*, Boston: Little, Brown, 1981; and Roger Burrows and Catherine Marsh (eds.), *Consumption and Class: Divisions and Change*, Houndmills, Hants: Macmillan, 1992.

44 See, for example, Lars Osberg (ed.), *Economic Inequality and Poverty: International Perspectives*, Armonk, NY: M. E. Sharpe, 1991; and Y. S. Brenner, Hartmut Kaelble, and Mark Thomas (eds.), *Income Distribution in Historical Perspective*, New York: Cambridge University Press, 1991. For more recent income distribution and inequality statistics, see *Poverty in the United States*, Washington, DC: US Department of Commerce, Bureau of the Census, 1995.

45 The wealthier, high income households were the "fortunate" as we earlier discussed: business people, owners and top managers of corporations, stars and celebrities of mass media.

46 Thorstein Veblen published his explorations into the conspicuous consumption behaviors of the rich, which he called "the leisure class," in 1899. His *The Theory of the Leisure Class*, New York: Macmillan, is a book that is still widely cited in the social sciences literatures.

47 For historical examples of such consumption in seventeenth- and eighteenth-century Europe, see *Consumption and the World of Goods*, op. cit.; and *Consumption and Class: Divisions and Change*, op. cit. For a similar exploration into the consumption ethic in America, see *Consumption and American Culture*, David E. Nye and Carl Pedersen (eds.), Amsterdam: VU University Press, 1991.

48 This can be discerned by the meanings culturally signified by the consumption items accumulated by the wealthy across American history. For examples of these accumulated goods, see Russell W. Belk, *Collecting in a Consumer Society*, London: Routledge, 1995.

49 As such, many of these products were called "time saving" devices, saving time from daily chores and providing freedom and free time. However, as many feminist scholars have demonstrated, the advent of such products did not reduce the housework time required by homemakers, while increasing the psychological pressures upon them to do a "better job." For discussion of such issues, see A. H. Stromberg and S. Harkess (eds.), *Women Working*, Palo Alto, CA: Mayfield, 1978.

50 Examples of these advertisements abound in advertising archives. For example, see Richard Pollay, *Information Sources in Advertising History*, Westport, CT: Greenwood Press, 1979.

51 We discussed these theories in the previous chapter.

52 See Chapter 2 for a discussion of this issue.

53 For information on corporate ownership in the United States, see Juvenal L. Angel, *Directory of Inter-Corporate Ownership*, New York: Simon & Schuster, 1974.

54 There are many sources which discuss the political and social influences of different interest groups in the United States. For some examples of these studies, see M. Nadel, "Economic Power and Public Policy: The Case of Consumer Protection," *Politics and Society*, vol. 1 (May), 1971, pp. 313–326; John E. Chubb, *Interest Groups and the Bureaucracy: The Politics of Energy*, Stanford, CA: Stanford University Press, 1983; and David C. Korten, *When Corporations Rule the World*, San Francisco: Berrett-Koehler Publishers, 1995.

55 Marxist economists have already illustrated that for capitalist economy to survive, market expansion is a must, because without market expansion a conclusive depression is inevitable. See, for example, Paul Sweezy, *The Theory of Capitalist Development*, London: Dobson, 1949; Ernest Mandel, *Marxist Economic Theory*, vols. 1 and 2, New York: Modern Reader, 1970 and 1971; and Karl Marx, *Capital Volume 1*, New York: Penguin, 1976.

56 The American literature abounds with the stories of entrepreneurs and professionals who worked in the development of new technologies and their profound loyalty and support for these technologies. For example, see Carroll W. Pursell, Jr. (ed.), *Technology in America: A History of Individuals and Ideas*, Cambridge, MA: MIT Press, 1990.

57 The interest in these products by state agencies, such as the Bureau of Labor Statistics, and by organizations who were the major beneficiaries of such information (corporations and commercial and industrial boards) was coincidental because they were the products most identified with the modern idea of progress and affluence.

58 See a compilation of these statistics in A. Fuat Fırat, *The Social Construction of Consumption Patterns*, PhD Dissertation completed at Northwestern University, Evanston, IL, 1978, pp. 155–161, Tables 23–29.

59 As we mentioned earlier in Chapter 1, there may clearly have been a political intent in stopping the publication of these statistics.

60 Chronological data on ownership of durables by income are surprisingly difficult to come by. Whenever data are available, the patterns we have discussed hold. In a recent study, it was found that a "college graduate with a family income of $50,000 [and above] a year is three times more likely to own a video camera than a non-graduate who earns less than $30,000. The gap is nearly *five to one* for personal computer ownership and an enormous *10 to 1* for on-line capability within the home" (emphasis in the original). From *The Role of Technology in American Life*, Times Mirror Center for the People and the Press, May, 1994, p. 8.

61 It is interesting to observe that societies with wide disparities in income, such as the United States, India, and Brazil, exhibit far more product differentiation in terms of what is available in the market than societies with lower income disparities such as Norway and Japan.

6 (POST)MODERNITY AND CONSUMPTION

1 The "imaginary" is used in this context as it generally is in postmodern litera-

ture, and refers to the totality of the vision that captures the meanings of a life-world for a sociopolitical group.

2 Metanarratives are usually defined as totalizing idea systems which seek complete inner consistency to present a universalizing perspective, or ideologies that determine a society's ideas about reality and its overall world view. Modernism is generally identified by the commitment to a metanarrative that is considered to be the only true way to view the world.

3 That many people do not know how to use the advanced functions on their video-cassette recorders and other technological appliances, a fact that finds many humorous expressions in the mass media, is a good indication of this alienated consumption.

4 Many women's studies researchers have illustrated that the abundance of "time saving" products in the home has not, in fact, reduced women's work at home, but increased the many psychological and social pressures on home-makers to do more cleaning, cooking, etc., by increasing the expectations of cleanliness, varied meals, etc. See, for example, Arlie Hochschild, *The Second Shift: Working Parents and the Revolution at Home*, New York: Viking, 1989; and A. H. Stromberg and S. Harkess (eds.), *Women Working*, Palo Alto, CA: Mayfield, 1978.

5 See Jürgen Habermas, "Modernity—An Incomplete Project," in *The Anti-Aesthetic: Essays on Postmodern Culture*, H. Foster (ed.), Seattle, WA: Bay Press, 1983.

6 See Emilia Steuerman, "Habermas vs Lyotard: Modernity vs Postmodernity?" in A. Benjamin (ed.), *Judging Lyotard*, London: Routledge, 1992, pp. 99–118.

7 See Hal Foster, "Postmodernism: A Preface," in *The Anti-Aesthetic*, op. cit., pp. ix–xvi.

8 See R. R. Reiter, *Toward an Anthropology of Women*, New York: Monthly Review Press, 1975, esp. pp. 252–282; Karen Sacks, *Sisters and Wives*, Urbana, IL: University of Illinois Press, 1975; and H. I. B. Saffioti, *Women in Class Society*, New York: Monthly Review Press, 1978.

9 See Immanuel Wallerstein, "Culture as the Ideological Battleground of the Modern World-System," in M. Featherstone (ed.), *Global Culture: Nationalism, Globalization and Modernity*, London: Sage, 1990, pp. 31–55.

10 We are using (post)modernity with the "post" in parentheses to indicate the transitional period in contemporary western culture we have just discussed. It represents this period when postmodernism has not become fully entrenched and the modern market is still dominant.

11 Adultery, for example, is considered unacceptable, yet rarely punished or acted upon, especially when committed by males.

12 *CNN News*, May 28, 1994.

13 Such feelings among the electorate may partially explain the very low voting turnout, especially in the United States. Only 39 percent voted in the 1994 mid-term elections in the United States (*The Nation*, November 28, 1994, p. 633).

14 Both the structure and forms of the modern family are being questioned, criticized, and changed. See, for example, Kath Weston, *Families We Choose: Lesbians, Gays, Kinship*, New York: Columbia University Press, 1991.

15 The same can be said for religious institutions, for example, the Church, where more and more incidents of abuse are being heard.

16 The modern project has been defined as the improvement of human lives by controlling nature through scientific technologies. This idea and ideal was what largely guided all modern thought. See Ian Angus, "Circumscribing Postmodern Culture," in I. Angus and S. Jhally (eds.), *Cultural Politics in Contemporary America*, New York: Routledge, 1989, 96–107.

17 These labels have been used in both the popular and the scholarly media. See, for example, *Business Week*, "Move Over Boomers," cover story, December 14, 1992, pp. 74–82; and E. Ann Kaplan, *Rocking Around the Clock: Music Television, Postmodernism, and Consumer Culture*, New York: Methuen, 1987. For an interpretation of postmodern tendencies from a Generation-X perspective, see Douglas Rushkoff, *Playing the Future: How Kids' Culture Can Teach Us to Thrive in an Age of Chaos*, New York: HarperCollins, 1996.

18 We are referring here to the Gulf War of 1991.

19 Later, it was revealed, especially in the alternative media, that these smart bombs were not so "smart" after all, a similar experience that consumers have with many promotional campaigns.

20 From *The Public Mind*, Part I, "Consuming Images: Image and Reality in America," broadcast on November 8, 1989, on the Public Broadcasting Service.

21 Among these scholars, it is possible to count Jürgen Habermas, Jean-François Lyotard, Richard Rorty, Jean Baudrillard, Fredric Jameson, and Daniel Bell. Some of the many sources that can be mentioned for an introduction to the postmodern phenomenon are *The Anti-Aesthetic*, op. cit.; Mike Featherstone, *Consumer Culture and Postmodernism*, London: Sage, 1991; Fredric Jameson, *Postmodernism: Or, the Cultural Logic of Late Capitalism*, Durham, NC: Duke University Press, 1991; Douglas Kellner, *Jean Baudrillard: From Marxism to Postmodernism and Beyond*, Stanford, CA: Stanford University Press, 1989; and Jean-François Lyotard, *The Postmodern Condition: A Report on Knowledge*, Minneapolis, MN: University of Minnesota Press, 1984.

22 There is, of course, in this idea the influence of the fact that scientific thought and its conception of reality were originally constructed in the context of natural and, specifically, physical events, such as the solar system, properties of water, and the like, rather than social events. However, the ideas that were constructed in physical sciences have historically reflected themselves in the social sciences as well.

23 Any parent with children in school encounters these demands for brand name products because of the pressures of such reality on the children, and the mass media has been replete with stories of the importance of wearing the right brand names, at times to the extent that people have been killed in order to get their brand name shoes.

24 This may best be represented in Las Vegas, formerly the gambling center of North America, but now generally regarded as a fantasy town where people of all ages go to play games. Yet, as portrayed in *Time* magazine, it is the "All American City" replete with visions of tomorrow's city life. Currently, Las Vegas is the largest tourist destination, having recently surpassed Orlando, Florida (*Going Places: Las Vegas*, Public Broadcasting Service, 1997). It is also the city in the United States to which the largest numbers of job seekers move.

25 Michael Sorkin (ed.), *Variations on a Theme Park*, New York: The Noonday Press, 1992.

26 Consider, for example, the Borgata, in Phoenix, Arizona, which simulates an *authentic* Italian market town, or the Via Rodeo (Rodeo Drive) in Beverly Hills, California, which simulates a Roman *original*. Also, see M. Gottdiener, *Postmodern Semiotics: Material Culture and the Forms of Postmodern Life*, Oxford: Blackwell, 1995.

27 Disney thoroughly understands that in contemporary society, fantasy and reality merge into each other. At the Walt Disney World complex in Florida, a residential community called Celebration is shaping up. People can now be born into, live their lives in, and die in a theme park.

28 Michel Foucault, *Power/Knowledge: Selected Interviews and Other Writings 1972–77*, C. Gordon (ed.), New York: Pantheon, 1980.
29 This does not mean, however, that all regimes of truth have to be equally liked or admired. According to postmodernist way of thinking we can prefer one to the other, we just cannot argue for one's superiority or inferiority, or rightness or wrongness on some absolute or fundamental basis.
30 Discussions of this perspective from an anthropological angle, for example, can be found in Arjun Appadurai (ed.), *The Social Life of Things*, Cambridge: Cambridge University Press, 1986.
31 T. M. Williams (ed.), *The Impact of Television*, Orlando, FL: Academic Press, 1986; Lynn Spiegel, "The Suburban Home Companion: Television and the Neighborhood Ideal in Postwar America," in B. Colomina (ed.), *Sexuality and Space*, Princeton Papers on Architecture Series, vol. 1, New York: Princeton Architectural Press, 1992, pp. 184–217; Jean Baudrillard, "The Ecstasy of Communication" (trans. by J. Johnston), in *The Anti-Aesthetic*, op. cit., pp. 126–134.
32 See Jean Baudrillard, *Seduction* (trans. by B. Singer), New York: St Martin's Press, 1990.
33 The contemporary success of "How to" books and magazine articles attests to this fact.
34 Bill Moyers, *The Public Mind: Image and Reality in America—Consuming Images*, Public Broadcasting Service, 1989.
35 See Roy Porter, "Consumption: disease of the consumer society?" in J. Brewer and R. Porter (eds.), *Consumption and the World of Goods*, London: Routledge, 1993, pp. 58–81.
36 See Jean Baudrillard, *For A Critique of the Political Economy of the Sign* (trans. by C. Levin), St. Louis, MO: Telos Press, 1981; and Mark Poster, "Translator's Introduction," in Jean Baudrillard, *The Mirror of Production*, St. Louis, MO: Telos Press, 1975, pp. 1–15.
37 See, for example, Mary Ann Doane, "The Economy of Desire: The Commodity Form in/of the Cinema," *Quarterly Review of Film and Video*, 11, 1989, pp. 23–33.
38 For discussions of the role of the female in the home, see Mary Ann Doane, op. cit.; Jane Flax, "Postmodernism and Gender Relations in Feminist Theory," *Signs*, 12, 4, 1987, pp. 621–643; Heleieth I. B. Saffioti, *Women in Class Society*, New York: Monthly Review Press, 1978; and Susan Rubin Suleiman (ed.), *The Female Body in Western Culture*, Cambridge, MA: Harvard University Press, 1986.
39 Maslow's hierarchy of needs, a model used to explain human needs and their satisfaction had self-actualization as the final stage, has been a cornerstone in sociological, psychological and marketing textbooks in modern education. For a critique of such modern, and very much western, models, see Alladi Venkatesh, "Ethnoconsumerism: A New Paradigm to Study Cultural and Cross-Cultural Consumer Behavior," in J. A. Costa and G. J. Bamossy (eds.), *Marketing in a Multicultural World: Ethnicity, Nationalism, and Cultural Identity*, Thousand Oaks, CA: Sage, 1995, pp. 26–67.
40 For a discussion of the impacts of time and labor saving household durables on the lives of home-maker women, see Joan Acker, "Issues in the Sociological Study of Women's Work," in A. H. Stromberg and S. Harkess (eds.), *Women Working*, Palo Alto, CA: Mayfield Publishing Company, 1978, 134–161; Barbara Ehrenreich and Deirdre English, *For Her Own Good: 150 Years of the Experts' Advice to Women*, New York: Anchor, 1979; Kristin A. Moore and Isabel V. Sawhill, "Implications of Women's Employment for Home and Daily

Life," in *Women Working*, op. cit., pp. 201–225; and Joann Vanek, "Housewives as Workers," in *Women Working*, op. cit., pp. 392–414.

41 It is important to note here that from here on the reader should recognize the different nature and meaning of consumption in the postmodern. As will be discussed at greater length at the beginning of the next chapter, postmodern consumption does not necessarily have the modern "consumptive" urge of an ever increasing use or destruction and devouring of objects, resources, etc. Consumption in its postmodern form is a productive activity and may be constructed to produce, for example, ecologically prudent, less materialistic and more social forms of life styles and patterns of existence.

42 While postmodernist insights point to the uniformity of consumption and production, it is interesting that postmodernists have elected not to make this an issue and have generally continued to use the two terms indiscriminately, arguing, in a sense, for the importance of consumption over production.

43 This is, arguably, a sexist title indicating that even if we are very tolerant in certain respects, we may not recognize our intolerance in other respects when we get caught up in our narrative terminologies, such as, "Man."

44 See Thomas S. Kuhn, *The Structure of Scientific Revolutions*, Chicago: University of Chicago Press, 1962; Paul Feyerabend, *Against Method*, Thetford: Lowe and Brydone, 1975; and *Farewell to Reason*, London: Verso, 1987.

45 The youth movements of the 1960s in America and Europe, anti-war movements, flower children, Woodstock, and the like, are examples of these.

46 A good example of this trend in the case of gay and lesbian life styles is provided by Amy Gluckman and Betsy Reed in "The Gay Marketing Moment: Leaving Diversity in the Dust," *Dollars and Sense*, no. 190, November/December, 1993, pp. 16–35.

47 The feminist deconstruction of the modern patriarchal structures was as influential in this development as the postmodernist attitudes. See, for example, L. J. Nicholson (ed.), *Feminism/Postmodernism*, New York: Routledge, 1990; and J. Butler and J. W. Scott (eds.), *Feminists Theorize the Political*, New York: Routledge, 1992.

48 See Kenneth Frampton, "Towards a Critical Regionalism: Six Points for an Architecture of Resistance," in *The Anti-Aesthetic*, op. cit.; Robert Venturi, Denise Scott Brown, and Steven Izenour, *Learning from Las Vegas: The Forgotten Symbolism of Architectural Form*, Cambridge, MA: MIT Press, 1977.

49 See, for example, two books by William Ouchi, *Theory Z: How American Business Can Meet the Japanese Challenge*, Reading, MA: Addison-Wesley, 1981; and *The M-form Society: How American Teamwork Can Recapture the Competitive Edge*, Reading, MA: Addison-Wesley, 1984. Also see two books by Tom Peters, *Liberation Management: Necessary Disorganization for the Nanosecond Nineties*, New York: Alfred A. Knopf, 1992; and *The Pursuit of WOW!: Every Person's Guide to Topsy-Turvy Times*, New York: Vintage Books, 1994.

50 Among others, Disney and CNN Headline News commercials where many essentially unrelated images race across the screen, represent excellent examples of this phenomenon.

51 A powerful rendition of this blurring of boundaries between news and televisual entertainment can be found in the 1976 film *Network*, produced by Paddy Chayefsky and directed by Sidney Lumet.

52 Todd Gitlin, "Postmodernism: Roots and Politics," in ·I. Angus and S. Jhally (eds.), *Cultural Politics in Contemporary America*, New York: Routledge, 1989, pp. 347–360.

53 For a discussion of the concept of the bricolage, see Michael Newman,

"Revising Modernism, Representing Postmodernism: Critical Discourses of the Visual Arts," in L. Appignanesi (ed.), *Postmodernism*, Croydon: ICA Documents, Cranford Press Group, 1986, pp. 32–51.

54 See, for example, U. Eco and T. A. Sebeok (eds.), *The Sign of Three: Dupin, Holmes, Pierce*, Bloomington, IN: Indiana University Press, 1983; and M. Santambrogio and P. Violi (eds.), *Meaning and Mental Representations*, Bloomington, IN: Indiana University Press, 1988.

55 See Kirk Varnedoe and Adam Gopnik, *High and Low: Modern Art and Popular Culture*, New York: Museum of Modern Art, 1990. It is surely a sign of advancing postmodernity that Campbell Soup Company, once the unwitting subject of Andy Warhol's art, now *sponsors* an art contest where artists are invited to submit works of art featuring Campbell soup products.

56 Russell W. Belk, Melanie Wallendorf, and John F. Sherry, Jr., "The Sacred and the Profane in Consumer Behavior: Theodicy on the Odyssey," *Journal of Consumer Research*, vol. 16, no. 1, June 1989, pp. 1–38.

57 During non-prime time slots and on secondary cable television channels, marketers tout the virtues of exercise products such as "8-minute Abs," "8-minute Buns," "Thigh Master," and the "Abdominizer."

58 Bill Moyers, *The Public Mind: Image and Reality in America—Consuming Images*, op. cit.

59 See, A. Fuat Fırat, "The Consumer in Postmodernity," in R. H. Holman and M. R. Solomon (eds.), *Advances in Consumer Research*, vol. 27, Provo, UT: Association for Consumer Research, 1990, pp. 70–76; and A. Fuat Fırat, "Postmodern Culture, Marketing, and the Consumer," in T. Childers (ed.), *Marketing Theory and Application*, Chicago, IL: American Marketing Association, 1991, pp. 237–242.

60 Gilles Deleuze and Félix Guattari, *Anti-Oedipus: Capitalism and Schizophrenia*, Minneapolis, MN: University of Minnesota Press, 1983; and Fredric Jameson, "Postmodernism and Consumer Society," in *The Anti-Aesthetic*, op. cit., pp. 111–125.

61 See, for example, R. D. Laing, *The Divided Self*, London: Penguin Books, 1969. Also see Kenneth J. Gergen, *The Saturated Self: Dilemmas of Identity in Contemporary Life*, New York: Basic Books, 1991.

7 POSTMODERN CONSUMPTION

1 Examples of such consumption have been observed in the political arena, for example in women's movements, such as the Suffragist movement, but also in everyday rebellions. See, for example, T. H. Breen, "The Meanings of Things: Interpreting the Consumer Economy in the Eighteenth Century," in *Consumption and the World of Things*, J. Brewer and R. Porter (eds.), London: Routledge, 1993, pp. 249–260.

2 This history is well recounted in Lynn Spiegel, "The Suburban Home Companion: Television and the Neighborhood Ideal in Postwar America," in B. Colomina (ed.), *Sexuality and Space*, Princeton Papers on Architecture Series, vol. 1, New York: Princeton Architectural Press, 1992, pp. 184–217.

3 Of all the marketing concepts invented in the second half of the twentieth century, perhaps the most nebulous and yet the most powerful is the concept of "positioning." It would not be an exaggeration to say that those who are experts in positioning are the undisputed champions of the marketing world. For insightful treatments of positioning from a marketing perspective, see Al Ries and Jack Trout, *Positioning: The Battle for Your Mind*, New York: McGraw-Hill, 1986.

4 At least three postmodern approaches can be identified. These have been called, by different students of postmodernism, *celebratory* (or *affirmative*), *skeptical* (or *ambivalent*), and *critical*. Celebratory postmodernism, perhaps most associated with Lyotard, is fully in support of the fragmentation of narratives and of the conditions that define postmodern culture. For a discussion of postmodern conditions, see A. Fuat Fırat and Alladi Venkatesh, "Postmodernity: The Age of Marketing," *International Journal of Research in Marketing*, vol. 10, no. 3, 1993. Postmodernists who belong to this approach present no apologies for holding all schools of thought on an equal footing. Skeptical postmodernists, perhaps best represented by Baudrillard, recognize the omnipresence and omnipotence of the conditions and their positive aspects in comparison to modern, tyrannical idea systems and social orders, but are concerned with some of the social consequences of a culture based on these conditions. Among these consequences of concern, for example, are the loss of commitment to anything and everything, including humane and democratic ways, objectification and commodification of all, including the human individual, and a loss of general interest in intellectual and political pursuits and rights. Critical postmodernists, perhaps best represented by Jameson, generally agree with the concerns of the skeptical postmodernists, are critical of the political and social directions that postmodern conditions are causing, and call for the necessity of action to transcend postmodernity.

5 On the increasing concentration of control in media, see Ben H. Bagdikian, *The Media Monopoly* (3rd edn.), Boston: Beacon Press, 1990; and Herbert I. Schiller, *Culture Inc.: The Corporate Takeover of Public Expression*, New York: Oxford University Press, 1989.

6 In the United States, for example, several anti-trust laws were put into effect.

7 Many have criticized the workings of the market and its ineffectiveness in terms of social justice and fairness, but they have mostly gone unheeded in the heyday of capitalist development. For some recent and more effective treatments, see John Kenneth Galbraith, *The New Industrial State* (3rd edn.), Boston: Houghton Mifflin, 1978; Stephen Hymer, *The Multinational Corporation: A Radical Approach*, New York: Cambridge University Press, 1979; and Andrew Bard Schmookler, *The Illusion of Choice: How the Market Economy Shapes Our Destiny*, Albany, NY: State University of New York Press, 1993. The stock market, which in many ways is the ideal form of all markets, has periodically been rocked by major scandals that reveal its fragility and manipulability.

8 For example, Baudrillard still perpetuates the distinction between production and consumption in his work, even when he argues that value is created in consumption, not in production. See Jean Baudrillard, *Mirror of Production*, St. Louis, MO: Telos, 1975; and Jean Baudrillard, *For a Critique of the Political Economy of the Sign*, St. Louis, MO: Telos, 1981.

9 Clear separations between some activities as "production" and others as "consumption" were not made before modern organization of these activities in the public and private domains. See our discussion in Chapter 3.

10 With only about 5 percent of the world's population, the United States consumes about 30 percent of the world's resources. The number of homeless in the United States is estimated to be anywhere between 4.5 million and 9 million.

11 See, for example, Kath Weston, *Families We Choose: Lesbians, Gays, Kinship*, New York: Columbia University Press, 1991. The "coming out" of television star Ellen DeGeneres in April, 1997, as a lesbian, both on her TV show and in real life, became a major media event, splashed across TV programs and covers of major news magazines, indicative of the increasing need not just to tolerate but to promote and "market" tolerance. See Bruce Handy, "Roll over, Ward

Cleaver," *Time*, vol. 149, no. 15, April 14, 1997, pp. 78–85. Of course, there is also a strong rise in the feelings and incidents of intolerance, presaging the enormous struggle that lies ahead for postmodern ideas.

12 The Appalachian region of North Carolina, for example, is one part of the United States where such communities are growing.

13 This change in popular culture is highly observable in the changes in the treatments of such communities in films and television programs, as well as in other media, during the last four decades. See, for example, Bruce Handy, "Roll Over, Ward Cleaver," op. cit.

14 The term "weekend warrior" is increasingly being applied to the alternative life-mode activities of people during the weekend. This was initially used to refer to the activities of the United States armed forces reservists—people who had regular, civilian jobs during the day but played warriors during the training activities every few weekends. See Martin Binkin and William W. Kaufmann, *US Army Guard and Reserve: Rhetoric, Realities, Risks*, Washington, DC: Brookings Institution, 1989. Contemporary weekend warriors include anyone who leads an alternative weekend life that is fantastic in comparison to the mundane, weekday life. For the transforming role of the weekend over the ages, see Witold Rybczynski, *Waiting for the Weekend*, New York: Penguin, 1992.

15 The marketing strategy of Sustecal, a dietary supplement for mature adults, is interesting. The advertising slogan of the product was: "It may not add years to your life, but it will add life to your years." The television advertising campaign in 1997 positioned Sustecal aggressively against the rival product Ensure. Two elderly couples were portrayed. While the couple drinking Ensure relaxed in sedate settings, the couple toasting Sustecal was seen engaging in activities like riding in fast convertible cars, scuba diving, and racing fast motorboats.

16 Las Vegas, which has been proclaimed as "The New All-American City" by *Time* magazine (*Time*, January 10, 1994), has the fastest growing population among cities in the United States, has the highest number of people moving in looking for jobs, and has been enjoying an economic boom unlike any other city. As a city which (re)presents itself as a bundle of thematic entertainment environments, it has attracted the interest of many students of postmodern culture. See, for example, Robert Venturi, Denise Scott Brown, and Steven Izenour, *Learning From Las Vegas: The Forgotten Symbolism of Architectural Form*, Cambridge, MA: The MIT Press, 1977; Alan Hess, *Viva Las Vegas: After Hours Architecture*, San Francisco: Chronicle Books, 1993; and Norman K. Denzin, "*Rain Man* in Las Vegas: Where is the Action for the Postmodern Self?" *Symbolic Interaction*, vol. 16, no. 1, 1993, pp. 65–77. There have also been many television programs studying the Las Vegas phenomenon. See, for example, *Coming and Going*, Public Broadcasting Service, 1994; *Going Places: Las Vegas*, Public Broadcasting Service, 1997; and *Las Vegas: Gamble in the Desert*, A&E Television Networks, 1996.

17 As in the case of preparing for the "perfect" intimate encounter through the use of cosmetics, flower arrangements, candlelight dinners, etc.

18 See Bill Moyers, *The Public Mind: Image and Reality in America—Consuming Images*, Public Broadcasting Service, 1989.

19 This, of course, is much easier in the anonymity of cyberspace than in the lighted glare of physical space. See Sherry Turkle, *Life on the Screen: Identity in the Age of the Internet*, New York: Simon & Schuster, 1995.

20 See Gail Faurschou, "Fashion and the Cultural Logic of Postmodernity," *Canadian Journal of Political and Social Theory*, vol. 11, no. 1–2, 1987, pp. 68–83; and Roland Barthes, *The Fashion System*, Berkeley, CA: University of California Press, 1990.

21 For a good recent exposé of the fashion system, see *The Look*, Public Broadcasting Service, 1993.

22 The flip-side process, that of resignifying the entertaining and the playful as serious and economically productive, has already started. See Tom Peters, *Liberation Management*, New York: Alfred A. Knopf, 1992; and Douglas Rushkoff, *Playing the Future: How Kids' Culture Can Teach Us to Thrive in an Age of Chaos*, New York: HarperCollins, 1996.

23 See *Playing the Future*, op. cit.; and *Liberation Management*, op. cit.

24 In his book *Liberation Management*, op. cit., Peters provides examples of more "playful" and attractive work environments created in different companies, such as at DKD, an avant garde design firm (p. 168), and at Accolade, a Silicon Valley software house (p. 602). Other examples are provided by Ed McCracken, CEO of Silicon Graphics, in Steven E. Prokesch, "Mastering Chaos at the High-Tech Frontier: An Interview with Silicon Graphics's Ed McCracken," *Harvard Business Review*, November–December, 1993; and at the Walt Disney World Casting Center: see Narayana Currimbhoy, "A Touch of Magic," *Interiors*, January, 1990.

8 GLOBAL CONSUMPTION

1 See Bill Moyers, *The Public Mind: Image and Reality in America—Consuming Images*, Public Broadcasting Service, 1989.

2 Therefore, as Alladi Venkatesh, a professor of management at the University of California, Irvine, has articulated in our private discussions, we may need a Consumers International more than any other international body at the present.

3 Jean Baudrillard, *In the Shadow of the Silent Majorities*, New York: Semiotext(e), 1983.

4 Theodore Levitt, "The Globalization of Markets," *Harvard Business Review*, vol. 61, May–June, 1983, pp. 92–102. Also see, Kenichi Ohmae, *The Borderless World: Power and Strategy in the Interlinked Economy*, New York: HarperPerennial, 1991.

5 Richard J. Barnet and John Cavanagh, *Global Dreams: Imperial Corporations and the New World Order*, New York: Simon & Schuster, 1994.

6 *Utne Reader*, November–December, 1994.

7 This was the case particularly in the 1970s. See, for example, Jean Jacques Servan-Schreiber, *The American Challenge* (trans. by R. Steel), New York: Avon Books, 1972.

8 This, of course, is true. Cultural products are the second largest exports from the United States after airplanes (see *Utne Reader*, November–December, 1994).

9 In *Global Dreams*, op. cit., p. 113.

10 According to the US Bureau of the Census statistics, in 1992, 11.7 percent of all United States families were poor, up from 8.8 percent in 1973; 14.5 percent of all persons in the United States were poor in 1992, up from 11.1 in 1973. The proportions of poor for children was 21.9 percent and for African-Americans 33.3 percent in 1992. The percentage for the poor among single females with children in 1992 was 45.7. See US Bureau of the Census, "Poverty in the United States: 1992," *Current Population Reports* (Series P60–185), Washington, DC: Government Printing Office, 1993. According to the *Status Report on Hunger and Homelessness in America's Cities: 1995*, Washington, DC: US Conference of Mayors, 1995, in the previous year requests for emergency shelters in the surveyed cities increased by an average of 11 percent, with 63 percent of the

cities registering an increase. Requests for shelter by homeless families alone increased by 15 percent, with 71 percent of the cities reporting an increase. The count for homeless in the United States differs due to difficulties of counting the homeless, but President Clinton stated the homeless figure as 7 million (see Patricia Edmonds, "Homeless Plan: More Federal Aid," *USA Today*, February 18, 1994, p. A3).

11 For expressions of such concerns see *Introduction to the Sociology of "Developing Countries"*, Hamza Alavi and Teodor Shanin (eds.), New York: Monthly Review Press, 1982; Mike Featherstone, *Global Culture: Nationalism, Globalization and Modernity*, London: Sage, 1990; and J. Keane, *Media and Democracy*, London: Polity Press, 1990.

12 For example, at the Cultural Dimension of International Marketing Conference in Denmark, May 1993, the Lego Corporation's Marketing Vice President noted that in many respects they find greater similarities among groups of consumers across national boundaries than among groups within the same country.

13 In settings such as fancy hotels and restaurants, it is now difficult to tell social class differences from casual observations of attire. Waiters, doormen, bellhops, receptionists, concierges and other service personnel in such settings are now trained to look for minor clues—watches, jewelry, shoes, belts, handbags—to spot the real VIPs, to ensure that such *primus inter pares* people get the special treatment they are accustomed to.

14 See, for example, arguments by Theodore Levitt in "The Globalization of Markets," *Harvard Business Review*, 83 (May–June), 1983, pp. 92–102. Further evidence for globalization of markets is well presented in *Global Dreams*, op. cit.

15 A witness to this growing trend toward tolerance is the increasingly harsh reactions from groups with fundamentalist ideologies that fear the loss of the hegemony of their ideas or preferred way(s) of life all across the western cultures.

16 It is, however, a very prominent example of trends in contemporary consumption. Disney World, with 30.2 million visitors annually (*USA Today*, April 8, 1994, p. A3) was, until recently surpassed by Las Vegas, the third largest tourist attraction in the world following France and Italy.

17 This phenomenon is articulated well in two recent books: *Postsuburban California: The Transformation of Orange County Since World War II*, Rob Kling, Spencer Olin, and Mark Poster (eds.), Berkeley, CA: University of California Press, 1991; and *Variations on a Theme Park: The New American City and the End of Public Space*, Michael Sorkin (ed.), New York: The Noonday Press, 1992.

18 Kurt Andersen brings this point home in his article, "Las Vegas, USA" (pp. 42–51), which appears in *Time* magazine's January 10, 1994, issue that proclaims Las Vegas as "The New All-American City."

19 These spectacles create not just spectators but "participators." Consumers at EPCOT Center's World Showcase walk through the simulated streets of France, Morocco, Mexico, etc., and sample their food and sounds among other things, and can momentarily imagine themselves as part of these cultures and life styles.

20 A Roman Forum at Caesar's Palace, Pirateland at Treasure Island, Land of Oz at MGM Grand, Pyramids of Egypt at Luxor, the Manhattan skyline at New York-New York, and the French Riviera ambiance of Monaco.

21 The transformation of Japan after the Meiji restoration was a prime exemplar to the rest of the non-western world of the power of west-imitating moderniza-

tion. The reformers who came into power after the Meiji restoration argued that western-style, technology-driven modernization was the only feasible option for Japan to ward off western imperialist threats. The country embarked on a westernization program on a scale unprecedented in prior world history and unequaled since then, with the possible exception of Atatürk's Turkey. On Meiji Japan, see Akira Iriye, *Power and Culture: The Japanese–American War, 1941–1945*, Cambridge, MA: Harvard University Press, 1981; Michio Morishima, *Why Has Japan Succeeded? Western Technology and the Japanese Ethos*, New York: Cambridge University Press, 1982; and Eleanor D. Westney, *Imitation and Innovation: The Transfer of Western Organizational Patterns to Meiji Japan*, Cambridge, MA: Harvard University Press, 1987.

22 See Paul Virilio, *The Vision Machine*, Bloomington, IN: Indiana University Press, 1994.

23 *The Vision Machine*, op. cit.

24 In the three decades following the Second World War, the United States government played a major role in promoting America's products and American culture across the world, particularly in the countries that had not allied with it or the Soviet Union. The Soviets, in turn, peddled the benefits of their version of modernization, although they often lacked the marketing savvy of the US government agencies.

25 Although both Nike and Benetton are known for their advertising, which creates intense cultural imagery, these two brands have an opposite take on culture. Nike creates intense culture images of athletes, mostly minority and women, that are lyrical, spiritual, nearly reverential. Benetton, on the other hand, presents striking images of global cultural diversity but in an irreverent, often shocking fashion.

26 Although there is some tourist trading at the reservation, the quality and quantity of what is made available leaves the tourist with the distinct impression that the Hopis have made a differentiation between the "authentic" items (katsina dolls used for their own ceremonial purposes, for example) and the "touristic" ones. Most of the katsina dolls sold at touristic shops in Arizona cities are produced by other nations, such as the Dinne (Navaho), Zuni, etc.

27 Absentee land ownership in the Appalachian region is over 80 percent. See Patricia D. Beaver, *Rural Community in the Appalachian South*, Lexington, KY: University Press of Kentucky, 1986.

28 Examples of such markets are found around the world, whether it be bootlegging in the United States or sales of fake brand names—for sodas, shirts, watches, etc.—in Thailand. For examples, see Clement Cottingham (ed.), *Race, Poverty, and the Urban Underclass*, Lexington, MA: Lexington Books, 1982; Belinda Coote, *The Trade Trap: Poverty and the Global Commodity Markets*, Oxford: Oxfam, 1992; Scott Sernau, *Economies of Exclusion: Underclass Poverty and Labor Market Change in Mexico*, Westport, CT: Praeger, 1994.

29 Examples of such relationships can be found in United Nations Conference on Trade and Development, *Globalization and Liberalization: Effects of International Economic Relations on Poverty*, New York: United Nations, 1996; Maria L. Lagos, *Autonomy and Power: The Dynamics of Class and Culture in Rural Bolivia*, Philadelphia: University of Pennsylvania Press, 1994; Pranab K. Bardhan, *Land, Labor, and Rural Poverty: Essays in Development Economics*, New York: Columbia University Press, 1984; Charles D. Brockett, *Land, Power, and Poverty: Agrarian Transformation and Political Conflict in Central America*, Boulder, CO: Westview Press, 1990; Thomas Benjamin, *A Rich Land, a Poor People: Politics and Society in Modern Chiapas*, Albuquerque, NM: University of New Mexico Press, 1996.

30 ·An example of an ecological system that has deteriorated under the pressures of industrialization to serve the market can be found in Bali, Indonesia. The irrigation canal systems that served not only to irrigate, but also to provide water for the population's use in drinking and bathing, have been heavily polluted by industry. However, since new water delivery systems have not been developed in their place, many Balinese still have to use the polluted system for their daily needs—as can be seen by the numbers who bathe every evening in the canals.

31 Driven by dollars, the market of course responds to these concerns—making vine-ripened hothouse tomatoes from the Netherlands and fresh air-shipped vegetables from Israel available at superpremium prices to the most affluent section of the market-linked consumer sector.

32 *The Life Styles of the Rich and the Famous*, presented by Robin Leach, is apparently one of the most successful international television programs seen even in the People's Republic of China.

33 Politics and policies such as those that maintain an unequal distribution of wealth and incomes in order to sustain the necessary capital investments and business energy required in a market economy.

34 See, for example, the discussion by Mark Crispin Miller in *The Public Mind*, op. cit.

35 Hyperreality means that social reality is dependent upon the simulations and/or hypes that are powerfully represented, and, therefore, that any social reality is possible.

36 It is interesting to note here that when under tremendous political or armed pressure, the dominant ideology often has to relent and acknowledge alternative paths, which, though not fully compatible with the dominant mode, are less inimical to it than subversive, revolutionary options. When Peru faced the growing threat of the Maoist, subversive "Shining Path" (*Sendero Luminoso*) guerilla movement, the Peruvian business leader and author Hernando de Soto wrote the book *The Other Path* (*El Otro Sendero*). The book extols the virtues of the informal or underground economy, the economy of peddlers and minibus operators, as an option for youth who could not find a place in the dominant corporate economy and were therefore likely to be attracted to the Shining Path movement. Not only did Hernando de Soto's *The Other Path* become an international best seller, in Latin America and elsewhere, his themes were picked up and championed by international agencies such as the World Bank, agencies that would have scoffed at proposals to promote "informal and underground economy" in the past.

37 Arguments and struggles against multiplicity or diversity are evident in many fields; for example, in education, see Allan Bloom, *The Closing of the American Mind*, New York: Simon & Schuster, 1987; E. D. Hirsch, Jr., *Cultural Literacy: What Every American Needs to Know*, New York: Vintage Books, 1988; as well as in the discussions on the New World Order: Jack Nelson-Pallmeyer, *Brave New World Order: Must We Pledge Allegiance?*, Maryknoll, NY: Orbis Books, 1992; David Jablonsky, *Paradigm Lost?: Transitions and the Search for a New World Order*, Westport, CT: Praeger, 1995; Hans-Henrik Holm, *Whose World Order?: Uneven Globalization and the End of the Cold War*, Boulder, CO: Westview Press, 1995.

9 CONSUMING PEOPLE

1 A reminder that we use the term (post)modern with the "post" in parentheses to represent the present transformational period from the modern to the postmodern.

2 It is rare to find someone inside the television industry criticizing the impact of television on education and culture. For such an exceptional view, see Danny Schechter, *The More You Watch, The Less You Know: The Media Adventures of a Network Refugee*, New York: Seven Stories Press, 1997.

3 See Mark Crispin Miller, *Boxed In: The Culture of TV*, Evanston, IL: Northwestern University Press, 1988.

4 "Seeing is believing," "a picture is worth a thousand words" are some of the adages that evidence this superiority of the visual over other forms of information in modern society. Furthermore, the role of "observation" in science has been central.

5 By multidimensionality we mean that the visual media, such as television and films, have integrated the visual with sounds and the written word.

6 As we admitted early, this book is no exception in this regard, relying as it does on a modern, linear flow of verbal argument.

7 With the rise of new media, there is growing acceptance that information and entertainment, as well as education and entertainment, need not be oppositional. Terms such as "infotainment" and "edutainment" have come into vogue. See, for example, Ruby Roy Dholakia, Norbert Mundorf, and Nikhilesh Dholakia (eds.), *New Infotainment Technologies in the Home: Demand-Side Perspectives*, Mahwah, NJ: Lawrence Erlbaum Associates, 1996.

8 In postmodernity, literacy is not simply one of reading and writing—that is, command over and understanding of the written text—but one of sensing and constructing—that is, command over and understanding of the multiple and multilayered signs that impress upon all human senses. This could be called (multi)signefficacy. See A. Fuat Fırat, "Literacy in the Age of New Information Technologies," in *New Infotainment Technologies in the Home*, op. cit., pp. 173–193.

9 See A. Fuat Fırat and Alladi Venkatesh, "Liberatory Postmodernism and the Reenchantment of Consumption," *Journal of Consumer Research*, vol. 22, December, 1995, pp. 239–267.

10 See Hamish McRae, *The World in 2020: Power Culture and Prosperity*, Boston, MA: Harvard Business School Press, 1995.

11 *The World in 2020*, op. cit.

12 Timothy H. Breen, "The Meanings of Things: Interpreting the Consumer Economy of the Eighteenth Century," in J. Brewer and R. Porter (eds.), *Consumption and the World of Goods*, London: Routledge, 1993, pp. 249–260.

13 This phenomenon is much promulgated already in the public media and discourse—e.g. "money can't buy happiness" and similar sayings—but it does not become a practiced ideology in the contemporary world.

14 This was discussed extensively in Chapter 7.

15 See, for example, Lawrence Grossberg, *We Gotta Get Out of This Place*, New York: Routledge, 1992.

16 An interesting, though hardly novel, take on the perceived failures of the modern, capitalist market project was by George Soros, the multi-billion dollar investor-capitalist known for his savvy global investments as well as his extensive philanthropy. See George Soros, "The Capitalist Threat," *The Atlantic Monthly*, February, 1997, pp. 45–58.

17 *We Gotta Get Out of This Place*, op. cit.

18 Pareto was the economist who studied and contributed to classical economics the idea of preference curves that defined points of optimum satisfaction for each participant in the economy that could be maintained with increasing levels of welfare through a redistribution of wealth. See, Vilfredo Pareto, *Manual of*

Political Economy (trans. by A. S. Schwier), New York: Augustus M. Kelley, 1971.

19 An extensive philosophical treatment of the emerging "marketing democracy" and its legitimation processes can be found in Romain Laufer and Catherine Paradeise, *Marketing Democracy: Public Opinion and Media Formation in Democratic Societies*, New Brunswick, NJ: Transaction Publishers, 1990.

20 Aggressive promotion of milk powder formula for infants in developing countries was blamed for major health problems. Not only did the market-bought formula use up the meager discretionary incomes of the Third World poor, it supplanted established and very healthy practices of breast feeding. Furthermore, mixing of the formula with contaminated water led to widespread diarrhea, dehydration, even death. Activist groups in the developed world, cognizant of Nestlé's vast array of consumer products, launched a boycott campaign that lasted years, finally forcing Nestlé to change its aggressive infant-formula marketing techniques in Third World countries. See S. Prakash Sethi, *Promises of the Good Life: Social Consequences of Private Marketing Decisions*, Homewood, IL: R. D. Irwin, 1979.

21 For an account of the consumerist agenda, see Ralph Nader (ed.), *The Consumer and Corporate Accountability*, New York: Harcourt, Brace, Jovanovitch, 1973; and Ralph Nader, Mark Green, and Joel Seligman, *Taming the Giant Corporation*, New York: Norton, 1976.

22 Philip Kotler and Paul Bloom, "Strategies for High Market-Share Companies," *Harvard Business Review*, November–December, 1975, pp. 63–72.

10 THE NEW THEATER OF CONSUMPTION

1 See, for example, Yiannis Gabriel and Tim Lang, *The Unmanageable Consumer: Contemporary Consumption and its Fragmentations*, London: Sage, 1995; Daniel Miller, *Material Culture and Mass Consumption*, Oxford: Blackwell, 1987; John Fiske, *Television Culture*, London: Methuen, 1987; Colin Campbell, *The Romantic Ethic and the Spirit of Modern Consumerism*, Oxford: Macmillan, 1987; and John Kenneth Galbraith, *The Affluent Society*, Harmondsworth: Penguin.

2 See, for example, Stuart Ewen, *Captains of Consciousness*, New York: McGraw-Hill, 1976; John Kenneth Galbraith, *The New Industrial State*, New York: Signet, 1967; Neil Postman, *Amusing Ourselves to Death*, New York: Penguin, 1984; Herbert I. Schiller, *The Mind Managers*, Boston: Beacon Press, 1973; and Andrew Bard Schmookler, *The Illusion of Choice*, Albany, NY: State University of New York Press, 1993.

3 We discussed this process in some detail in Chapter 3.

4 Some call this tendency of modern nation states the "tyranny of the majority." Of course, it is not always the will of the majority—often it is the will of a minority—that dominates political choices in modern democracies.

5 See, for example, the books, Kenichi Ohmae, *The End of the Nation State*, New York: HarperCollins, 1995; Jean-Marie Guéhenno, *The End of the Nation-State*, Minneapolis, MN: University of Minnesota Press, 1995; and Michael Mann (ed.), *The Rise and Decline of the Nation State*, Cambridge, MA: Basil Blackwell, 1992. Many articles on the topic also exist. For example, Janos Kis, "Beyond the Nation State," *Social Research*, vol. 63, no. 1, 1995, pp. 191–245; Jan W. Van Deth, "Comparative Politics and the Decline of the Nation State in Western Europe," *European Journal of Political Research*, vol. 27, 1995, pp. 443–462; Vivien A. Schmidt, "The New World Order, Incorporated: The Rise of Business and the Decline of the Nation-State," *Daedalus*, vol. 124, no.

2, 1995, pp. 75–106; and Masao Miyoshi, "A Borderless World? From Colonialism to Transnationalism and the Decline of the Nation-State," *Critical Inquiry*, vol. 19, Summer. 1993, pp. 726–751.

6　Such as the use of marijuana and other substances.

7　See Nikhilesh Dholakia, "The Webs and the Web-Nots: Access Issues in the Information Age," *Telematics and Informatics*, May, 1997.

8　See A. Fuat Fırat, John F. Sherry, Jr., and Alladi Venkatesh, "Postmodernism, Marketing and the Consumer," *International Journal of Research in Marketing*, vol. 11, no. 4, 1994, pp. 311–316.

9　Zygmunt Bauman, "From Pilgrim to Tourist—or a Short History of Identity," in S. Hall and P. du Gay (eds.), *Questions of Cultural Identity*, London: Sage, 1996, pp. 18–36.

10　Michel Maffesoli, *The Time of the Tribes: The Decline of Individualism in Mass Society*, London: Sage, 1996.

11　Lawrence Grossberg, *We Gotta Get Out of This Place: Popular Conservatism and Postmodern Culture*, New York: Routledge, 1992, p. 369.

12　This was expressed colorfully and with some implied rage in a bumper sticker we saw in Phoenix, Arizona: "I am not a hyphenated anything."

13　Jean Baudrillard, *For a Critique of the Political Economy of the Sign*, St. Louis, MO: Telos, 1981.

14　See Georges Bataille, *Visions of Excess: Selected Writings, 1927–1939* (ed. and trans. by A. Stoekl), Minneapolis, MN: University of Minnesota Press, 1985; Jean Baudrillard, *Symbolic Exchange and Death* (trans. by H. Grant), London: Sage, 1993; and *The Transparency of Evil: Essays on Extreme Phenomena* (trans. by J Benedict), London: Verso, 1993.

15　In the discussion to follow, we are primarily referring to the following works of the authors discussed: Jürgen Habermas, *The Theory of Communicative Action—Volume One: Reason and the Rationalization of Society*, Boston: Beacon Press, 1984, and *The Theory of Communicative Action—Volume Two*, Boston: Beacon Press, 1987 (both volumes trans. by T. McCarthy); Michel Foucault, *Power/Knowledge: Selected Interviews and Other Writings 1972–77*, C. Gordon (ed.), New York: Pantheon, 1980; Ulrich Beck, Anthony Giddens, and Scott Lash, *Reflexive Modernization: Politics, Tradition and Aesthetics in the Modern Social Order*, Stanford, CA: Stanford University Press, 1994.

16　Thomas McCarthy, *Ideals and Illusions: On Reconstruction and Deconstruction in Contemporary Critical Theory*, Cambridge, MA: The MIT Press, 1993.

17　Karl-Otto Apel, *Towards a Transformation of Philosophy* (trans. by G. Adey and D. Frisby), London: Routledge & Kegan Paul, 1980, p. 229.

18　See, Michel Foucault, *Discipline and Punish: The Birth of the Prison* (trans. by A. Sheridan), New York: Pantheon, 1977; and *Power/Knowledge*, op. cit. Also see Friedrich W. Nietzsche, *The Portable Nietzsche* (ed. and trans. by Walter Kaufmann), Harmondsworth: Penguin, 1968.

19　Ulrich Beck, "Replies and Critiques—Self-Dissolution and Self-Endangerment of Industrial Society: What Does This Mean?" in *Reflexive Modernization*, op. cit., p. 176.

20　Anthony Giddens, "Replies and Critiques—Risk, Trust, Reflexivity," in *Reflexive Modernization*, op. cit., p. 187.

21　See, for example, two books by Richard Rorty, *Philosophy and the Mirror of Nature*, Princeton, NJ: Princeton University Press, 1979; and *Consequences of Pragmatism: Essays, 1972–1980*, Minneapolis, MN: University of Minnesota Press, 1982.

22　Pierre Bourdieu, *Distinction: A Social Critique of the Judgement of Taste*, Cambridge, MA: Harvard University Press, 1984. Also see C. Calhoun, E.

LiPuma, and M. Postone (eds.), *Bourdieu: Critical Perspectives*, Chicago: University of Chicago Press, 1993.

23 In late modernity, in the age of the "live television show," even the spontaneity of the audience was perceived as too unreliable. It was replaced by programmed responses such as the flashing "Applause" sign and canned laughter.

24 Here "outside" does not mean a physical separation but a practical separation.

25 At this juncture, of course, the market is at the forefront of providing transient, quick-immersion experiences to consumers. The resources required for such "experiential enclaves" are often large and the market provides a way of spreading the investment over masses of consumers, in return for making profits for the investors. We do not see this as problematic. The practices of establishing and maintaining experiential enclaves could evolve in a market setting, but there is no reason why such practices have to be contingent on a market setting.

26 Néstor Garcia Canclini, *Consumers and Citizens: Multicultural Conflicts in the Processes of Globalization*, Minneapolis, MN: University of Minnesota Press, forthcoming, cited in George Yúdice, "Civil Society, Consumption, and Governmentality in the Age of Global Restructuring: An Introduction," *Social Text*, vol. 14, no. 4, Winter, 1995, pp. 1–25.

27 Néstor Garcia Canclini, *Consumers and Citizens*, op. cit., p. 172, cited in George Yúdice, op. cit., p. 19.

28 George Yúdice, op. cit., p. 18.

29 Howard Rheingold already provides a preview of some of these possibilities in his book *The Virtual Community: Homesteading on the Electronic Frontier*, New York: HarperPerennial, 1994.

Index